Microsoft® EXCEL 97

Step by Step

Other titles in the *Step by Step* series:

*Microsoft Access 97 Step by Step

*Microsoft Excel 97 Step by Step, Advanced Topics

*Microsoft FrontPage 97 Step by Step

 Microsoft Internet Explorer 3.0 Step by Step

 Microsoft Office 97 Integration Step by Step

*Microsoft Outlook 97 Step by Step

*Microsoft PowerPoint 97 Step by Step

 Microsoft Team Manager 97 Step by Step

 Microsoft Windows 95 Step by Step

 Microsoft Windows NT Workstation version 4.0 Step by Step

*Microsoft Word 97 Step by Step

*Microsoft Word 97 Step by Step, Advanced Topics

Step by Step books are also available for the Microsoft Office 95 programs.

* These books are approved courseware for Certified Microsoft Office User (CMOU) exams. For more details about the CMOU program, see page xvii.

Microsoft® EXCEL 97

Step by Step

Microsoft Press

PUBLISHED BY
Microsoft Press
A Division of Microsoft Corporation
One Microsoft Way
Redmond, Washington 98052-6399

Copyright © 1996 by Catapult, Inc.

Library of Congress Cataloging-in-Publication Data
Microsoft Excel 97 Step by Step / Catapult, Inc.
        p.   cm.
    Includes index.
    ISBN 1-57231-314-5
    1. Microsoft Excel (Computer file)   2. Business--Computer
programs   3. Electronic spreadhseets.   I. Catapult, Inc.
HF5548.4.M523M51575   1997
005.369--dc20   96-38988
                                                           CIP

Printed and bound in the United States of America.

13 14 15 16   QWTQWT   5 4 3 2 1 0

Distributed in Canada by Penguin Books Canada Limited.

A CIP catalogue record for this book is available from the British Library.

Microsoft Press books are available through booksellers and distributors worldwide. For further information about international editions, contact your local Microsoft Corporation office or contact Microsoft Press International directly at fax (425) 936-7329. Visit our Web site at mspress.microsoft.com.

Intel is a registered trademark of Intel Corporation. AutoSum, Microsoft, Microsoft Press, MS-DOS, PivotTable, PowerPoint, Windows, Windows NT, and Visual Basic are either registered trademarks or trademarks of Microsoft Corporation in the United States and/or other countries. Other product and company names mentioned herein may be the trademarks of their respective owners.

The names of example companies, products, people, characters, and/or data mentioned herein are fictitious and are in no way intended to represent any real individual, company, product, or event, unless otherwise noted.

For Catapult, Inc.
Managing Editor: Diana Stiles
Writer: Julia Kelly
Project Editor: Armelle O'Neal
Technical Editor: John Cronan
Production/Layout Editor: Jeanne Hunt
Indexer: Julie Kawabata

For Microsoft Press
Acquisitions Editor: Casey D. Doyle
Project Editors: Laura Sackerman,
    Ina Chang

Catapult, Inc. & Microsoft Press

Microsoft Excel 97 Step by Step has been created by the professional trainers and writers at Catapult, Inc., to the exacting standards you've come to expect from Microsoft Press. Together, we are pleased to present this self-paced training guide, which you can use individually or as part of a class.

Catapult, Inc., is a software training company with years of experience in PC and Macintosh instruction. Catapult's exclusive Performance-Based Training system is available in Catapult training centers across North America and at customer sites. Based on the principles of adult learning, Performance-Based Training ensures that students leave the classroom with confidence and the ability to apply skills to real-world scenarios. *Microsoft Excel 97 Step by Step* incorporates Catapult's training expertise to ensure that you'll receive the maximum return on your training time. You'll focus on the skills that can increase your productivity the most while working at your own pace and convenience.

Microsoft Press is the book publishing division of Microsoft Corporation. The leading publisher of information about Microsoft products and services, Microsoft Press is dedicated to providing the highest quality computer books and multimedia training and reference tools that make using Microsoft software easier, more enjoyable, and more productive.

Table of Contents

Table of Contents

Table of Contents

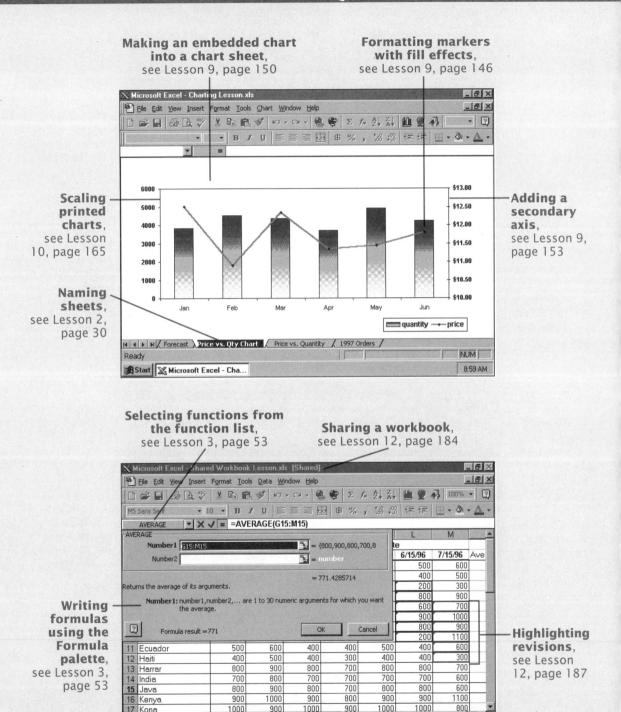

Making an embedded chart into a chart sheet, see Lesson 9, page 150

Formatting markers with fill effects, see Lesson 9, page 146

Scaling printed charts, see Lesson 10, page 165

Adding a secondary axis, see Lesson 9, page 153

Naming sheets, see Lesson 2, page 30

Selecting functions from the function list, see Lesson 3, page 53

Sharing a workbook, see Lesson 12, page 184

Writing formulas using the Formula palette, see Lesson 3, page 53

Highlighting revisions, see Lesson 12, page 187

Filtering records,
see Lesson 6, page 100

Writing formulas with AutoSum,
see Lesson 3, page 48

Undoing multiple actions,
see Lesson 1, page 16

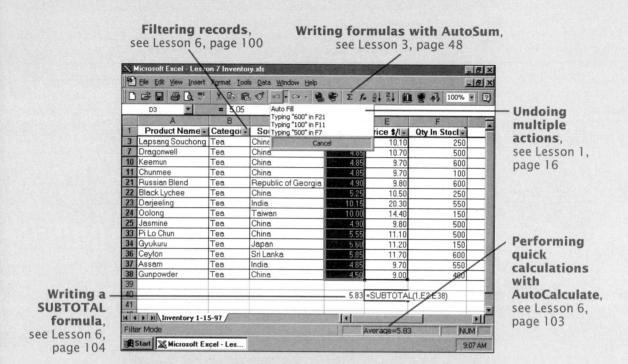

Writing a SUBTOTAL formula,
see Lesson 6, page 104

Performing quick calculations with AutoCalculate,
see Lesson 6, page 103

Applying conditional number formatting,
see Lesson 5, page 89

Copying worksheets by dragging and dropping,
see Lesson 5, page 87

Arranging multiple workbooks in multiple windows,
see Lesson 5, page 85

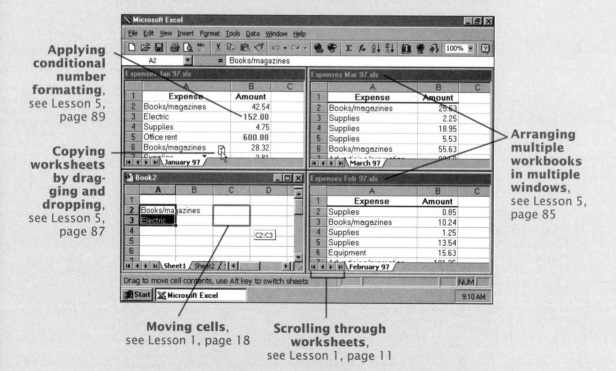

Moving cells,
see Lesson 1, page 18

Scrolling through worksheets,
see Lesson 1, page 11

Creating PivotTables,
see Lesson 8, page 129

Creating embedded charts,
see Lesson 9, page 145

Grouping dates into months,
see Lesson 8, page 130

Applying AutoFormats,
see Lesson 8, page 132

Getting help from the Office Assistant,
see Lesson 1, page 8

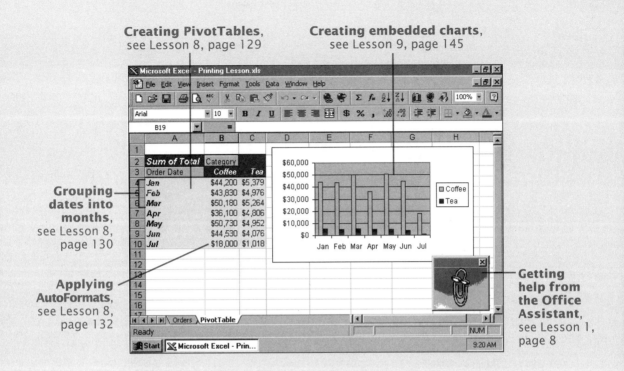

Viewing a worksheet in Page Break Preview,
see Lesson 10, page 159

Changing page printing order,
see Lesson 10, page 161

Changing page breaks by dragging,
see Lesson 10, page 159

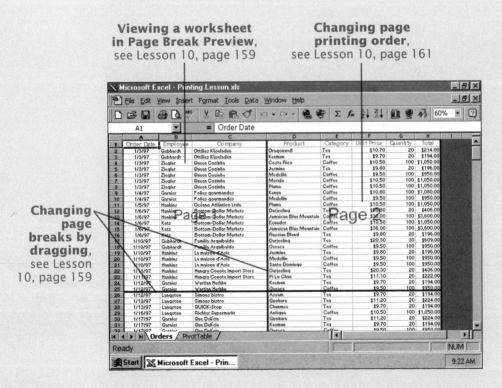

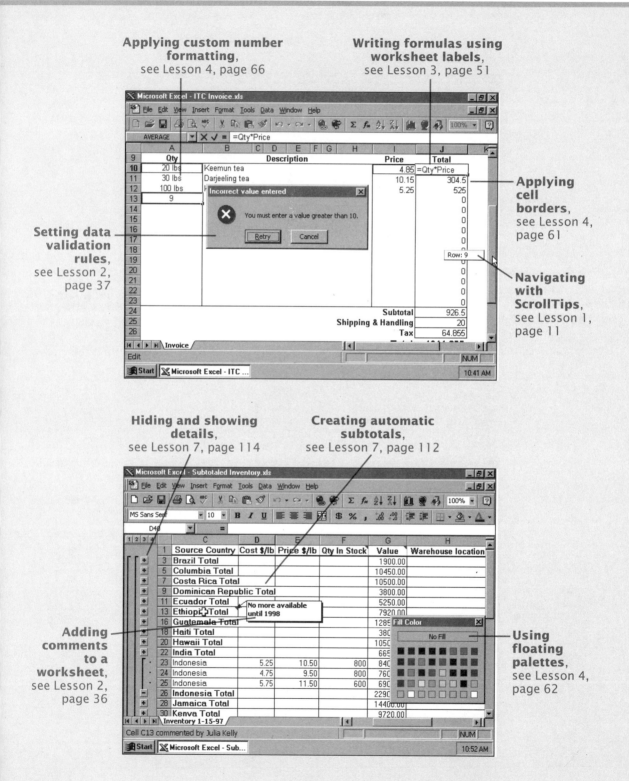

Applying custom number formatting, see Lesson 4, page 66

Writing formulas using worksheet labels, see Lesson 3, page 51

Applying cell borders, see Lesson 4, page 61

Setting data validation rules, see Lesson 2, page 37

Navigating with ScrollTips, see Lesson 1, page 11

Hiding and showing details, see Lesson 7, page 114

Creating automatic subtotals, see Lesson 7, page 112

Adding comments to a worksheet, see Lesson 2, page 36

Using floating palettes, see Lesson 4, page 62

Finding Your Best Starting Point

Microsoft Excel is a powerful spreadsheet program that you can use to efficiently store and work with lists of data, calculate numbers, and create reports and charts. With *Microsoft Excel 97 Step by Step*, you'll quickly and easily learn how to use Microsoft Excel to get your work done.

 IMPORTANT   This book is designed for use with Microsoft Excel 97 for the Windows 95 and Windows NT version 4.0 operating systems. To find out what software you're running, you can check the product package or you can start the program, click the Help menu at the top of the screen, and then click About Microsoft Excel. If your product is not compatible with this book, a Step by Step book for your program is probably available. Please visit our World Wide Web site at http://www.microsoft.com/mspress/ or call 1-800-MSPRESS for more information.

Finding Your Best Starting Point in This Book

This book is designed for readers learning Microsoft Excel for the first time and for more experienced readers who want to learn and use the new features in Microsoft Excel 97. Use the following table to find your best starting point in this book.

If you are	Follow these steps

New...

to computers

to graphical (as opposed to text-only) computer programs

to Windows 95 or Windows NT

1 Install the practice files as described in "Installing and Using the Practice Files.

2 Become acquainted with the Windows 95 or Windows NT operating system and how to use the online Help system by working through Appendix A, "If You're New to Windows 95, Windows NT, or Microsoft Excel."

3 Learn basic skills for using Microsoft Excel by working sequentially through Lessons 1 through 4. Then, you can work through Lessons 5 through 13 in any order.

Switching...

from Lotus 1-2-3

from QuattroPro

from Microsoft Works

1 Install the practice files as described in "Installing and Using the Practice Files."

2 Learn basic skills for using Microsoft Excel 97 by working sequentially through Lessons 1 through 4. Then, you can work through Lessons 5 through 13 in any order.

Upgrading...

from Microsoft Excel for Windows 95

1 Learn about the new features in this version of the program that are covered in this book by reading through the following section, "New Features in Microsoft Excel 97."

2 Install the practice files as described in "Installing and Using the Practice Files."

3 Complete the lessons that cover the topics you need. You can use the table of contents and the *Quick*Look Guide to locate information about general topics. You can use the index to find information about a specific topic or a feature from a previous version of Microsoft Excel.

Referencing...

this book after working through the lessons

1 Use the index to locate information about specific topics, and use the table of contents and the *Quick*Look Guide to locate information about general topics.

2 Read the Lesson Summary at the end of each lesson for a brief review of the major tasks in the lesson. The Lesson Summary topics are listed in the same order as they are presented in the lesson.

Certified Microsoft Office User Program

The Certified Microsoft Office User (CMOU) program is designed for business professionals and students who use Microsoft Office 97 products in their daily work. The program enables participants to showcase their skill level to potential employers. It benefits accountants, administrators, executive assistants, program managers, sales representatives, students, and many others. To receive certified user credentials for a software program, candidates must pass a hands-on exam in which they use the program to complete real-world tasks.

The CMOU program offers two levels of certification: Proficient and Expert. The table below indicates the levels available for each Office 97 program. (You can find out more about the certification levels by visiting the CMOU program Web site at http://www.microsoft.com/office/train_cert/)

Software	Proficient level	Expert level
Microsoft Word 97	✔	✔
Microsoft Excel 97	✔	✔
Microsoft Access 97		✔
Microsoft PowerPoint 97		✔
Microsoft Outlook 97		✔
Microsoft FrontPage 97		✔

Microsoft Press offers the following books in the *Step by Step* series as approved courseware for the CMOU exams:

Proficient level:
Microsoft Word 97 Step by Step, by Catapult, Inc. ISBN: 1-57231-313-7
Microsoft Excel 97 Step by Step, by Catapult, Inc. ISBN: 1-57231-314-5

Expert level:
Microsoft Word 97 Step by Step, Advanced Topics by Catapult, Inc.
   ISBN: 1-57231-563-6
Microsoft Excel 97 Step by Step, Advanced Topics by Catapult, Inc.
   ISBN: 1-57231-564-4
Microsoft Access 97 Step by Step, by Catapult, Inc. ISBN: 1-57231-316-1
Microsoft PowerPoint 97 Step by Step, by Perspection, Inc. ISBN: 1-57231-315-3
Microsoft Outlook 97 Step by Step, by Catapult, Inc. ISBN: 1-57231-382-X
Microsoft FrontPage 97 Step by Step, by Catapult, Inc. ISBN: 1-57231-336-6

Candidates may take exams at any participating Sylvan Test Center, participating corporations, or participating employment agencies. Exams have a suggested retail price of $50 each.

To become a candidate for certification, or for more information about the certification process, please visit the CMOU program World Wide Web site at http://www.microsoft.com/office/train_cert/ or call 1-800-933-4493 in the United States.

New Features in Microsoft Excel 97

The following table lists the major new features in Microsoft Excel 97 that are covered in this book. The table shows the lesson in which you can learn how to use each feature. You can also use the index to find specific information about a feature or a task you want to perform.

To learn how to	See
Get help with specific procedures from the Office Assistant	Lesson 1 and Appendix A
Enter lists of data in a worksheet efficiently using AutoReturn	Lesson 1
Undo multiple actions and redo multiple undone actions	Lesson 1
See the range reference where dragged cells will be dropped using ScreenTips	Lesson 1
Write formulas using the Formula palette	Lesson 1
Select formulas from the formula list in the Name box	Lesson 1
See which cells a formula refers to by looking at the color-coded cell references in a formula	Lesson 1
Use the new interface to name a worksheet	Lesson 2
Add worksheet comments with an automatic user name	Lesson 2
Ensure entry of valid data using data validation	Lesson 2
Use worksheet labels in formulas	Lesson 3
Use conditional number formatting to apply cell formatting that changes depending on the value in the cell	Lesson 5
Open a file using Microsoft Outlook	Lesson 6
Apply new fill effects to chart elements	Lesson 9
Switch an embedded chart to a chart sheet and vice versa	Lesson 9
View a worksheet's page layout using Page Break Preview	Lesson 10
Set and change page breaks easily using Page Break Preview	Lesson 10
Track changes and review revisions made to a shared workbook	Lesson 12
Print a history of changes made to a shared workbook	Lesson 12
Work with other Microsoft Office 97 programs	Lesson 13

Corrections, Comments, and Help

Every effort has been made to ensure the accuracy of this book and the contents of the practice files disk. Microsoft Press provides corrections and additional content for its books through the World Wide Web at:

http://www.microsoft.com/mspress/support/

If you have comments, questions, or ideas regarding this book or the practice files disk, please send them to us.

Send e-mail to:
mspinput@microsoft.com

Or send postal mail to:
Microsoft Press
Attn: Step by Step Series Editor
One Microsoft Way
Redmond, WA 98052-6399

Please note that support for the Microsoft Excel 97 software product itself is not offered through the above addresses. For help using Microsoft Excel 97, you can call Microsoft Excel 97 AnswerPoint at (425) 635-7070 on weekdays between 6 a.m. and 6 p.m. Pacific time.

Visit Our World Wide Web Site

We invite you to visit the Microsoft Press World Wide Web site. You can visit us at the following location:

http://www.microsoft.com/mspress/

You'll find descriptions for all of our books, information about ordering titles, notices of special features and events, additional content for Microsoft Press books, and much more.

You can also find out the latest in software developments and news from Microsoft Corporation by visiting the following World Wide Web site:

http://www.microsoft.com/

We look forward to your visit on the Web!

Installing and Using the Practice Files

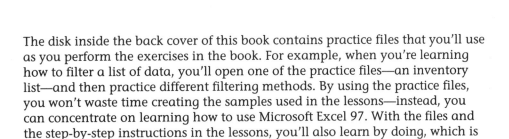

The disk inside the back cover of this book contains practice files that you'll use as you perform the exercises in the book. For example, when you're learning how to filter a list of data, you'll open one of the practice files—an inventory list—and then practice different filtering methods. By using the practice files, you won't waste time creating the samples used in the lessons—instead, you can concentrate on learning how to use Microsoft Excel 97. With the files and the step-by-step instructions in the lessons, you'll also learn by doing, which is an easy and effective way to acquire and remember new skills.

IMPORTANT Before you break the seal on the practice disk package, be sure that this book matches your version of the software. This book is designed for use with Microsoft Excel 97 for the Windows 95 and Windows NT version 4.0 operating systems. To find out what software you're running, you can check the product package or you can start the program, and then on the Help menu at the top of the screen, click About Microsoft Excel. If your product is not compatible with this book, a Step by Step book matching your program is probably available. Please visit our World Wide Web site at http://www.microsoft.com/mspress/ or call 1-800-MSPRESS for more information.

Install the practice files on your computer

Follow these steps to install the practice files on your computer's hard disk so that you can use them with the exercises in this book.

 NOTE If you are new to Windows 95 or Windows NT, you might want to work through Appendix A, "If You're New to Windows 95, Windows NT, or Microsoft Excel," before installing the practice files.

In Windows 95, you will be prompted for a username and password if your computer is configured for user profiles.

Close

1   If your computer isn't on, turn it on now.

2   If you're using Windows NT, press CTRL+ALT+DEL to display a dialog box asking for your username and password. If you are using Windows 95, you will see this dialog box if your computer is connected to a network or is configured for user profiles.

3   Type your username and password in the appropriate boxes, and then click OK. If you see the Welcome dialog box, click the Close button.

4   Remove the disk from the package inside the back cover of this book.

5   Insert the disk in drive A or drive B of your computer.

6   On the taskbar at the bottom of your screen, click the Start button.

The Start menu appears.

7   On the Start menu, click Run.

The Run dialog box appears.

Click Start...   ...and then click Run.

8   In the Open box, type **a:setup** (or **b:setup** if the disk is in drive B). Don't add spaces as you type.

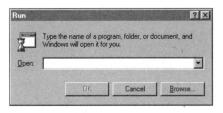

9 Click OK, and then follow the directions on the screen.

The setup program window appears with recommended options pre-selected for you. For best results in using the practice files with this book, accept these preselected settings.

10 When the files have been installed, remove the disk from your drive and replace it in the package inside the back cover of the book.

A folder called Excel SBS Practice has been created on your hard disk, and the practice files have been put in that folder.

Microsoft
Press
Welcome

Camcorder
Files On The
Internet

NOTE In addition to installing the practice files, the Setup program has created two shortcuts on your Desktop. If your computer is set up to connect to the Internet, you can double-click the Microsoft Press Welcome shortcut to visit the Microsoft Press Web site. You can connect to the Web site directly at http://www.microsoft.com/mspress/

You can double-click the Camcorder Files On The Internet shortcut to connect to the *Microsoft Excel 97 Step by Step* Camcorder files Web page. You can copy this page to your computer to view audiovisual demonstrations of how to do a number of tasks in Excel. You can connect to the Web site directly at http://www.microsoft.com/mspress/products/340

Using the Practice Files

Each lesson in this book explains when and how to use any practice files for that lesson. When it's time to use a practice file, the book will list instructions for how to open the file. The lessons are built around scenarios that simulate a real work environment, so you can easily apply the skills you learn to your own work. For the scenarios in this book, imagine that you're the office manager for the Island Tea & Coffee Company, a small company that imports and sells gourmet coffees and teas from around the world.

The screen illustrations in this book might look different than what you see on your screen, depending on how your computer has been set up. To help make your screen match the illustrations in this book, please follow the instructions in Appendix B, "Matching the Exercises."

For those of you who like to know all the details, here's a list of the files included on the practice disk:

Filename	Description
Lesson 1	
Customer List	A list of the Island Tea & Coffee Company's customers
Lesson 2	
No practice file	This lesson begins with a new workbook
Lesson 3	
03 Lesson	A copy of the partially completed workbook from Lesson 2 (or you can open the workbook you saved at the end of Lesson 2, ITC Invoice)
Lesson 4	
04 Lesson	A copy of the partially completed workbook from Lesson 3 (or you can open the workbook you saved at the end of Lesson 3, ITC Invoice)
Review & Practice 1	
No practice file	This Review & Practice begins with a new workbook
Lesson 5	
Expenses Jan 97	An Island Tea & Coffee Company expenses list for January 1997
Expenses Feb 97	An Island Tea & Coffee Company expenses list for February 1997
Expenses Mar 97	An Island Tea & Coffee Company expenses list for March 1997
Lesson 6	
Lesson 6 Inventory	An inventory list for practicing filtering data
Lesson 7	
Lesson 7 Inventory	An inventory list for practicing subtotaling
Inventory Report.doc	A short Microsoft Word document you'll paste a subtotaled Microsoft Excel list into
Review & Practice 2	
R&P 2	Expenses lists for four employees, and a long list that combines all four expenses lists
Lesson 8	
1996order.txt	A text file containing a list of 1996 sales information

Filename	Description
Lesson 9	
Current Orders	A workbook with two short lists and a PivotTable of sales figures for practicing charting
Lesson 10	
1997 Orders	A long list of 1997 sales orders, a PivotTable, and a chart, for practicing printing
Review & Practice 3	
1996exp.txt	A text file containing a list of 1996 expenses
Lesson 11	
1997 Budget	The Island Tea & Coffee Company 1997 budget
Lesson 12	
Shared Inventory List	An inventory history, containing monthly inventory figures for six months
Lesson 13	
Sales Analysis.doc	Microsoft Word document, containing sales analysis
Sales Report.xls	Microsoft Excel document, containing sales data
Review & Practice 4	
R&P 4	A list of the expenses for the 2nd quarter of 1997, and a consolidation of the same list
SUAA Newsletter	A short Microsoft Word file that you'll paste into a Commentary.doc worksheet
Appendix C	
Price list	A price list of available goods

Need Help with the Practice Files?

Every effort has been made to ensure the accuracy of this book and the contents of the practice files disk. If you do run into a problem, Microsoft Press provides corrections for its books through the World Wide Web at:

> http://www.microsoft.com/mspress/support/

We also invite you to visit our main Web page at:

> http://www.microsoft.com/mspress/

You'll find descriptions for all of our books, information about ordering titles, notices of special features and events, additional content for Microsoft Press books, and much more.

Conventions and Features in This Book

You can save time when you use this book by understanding, before you start the lessons, how instructions, keys to press, and so on, are shown in the book. Please take a moment to read the following list, which also points out helpful features of the book that you might want to use.

 NOTE   If you are unfamiliar with Windows 95, Windows NT, or mouse terminology, see Appendix A, "If You're New to Windows 95, Windows NT, or Microsoft Excel."

Conventions

- Hands-on exercises for you to follow are given in numbered lists of steps (1, 2, and so on). An arrowhead bullet (➤) indicates an exercise with only one step.
- Text that you are to type appears in **bold**.
- A plus sign (+) between two key names means that you must press those keys at the same time. For example, "Press ALT+TAB" means that you hold down the ALT key while you press TAB.

The following icons identify the different types of supplementary material:

	Notes labeled	Alert you to
	Note	Additional information for a step.
	Tip	Suggested additional methods for a step or helpful hints.
	Important	Essential information that you should check before continuing with the lesson.
	Troubleshooting	Possible error messages or computer difficulties and their solutions.
	Warning	Possible data loss and tell you how to proceed safely.
	Demonstration	Skills that are demonstrated in audiovisual files available on the World Wide Web.

Other Features of This Book

- You can learn how to use other Microsoft products, such as Outlook and FrontPage, with Excel by reading the shaded boxes throughout the book.

- You can learn about techniques that build on what you learned in a lesson by trying the optional "One Step Further" exercise at the end of the lesson.

- You can get a quick reminder of how to perform the tasks you learned by reading the Lesson Summary at the end of a lesson.

- You can quickly determine what online Help topics are available for additional information by referring to the Help topics listed at the end of each lesson. To learn more about online Help, see Appendix A.

- You can practice the major skills presented in the lessons by working through the Review & Practice sections at the end of each part.

- If you have Web browser software and access to the World Wide Web, you can download audiovisual demonstrations of how to perform some of the more complicated tasks in Excel. Double-click the Camcorder Files On The Internet shortcut that was created on your Desktop when you installed the practice files for this book, or connect directly to http://www.microsoft.com/mspress/products/340/. The Web page that opens contains full instructions for copying and viewing the demonstration files.

Accomplishing Basic Tasks

Working in the Excel Environment

In this lesson you will learn how to:

Estimated time
45 min.

- Open and save a workbook file.
- Navigate through a workbook and a worksheet.
- Enter, edit, and delete data.
- Use AutoComplete and AutoCorrect to speed data entry.
- Move and copy cells and sheets.
- Write and edit simple formulas.

The basic working environment in Microsoft Excel is a workbook file that can contain one or more worksheets. A worksheet is similar to an accountant's ledger, with numbers, text, and calculations lined up in columns and rows. But, unlike in an accountant's ledger, when you type the numbers in Microsoft Excel, the program performs the calculations for you.

With Microsoft Excel, it's easy to enter information into a worksheet, and then change, delete, or add to the information. You don't need to worry about entering your data perfectly or completely the first time; you can always edit it later. You can arrange multiple worksheets within a workbook (for example, you might place all the worksheets for a single client or a single project into one workbook), and then name them so that you can locate the information you need quickly.

In this lesson, you'll learn how to work with worksheets and workbooks; open, save, and close a workbook; and enter and edit data in a worksheet. You'll also learn how to work more efficiently by using features like AutoComplete and AutoCorrect to do some of your work for you, and by writing simple formulas.

Starting the Lesson

If you have not yet started Microsoft Excel or installed the Excel SBS Practice files, refer to "Installing and Using the Practice Files," earlier in this book.

In the following exercises, you'll open the practice file called Customer List, and then save the file with a different name, Lesson 01. This process creates a duplicate of the practice file, which you can work on and modify during the lesson. The original file, Customer List, will remain unchanged and will be used again later in this book.

Open

Open a workbook

1 On the Standard toolbar, click the Open button.

The Open dialog box appears. In this dialog box, you select the folder and the document you want to open. The box labeled Look In shows the folder that is currently selected.

Look In Favorites

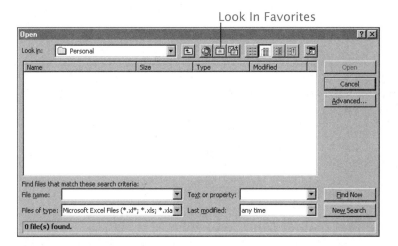

2 Click the Look In Favorites button.

The names of all folders and files that are contained within the selected folder are listed.

3 Be sure that the Excel SBS Practice folder appears in the Look In box. Scroll the window, if necessary.

4 Double-click the folder named Excel SBS Practice.

The list of practice files appears.

5 In the file list, double-click the Customer List file.

The Open dialog box closes, and the Customer List file appears in the document window.

Save the practice file with a new name

When you save a practice file, you give it a name and specify where you want to store it. For each file you use in this book, you'll usually save it in the Excel SBS Practice folder with a new name so that the original practice file will remain unchanged.

 IMPORTANT For the purposes of this book we have elected to show the file extensions. To match the illustrations in this book, click the Start button, point to Programs, and then click Windows Explorer. On the View menu, click Options. On the View tab, clear the Hide MS-DOS File Extension For File Types That Are Registered check box. Click OK.

---

1 On the File menu, click Save As.

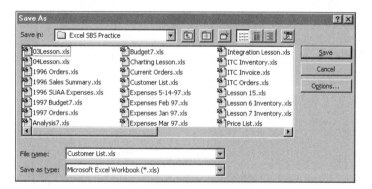

2 Be sure that Excel SBS Practice appears in the Save In box.

If the Excel SBS Practice folder does not appear, repeat steps 2 through 4 of the previous exercise to select the folder.

3 In the File Name box, type **Lesson 01**

4 Click the Save button or press ENTER to close the dialog box and save the file.

Getting Around in a Workbook

In Microsoft Excel, files are called *workbooks*. Workbooks can contain multiple worksheets, as well as chart sheets. You'll learn more about charts and chart sheets in Lesson 9, "Charting to Assess Trends and Relationships." In this lesson, you'll learn about moving around in a worksheet as well as in a workbook that contains worksheets.

Moving Around in a Workbook

The practice file you opened in the previous exercise contains customer information for the Island Tea & Coffee Company. The first worksheet, as shown in the following illustration, contains a list of customer names and addresses, and the remainder of the worksheets are blank. You can select different sheets in a workbook by clicking the Sheet tabs (also called "tabs") that are located at the bottom of each sheet. You can use the Sheet tab scroll buttons to bring hidden sheet tabs into view so that you can select them. The selected sheet is called the *active* sheet.

Sheet tab
scroll buttons   Sheet tabs

Additionally, you can select several sheets at a time, even if they are non-adjacent sheets, and enter the same data on all the active sheets at once. This is particularly useful if you need to set up several worksheets that are identical in some respect (for example, adding common labels to a monthly report).

Select worksheets in a workbook

In this exercise, you select different sheets in the workbook.

1   Click the Sheet tab labeled Sheet2.

Sheet2 becomes the active sheet.

2   Click the tab labeled Customers.

Last Tab Scroll

3 Click the Last Tab Scroll button.

The sheet tabs scroll so that you can see the last tab in the workbook, which is Sheet10. The Customers sheet is still the active sheet.

4 Click the tab labeled Sheet10.

Sheet10 becomes the active sheet.

5 Use the right mouse button to click a Sheet tab scroll button.

A shortcut menu appears, listing the names of all the sheets contained in the workbook.

6 On the shortcut menu, click Customers.

The Customers sheet becomes the active sheet.

Select several worksheets at once

In this exercise, you select several sheets at the same time. All the selected sheets become active and, if you enter data in one of the sheets, the data is automatically entered in all of the other active sheets.

To select a group of non-adjacent sheets, hold down CTRL while you click the Sheet tabs.

1 Click the tab for Sheet2.

2 Hold down SHIFT and click the Sheet4 tab.

Sheet2, Sheet3, and Sheet4 are all selected and active. The word [Group] appears in the title bar next to the filename.

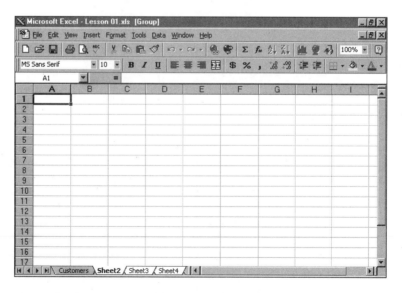

3 Use the right mouse button to click the Sheet2 tab.

4 On the shortcut menu, click Ungroup Sheets.

Only Sheet2 remains active.

7

Ask the Office Assistant for help

If you want to know more about moving around in worksheets, you can enlist help from the Office Assistant.

An Introduction to the Office Assistant

While you are working with Microsoft Office 97, an animated character called the *Office Assistant* pops up on your screen to help you work productively. As you work, you can ask the Office Assistant questions by typing your question, then clicking Search. The Office Assistant then shows you the answer to your question.

You will sometimes see a light bulb next to the Office Assistant—clicking the light bulb displays a tip about the action you are currently performing. You can view more tips by clicking Tips in the Office Assistant balloon. In addition, the Office Assistant is tailored to how you work—after you master a particular skill, the Office Assistant stops offering tips.

You can close any Office Assistant tip or message by pressing ESC.

Clippit, an Office Assistant, in action

The Office Assistant appears in the following situations:

- When you click the Office Assistant button on the Standard toolbar.
- When you choose Microsoft Excel Help on the Help menu or press F1.
- When you type certain phrases.

Office Assistant

The Office Assistant is a shared application—any settings that you change will affect the Office Assistant in other Office 97 programs. You can customize the Office Assistant in two ways. You can:

Determine under what circumstances you want to see the Office Assistant

You can use the right mouse button to click the Office Assistant and click Options to open the Office Assistant dialog box. You can then define when you want the Office Assistant to appear, and what kind of help you want it to offer.

Change your Office Assistant character

You can use the right mouse button to click the Office Assistant and click Options to open the Office Assistant dialog box. Click the Gallery tab.

IMPORTANT If the Office Assistant appears, click the Start Using Microsoft Program option. If the User Name dialog box appears, fill in your name and initials, and then click OK. In the Office Assistant, click the Close button.

For the purposes of this book, the Office Assistant will not appear in the illustrations. If you want to match the illustrations, any time the Office Assistant appears, use the right mouse button to click the Office Assistant, and then click Hide Assistant. If you want to leave Office Assistant on top to help guide you, but it is in your way, simply drag it to another area on the screen.

1 Click the Office Assistant button.

2 In the What Would You Like To Do area, type **Learn about moving around in a worksheet**, and then click Search.

3 Click the Change Options For Entering And Editing Data topic.

Close

4 Read the Help topic, and then click the Close button in the Help window.

Moving Around in a Worksheet

Column headers are also referred to as column letters. Row headers are also referred to as row numbers.

A worksheet consists of *columns* and *rows*. Columns run vertically and are identified by letters, called *column headers*, which run across the top of a worksheet. Rows run horizontally and are identified by numbers, called *row headers*, which run down the left side of a worksheet. The intersection of a row and a column is called a *cell*. Cells are identified according to their positions in the rows and columns. The combination of the column letter and row number for a cell is called the *cell reference*. For example, the cell reference for the cell located in column A and row 1 is A1.

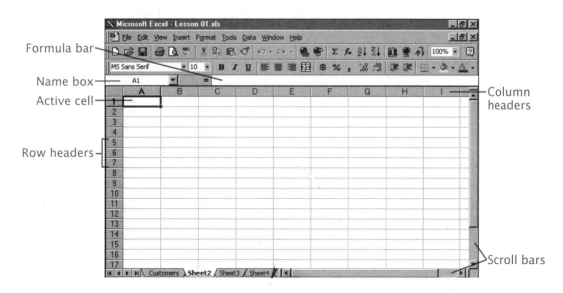

When you select a cell by clicking it, that cell becomes the *active cell* and you can enter data in it. The active cell is surrounded by a heavy border. The cell reference for the active cell appears in the Name box, on the left side of the formula bar, and the corresponding row and column headers become bold and raised. You can also change the active cell by pressing the ENTER key, the TAB key, or the arrow keys.

Scroll bars appear on the right and bottom side of the worksheet, and are used to view different parts of a worksheet quickly when it contains more information than can be displayed on one screen. When you change the view of a worksheet using the scroll bars, the active cell does not change; only your view of the worksheet changes. You can only see a small portion of your worksheet in the Microsoft Excel window (an entire worksheet is 256 columns by 65536 rows), but the scroll bars help you to move around quickly to view any part of the worksheet.

In the following exercises, you'll learn how to select cells and view worksheets.

Select cells on a worksheet

In this exercise, you practice moving around in a worksheet and selecting data.

1 Click the Customers sheet tab to select it.

2 Click the cell at the intersection of column B and row 2.

Cell B2 is selected.

B2		=	Alfreds Futterkiste		
	A	B		C	D
1	Customer ID	Company Name		Contact Name	Contac
2	ALFRE	Alfreds Futterkiste		Maria Anders	Sales Represen
3	ANATR	Ana Trujillo Emparedados y helados		Ana Trujillo	Owner
4	ANTON	Antonio Moreno Taquería		Antonio Moreno	Owner

Because it is the active cell, B2 is surrounded by a heavy border. The cell reference, B2, appears in the Name box, and the headers for column B and row 2 are bold and raised. The contents of the cell appear in the formula bar.

3 Press the down arrow key.

The active cell is now B3.

To drag, point to the first cell, then hold down the mouse button as you move the pointer, and release when the pointer is over the last cell.

4 Press CTRL+HOME.

The active cell moves to the beginning of the worksheet, cell A1.

5 Drag from cell A1 to cell C3.

A rectangular *range* of cells is selected.

Cell A1 is the active cell within the selected range, and the headers for the range (columns A through C and rows 1 through 3) are highlighted.

6 Press ENTER repeatedly.

The active cell moves around within the selected range.

Pressing the TAB key will also move the active cell around within a selected range, from left to right instead of top to bottom.

7 Click cell A5.

Cell A5 becomes the active cell and the range A1 to cell C3 is no longer highlighted.

8 Move the mouse over the bottom border of the cell until the pointer becomes a white arrow, and then double-click the bottom border of the cell.

Double-click this border.

3	ANATR	Ana Trujillo Empa
4	ANTON	Antonio Moreno T
5	AROUN	Around the Horn
6	AUXJO	Aux joyeux ecclé
7	BERGL	Berglunds snabbl

The active cell moves to the bottom of the list of data (cell A119 is selected).

9 Double-click the top border of the active cell.

The active cell moves to the top of the list (cell A1 is selected).

View different areas of the worksheet

You can use the scroll bars to see different areas of your worksheet. In this exercise, you move around your worksheet to familiarize yourself with its different areas.

1 Move the mouse pointer over the vertical scroll box (the box that moves within the vertical scroll bar), and press and hold down the mouse button.

A ScrollTip appears that contains the number of the row at the top of your worksheet window (Row: 1).

2   Drag the scroll box downward as far as it will go.

The ScrollTip displays the number of the row that will be visible at the top of your worksheet window when you release the mouse button.

3   Release the mouse button.

You can now see the data at the end of the list.

4   Drag the horizontal scroll box until the ScrollTip reads Column: D, then release the mouse button.

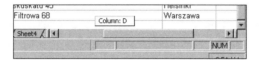

Column D is the leftmost visible column in the worksheet.

5   Press CTRL+HOME to return to cell A1, the first cell of the worksheet.

Display helpful tips

In addition to ScrollTips, there are ScreenTips to help you identify buttons on the toolbars, and comments to add extra information to your worksheet. You'll learn how to add comments to cells in your worksheet in Lesson 2, "Setting Up a Worksheet."

If the ScreenTips do not appear, use the right mouse button to click a toolbar, and then click Customize. Click the Options tab, and then select the Show ScreenTips On Toolbars check box.

1   Move the pointer over any tool on a toolbar.

A ScreenTip will appear below the pointer and will display the name of the button.

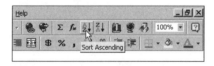

If comment indicators do not appear, on the Tools menu, click Options. On the View tab, click the Comment Indicator Only option button.

2   Move the pointer over cell A1.

A comment appears and displays information entered by the workbook's author. A cell containing a comment is identified by a small red triangle in its upper right corner.

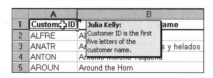

Entering and Editing Data

You can enter text, numbers, and formulas into any cell on a worksheet. When you enter data, Microsoft Excel recognizes it as either text, a date, a number that can be calculated, or a formula. You can also edit or delete anything that you have entered. Whatever you type appears in both the active cell and the formula bar, and can be edited in either location.

Entering Data

Entering data is simple. You first select the cell in which you want the information to appear, type the text or numbers you want, and then press ENTER or TAB to enter what you typed. You can also press an arrow key or click another cell to enter typed information.

You can cancel an entry before you enter it (for example, if you entered it in the wrong cell or misspelled it) by pressing ESC. If you make a mistake while typing, you can use the BACKSPACE key to undo the mistake.

When you first create a worksheet, you'll start by typing in your data. After a while, your worksheet will start to fill up with information, and you might not be able to see all your data on your screen. When you are revising a large worksheet, you can make your editing tasks easier by controlling what you can see on the worksheet.

For example, the customers list is too long to see in one window, so when you enter data at the bottom of the list, you can't see the column headings at the top of the list. You can *freeze* the first row (the row with the column headings) so that it remains visible regardless of where you are working in the list.

Another way to make your editing tasks easier and speed up data entry is by using AutoComplete to type recurring entries in a column. For example, in the customers list, contact titles are repeated for many customers. AutoComplete can save you time by entering these repeated entries for you.

Freeze panes to keep column headings visible

In this exercise, you freeze row 1 so that the column labels will remain visible while you enter new data at the bottom of the list.

If you select cell B2, both row 1 and column A will be frozen.

1 On the Customers sheet, click cell A2.

2 On the Window menu, click Freeze Panes.

The top row, row 1, is frozen. You can scroll down the worksheet, and row 1 will remain in view.

Enter text

A new customer of the Island Tea & Coffee Company needs to be added to the customers list. In this exercise, you enter the Company Name, Contact

Name, and Contact Title of the new customer. Microsoft Excel recognizes text entries as text, and aligns them automatically on the left side of the cell.

1 Click cell B1.

2 Double-click the bottom border of cell B1 to move quickly to the last entry in the column.

The cell containing the last entry in the Company Name column is selected.

3 Click cell B120.

4 Type **Hanari Carnes**, then press TAB.

The new company name is entered, and the next cell on the right is selected.

5 Type **Mario Pontes**, and then press TAB.

The new contact name is entered, and the next cell on the right is selected.

6 Type **Ac**

AutoComplete has guessed, based on the closest match to previous entries in the D column, that you want to enter Accounting Manager and has inserted it for you.

118	Matti Karttunen	Owner/Marketing Assistant	Keskuskat
119	Zbyszek Piestrzeniewicz	Owner	ul. Filtrowa
120	Mario Pontes	Accounting Manager	
121			
122			

7 Press ENTER to complete the entry.

A feature called AutoReturn returns the active cell to the next cell in which you have started to type—in this case cell B121, the next company name.

 TIP In a column of repeated entries, such as the Contact Title column, you can use the right mouse button to click the cell, and then click the Pick From List command on the shortcut menu. A list of all entries available in the column will appear. You can then click the entry you want to enter in the cell.

Enter numbers

In this exercise, you practice entering numbers on a blank worksheet. You enter numbers the same way you enter text: type the number, then press ENTER. Microsoft Excel recognizes numbers and aligns them automatically on the right side of the cell.

1   Click the tab for Sheet2.

Sheet2, a blank worksheet, is the active sheet.

2   In cell B2, type **12**, then press ENTER.

The value 12 is entered in cell B2, and B3 becomes the active cell.

3   In cell B3, type **100**, then press ENTER.

The value 100 is entered in cell B3, and B4 becomes the active cell. Your screen should look similar to the following illustration.

B4	▼	=	
	A	B	C	D
1				
2		12		
3		100		
4				
5				

Making Changes

You can change or edit data in a worksheet by deleting the data, typing a new entry over an existing entry, or changing a few characters in an entry. In the following exercises, you will change data, then practice undoing and redoing deletions and entries.

Delete data

To delete an entry and leave the cell blank, click the cell, and then press DELETE.

1   Click cell B3, type **200**, and then press ENTER.

Your new entry replaces your previous entry.

2   Double-click cell B2.

The data contained in cell B2 is ready to be edited.

B2	▼ X ✓ =	12	
	A	B	C	D
1				
2		12		
3		200		
4				
5				

3   Click between the 1 and the 2 to place the insertion point there, and then press BACKSPACE to erase the 1.

4   Type **5**, then press ENTER.

Cell B2 now contains the number 52.

Undo a previous action

➤ Click the Undo button on the Standard toolbar.

The change you just made to cell B2 is undone, and the value is 12 again.

Undo several previous actions

Undo

1 Point to the Undo button on the Standard toolbar, and then click the down arrow that appears on the right side of the button.

A list of recent actions appears.

2 Drag down the list of actions until the first three actions are highlighted, and then release the mouse button.

Your last three actions are undone. All the numbers you entered in Sheet2 are deleted.

Redo previous actions

Redo

1 Point to the Redo button on the Standard toolbar, and then click the down arrow that appears on the right side of the button.

A list of recently undone actions appears.

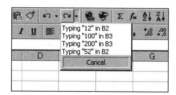

2 Click the fourth action in the list.

All of the actions you had undone in the previous exercise are redone. The number in cell B2 is 52, and the number in B3 is 200.

Making Corrections Using AutoCorrect

To turn off AutoCorrect, on the Tools menu, click AutoCorrect, and then clear the Replace Text As You Type check box.

To undo an AutoCorrect change without turning off AutoCorrect, click the Undo button as soon as the AutoCorrect change is made.

AutoCorrect corrects typing mistakes for you as you type. You don't have to do anything extra, and you might not even be aware that you made a mistake and that it was corrected. AutoCorrect includes an extensive list of commonly misspelled words, but you can customize it by adding your own words to the list. You can also customize AutoCorrect to insert long words or phrases when you type a short abbreviation or acronym.

In the following exercises, you will see how AutoCorrect works, and then customize AutoCorrect to insert the company name, Island Tea & Coffee, when you type the acronym "itc."

Correct commonly misspelled words

1 Click cell B14.

2 Type **teh** followed by a space, type **adn**, and then press ENTER.

When you press SPACEBAR or ENTER, the spelling of the word you just typed is corrected.

Customize AutoCorrect to type long words

1 On the Tools menu, click AutoCorrect.

The AutoCorrect dialog box appears.

2 In the Replace box, type **itc**

3 In the With box, type **Island Tea & Coffee**

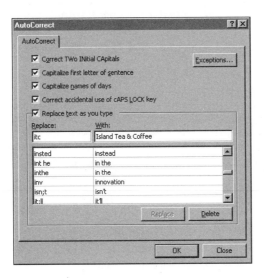

If you have more words to add to the list, click Add, add the desired acronyms and terms, and then click OK to close the dialog box when you are finished.

4 Click OK.

5 Click cell B14.

6 Type **itc**, and then press ENTER.

Island Tea & Coffee is entered in the cell.

Rearranging a Worksheet by Moving and Copying Cells

Sometimes you might enter information in the wrong cells, or you might want to enter the same information in three different places in a workbook. Instead of deleting and re-entering the information, or entering the same information several times, you can move or copy it easily. In the following exercise, you will practice moving and then copying cells.

NOTE Although what you will be doing in the following exercises is commonly referred to as "moving" and "copying" cells, you are actually moving and copying the entries in cells, rather than the cells themselves.

Move cells to a new location on the same worksheet

In this exercise, you move cells by dragging them to another location on your worksheet.

1 On Sheet2, select the B2:B3 range.

2 Point to a border of the selection, and then hold down the mouse button while you drag the selected range to cells D2:D3.

While you drag the selected cells, a tip appears next to the pointer to tell you what range of cells your selection is in.

	A	B	C	D	E	F
1						
2		52				
3		200				
4				D2:D3		
5						

3 When the D2:D3 range is selected, release the mouse button.

The cells are moved to the D2:D3 range.

Move cells to a different worksheet

Dragging cells to move them works well when you are moving the cells short distances on the same worksheet, but if you want to move cells to a different area of the worksheet or to another worksheet, using the toolbar buttons is easier.

Cut

1 On Sheet2, verify that the D2:D3 range is still selected.

2 On the Standard toolbar, click the Cut button.

A moving border appears around the cut selection.

3 Select Sheet3.

4 On Sheet3, select cell B2, and then click the Paste button.

The cut cells are pasted onto Sheet3. The upper-left corner of the cut selection is pasted into the cell you selected on the new sheet.

Paste

Copy cells to another location on the same worksheet

There are many ways to copy cells. In this exercise, you practice two of the easiest methods.

1 On Sheet3, verify that the B2:B3 range is selected.

2 Point to a selection border, and then hold down CTRL while you drag the selection to the F2:F3 range.

While you are dragging the selection, a small plus sign (+) appears next to the pointer to tell you that you are dragging a copy of the selection.

3 Release the mouse button, and then release CTRL.

The cells are copied to a new location.

4 Select the B2:B3 range.

5 Point to a selection border, and then use the right mouse button to drag the selection to the C7:C8 range.

A shortcut menu appears after you release the right mouse button.

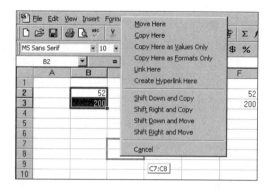

6   On the shortcut menu, click Copy Here.

The cells are copied to the new location.

Move cells to a different worksheet

As with moving cells, dragging cells to copy them works well when you copy the cells across short distances on the same worksheet, but if you want to copy cells to another area of the worksheet or to another worksheet, using the toolbar buttons is easier.

1   On Sheet3, select the range F2:F3.

2   On the Standard toolbar, click the Copy button.

A moving border appears around the copied selection.

Copy

3   Select Sheet2.

4   On Sheet2, select cell C4, and then click the Paste button.

The copied cells are pasted onto Sheet2. The upper-left corner of the copied selection is pasted into the cell you selected on the new sheet.

Paste

Rearranging a Workbook by Moving and Copying Sheets

Now you know how to move and copy cells in a workbook, but suppose you want to rearrange your workbook by moving or copying an entire sheet. This is even simpler than moving and copying cells. In the following exercises, you rearrange your workbook by moving a worksheet, and then copying it.

Move a sheet to a new location in the same workbook

In this exercise, you move Sheet2 behind Sheet3.

1   Click the Sheet2 tab.

2 Drag the Sheet2 tab to the right, until the small triangle appears on the right of the Sheet3 tab. Your screen should look similar to the following illustration.

3 Release the mouse button.

Sheet2 is now behind Sheet3 in the workbook.

Copy a sheet in the same workbook

Suppose you have spent time creating a worksheet, and would like to re-use it as a starting point for another worksheet. Instead of recreating the worksheet, you can just make a copy of it. In this exercise, you create a copy of Sheet2.

1 Click the Sheet2 tab.

2 Hold down CTRL while you drag the Sheet2 tab to the right.

3 When the small triangle appears on the right of the Sheet2 tab, release the mouse button, and then release CTRL.

Sheet2 is now copied, and the copy is named Sheet2 (2).

NOTE You will learn about moving or copying sheets between workbooks in Lesson 5, "Consolidating Multiple Lists."

Writing Simple Formulas

Microsoft Excel was specifically created to calculate numbers. You can place raw data (numbers) in a worksheet, and then tell Microsoft Excel how to calculate the numbers to give you the results you want. You tell Microsoft Excel how you want the numbers calculated by writing a formula. In its simplest form, a formula might be used to add two numbers together. One of the main advantages of using a powerful spreadsheet program like Microsoft Excel is that you can insert a formula in a cell and have it perform a calculation on values that are in other cells. For example, you can enter a formula in a cell to total the values in another range of cells, such as the cells above the formula. Regardless

You'll learn more about the Formula Palette in Lesson 3.

of what numbers you place in the specified range, the correct total will appear in the cell containing the formula.

You can perform calculations with your data using arithmetic operators (such as +, -, and *) and with *functions*, which are built-in formulas. Microsoft Excel comes with hundreds of functions that you can use in formulas to save you time. For example, there are functions that calculate the periodic payment on a loan or annuity (the PMT function), the standard deviation based on a sample (the STDEV function), and the square root of a number (the SQRT function). The Formula Palette makes it easy to write formulas that use these and other functions.

In Microsoft Excel, all formulas begin with an equal sign (=). After the equal sign, you type the formula, and then press ENTER. After the formula has been entered, the cell will display the results of the calculation. You can easily edit the formula to change any part of it.

In the following exercises, you will practice writing and editing simple formulas.

Write a simple formula

In this exercise, you write a formula to add two numbers.

1   On Sheet2, select cell E4.

2   Type **=52+200**, and then press ENTER.

The formula is entered in the cell, and the result of the addition appears.

3   Select cell E4.

The formula appears in the formula bar, and the result appears in the cell.

E4	▼	=	=52+200		
A	B	C	D	E	F
1					
2					
3					
4			52		252
5			200		

4   Select cell E5.

5   Type **=**, and then click cell C4.

The cell reference is entered in the formula.

SUM	▼	X ✓ =	=C4		
A	B	C	D	E	F
1					
2					
3					
4			52		252
5			200		=C4
6					

6   Type **+**, click cell C5, and then press ENTER.

The formula, which adds the contents of cells C4 and C5, is entered in the cell. The result of the addition appears in the cell.

7 Click cell C4, type **100**, and then press ENTER.

The formula in cell E5 displays the result of the addition.

 NOTE You can also write formulas that use a combination of cell references and numbers. For example, you can write a formula that calculates a sales tax of 7% on a price by multiplying .07 times a cell reference.

Edit an existing formula

You can edit a formula by selecting the cell that contains it, and then making changes in the formula bar. You can also double-click the cell and make changes to the formula directly in the cell. In this exercise, you change the operator, and then modify a reference in the formula.

1 Double-click cell E5.

Cell E5 is opened for editing. The cell references in the formula and the cells that are referred to are color-coded to help you see which cells the formula refers to.

2 Select the plus sign (+) by dragging the insertion point over it, type an asterisk (*), and then press ENTER.

The formula multiplies the two cells and displays the result of the multiplication.

3 Double-click cell E5, and then double-click the reference to cell C5 in the formula.

The reference to cell C5 is selected.

SUM	▼ X ✓ =	=C4*C5			
A	B	C	D	E	F
1					
2					
3					
4			100		252
5			200		=C4*C5
6					

4 Click cell E4, and then press ENTER.

The formula now multiplies the value in cell C4 by the value in cell E4. The result is 25200.

 NOTE If you'd like to build up on the skills you learned in this lesson, you can do the One Step Further. Otherwise, skip to "Finish the Lesson."

One Step Further: Creating a Form to Enter Data Easily

In this lesson, you entered data in the Customers sheet by typing text directly in the cells, but it can be time-consuming to move from cell to cell in a worksheet, and you might enter data in the wrong cells. Sometimes it's easier to enter data in a form because you don't have to scroll around in the worksheet or move from cell to cell. By using a form, you can make certain that you're entering the right data in the right place. You can create a data form quickly for any worksheet.

1 Select the Customers sheet, and be sure that a cell within the customer list table is selected.

2 On the Data menu, click Form.

A data entry form is created for the Customers sheet. The column headings in the worksheet become field names on the left side of the form. The form opens with the first record in the worksheet showing.

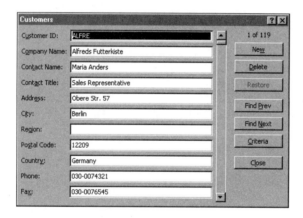

3 On the data form, click New.

The form displays a new blank record, and you can enter data for a new customer. You can move from box to box in the data form by pressing TAB.

4 When you are finished using the data form, click Close.

Finish the lesson

1 On the File menu, click Save.

2 To continue to the next lesson, on the File menu, click Close.

3 If you are finished using Microsoft Excel for now, on the File menu, click Exit.

Lesson Summary

To	Do this	Button
Open a file	On the Standard toolbar, click the Open button. Locate the folder that contains the file you want to open, and then double-click the filename.	
Save a file with another name	On the File menu, click Save As. Open the folder in which you want to save the file, type the new name in the File Name box, and then click Save.	
Select a worksheet	Click the sheet tab.	
Select multiple worksheets	Click the sheet tab for the first worksheet you want to select, hold down SHIFT, and then click the sheet tab for the last worksheet you want to include (hold down CTRL to select non-adjacent sheets).	
Select a cell	Click the cell.	
Select a range of cells	Hold down the mouse button and drag from one corner to the opposite diagonal corner of the range you want.	
Enter data	Select a cell. Type the data, and then press ENTER or select another cell.	
Freeze panes	Select a cell immediately below or to the right of the row or column, and then, on the Window menu, click Freeze Panes.	
Change data	Select the cell containing the data you want to change. Type the new data, and then press ENTER or select another cell.	
Delete data	Select the cell (or range of cells) containing the data you want to delete, and then press DELETE.	

25

To	Do this	Button
Undo an action	On the Standard toolbar, click the Undo button. To undo several actions, click the Undo down arrow, and then select the actions you want to undo.	
Redo an undone action	On the Standard toolbar, click the Redo button. To redo several undone actions, click the Redo down arrow, and then select the actions you want to redo.	
Customize AutoCorrect	On the Tools menu, click AutoCorrect. Type the misspelled word or the acronym in the Replace box, type the correct spelling or long phrase in the With box, and then click OK.	
Move cells	Drag a cell or range of cells by its border.	
Copy cells	Hold down CTRL while you drag a cell or range of cells by its border.	
Move a worksheet	Drag the sheet tab.	
Copy a worksheet	Hold down CTRL while you drag the sheet tab.	
Write a formula	Type =, type the rest of the formula, and then press ENTER.	
Edit a formula	Double-click the cell containing the formula. Select the part of the formula you want to change, type your changes, and then press ENTER.	

For online information about	**On the Help menu, click Contents And Index, click the Index tab, and then type**
Opening and saving files	**opening, files; documents, saving**
Using workbooks	**workbooks**
Using worksheets	**worksheets**
Selecting cells	**selecting, cells**
Changing data	**changing data**
Entering formulas	**entering formulas**
Using data forms	**data forms**

Setting Up a Worksheet

Estimated time

30 min.

In this lesson you will learn how to:

- Add a keyword to a file to quickly find it later.
- Name a worksheet.
- Delete worksheets.
- Set column widths.
- Add comments to a worksheet to document it.
- Control data entry with Data Validation.
- Print a worksheet.

In the next few lessons, you'll learn how to perform many basic Microsoft Excel tasks while creating a template. Templates are great time-savers. When you open a copy of a template, such as the invoice template you are about to create, all the labels, formulas, and formatting are in place and ready for you to build upon. You simply enter your new data and change any formatting that you want, and you're finished.

To find the templates supplied with Microsoft Excel, on the File menu, click New.

To create a template, you can use any workbook that contains formatting and data that you use repeatedly, such as a time sheet, a weekly task list, an inventory form, an order form, or a tax-estimation worksheet, and then simply save your workbook as a template, as you'll do later in this book.

In this lesson, you'll create a new workbook and build the structure of the Island Tea & Coffee Company invoice. You'll add and position text entries, add instructions for users, set data validation rules so that only the appropriate data can be entered in specific cells, and then you'll preview and print a copy of the new (unfinished) invoice. This invoice, which you'll continue to build in Lessons 3 and 4, will be the basis for the template that you'll create in Lesson 4.

 NOTE Although you are starting to build your template in this lesson, you won't save your workbook as a template until the end of Lesson 4, when the template has been completed with formulas and formatting. Until then, the file you work on will be a workbook file like any other.

Setting Up a New Workbook

The first task in setting up a workbook is to open a new workbook and save it with a name that makes sense to you and that will remind you of its contents. Next, you can add a keyword to the file properties (file properties include such things as the title, author, subject, date saved, and so on) so that, in the future, you can find the file quickly by searching for the keyword.

The invoice template that you will be creating will only require one worksheet. In the following exercises, you will open and save a new workbook, name the worksheet that will become the invoice, and then delete all the remaining worksheets in the workbook.

Open a new workbook

Microsoft Excel opens with a new, unsaved workbook ready for you to start using. If you have already been working in Microsoft Excel, however, you might need to open a new workbook to use in this lesson.

If you need to open a new workbook, follow this exercise. If you have just started Microsoft Excel and a new, blank workbook is already open, skip to the next exercise, "Save a new workbook."

New

➤ On the Standard toolbar, click the New button.

A new workbook appears. It will display an unsaved workbook name, such as Book1 or Book2, in the title bar.

Save a new workbook

You are ready to start working on your invoice template. The first step is to save your workbook under a name that describes its contents. In this exercise, you name the new workbook "ITC Invoice" and save it in the Excel SBS Practice folder.

Save

1   On the Standard toolbar, click the Save button.

    The Save As dialog box appears.

2   In the Save As dialog box, click the Look In Favorites button.

    The Favorites folder appears in the Save In box. The Excel SBS Practice folder appears in the list of folders and files.

3   Double-click the Excel SBS Practice folder.

    Excel SBS Practice appears in the Save In box, and the names of the practice files appear in the file list.

4   In the File Name box, drag over the default book name to select it, and then type **ITC Invoice**

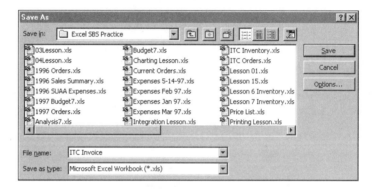

5   Click Save.

    The file is saved with the name ITC Invoice in the Excel SBS Practice folder. The new file name, ITC Invoice, appears in the title bar.

Add a keyword to easily find the file later

The Island Tea & Coffee Company creates many files in the course of conducting business, and it can be tedious to find the specific file or files you need among hundreds of filenames in a list. Microsoft Excel speeds up the process by letting you search for specific files based on *file properties.*

You can add as many file properties as you want.

There are many file properties you can base your search on, including title, author, date last saved, or subject. Some properties, such as date last saved and author, are automatically recorded as file properties, but others, like subject and keyword, must be specifically entered before you can use them in a file search. For example, if you create monthly budget workbooks, you can add the keyword "budget" to each of those files. Later, you can search for the keyword "budget," and Microsoft Excel will find all the files that have that keyword as a file property.

In this exercise, you add the keyword "invoice" to your invoice worksheet. When you create a template from this worksheet, all copies of the template will contain this keyword.

1 On the File menu, click Properties.

The Properties dialog box appears.

2 On the Summary tab, click in the Keywords box, type **invoice**, then click OK.

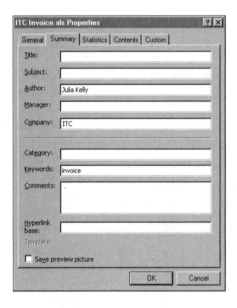

Save

3 On the Standard toolbar, click the Save button.

The new keyword is saved with the file.

Name a worksheet

If a workbook contains several sheets, the sheet names (on the sheet tabs) are important for identification purposes. Even if, as in this case, there will only be one sheet in the workbook, the sheet name is important because it might be used in formulas and it provides the default header for the printed page.

You can easily give your worksheets names that make more sense than "Sheet1." In this exercise, you name the invoice worksheet "Invoice."

1 Double-click the Sheet1 tab.

The sheet name is highlighted.

2 Type **Invoice**, and then press ENTER.

The sheet is renamed "Invoice."

Delete unnecessary sheets to streamline your workbook

By default, new workbooks contain three worksheets. If you don't need the extra sheets, you can streamline your workbook by deleting them—you can always add worksheets later if you need them. In this exercise, you delete the two extra worksheets you won't be needing.

1 Click the Sheet2 tab, hold down SHIFT, and then click the Sheet3 tab.

Sheet2 and Sheet3 are selected.

2 Use the right mouse button to click one of the selected tabs.

A shortcut menu appears.

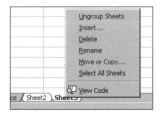

3 Click Delete.

A message box appears, prompting you to confirm the deletion of the worksheets.

4 Click OK.

The extra sheets are deleted.

TIP If you need to insert a worksheet, use the right mouse button to click a sheet tab, click Insert on the shortcut menu, and then double-click the Worksheet icon.

Building a Template

Your invoice template will be a standard form that the Island Tea & Coffee Company sales staff can fill out online, print, and then mail or fax to customers along with their orders.

31

You will create the invoice template in stages. First, you'll build the structure of the invoice by entering labels on the worksheet and arranging them to create a useful layout on the invoice printed page. Then, you'll add formulas to the template so that calculations are automatic, and finally, you'll apply formatting to the template for a professional appearance.

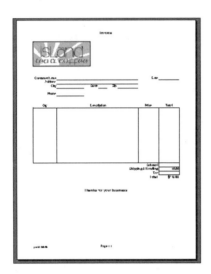

Entering Data to Build the Invoice

In the following exercises, you'll enter text labels that will identify the cells where the sales staff will enter data.

Enter labels for the customer information cells

In this exercise, you enter labels for the customer information cells.

1 In cell A1, type **Customer Name**, and then press ENTER.

2 In cell I1, type **Date**, and then press ENTER.

3 In cell A2, type **Address**, and then press ENTER.

4 In cell A3, type **City**, and then press ENTER.

5 In cell D3, type **State**, and then press ENTER.

6 In cell G3, type **Zip**, and then press ENTER.

7 In cell A5, type **Phone**, and then press ENTER.

Enter labels for the order information area

In this exercise, you enter labels for the order information area.

1 In cell A8, type **Qty**, and then press ENTER.

2 In cell B8, type **Description**, and then press ENTER.

3 In cell I8, type **Price**, and then press ENTER.

4 In cell J8, type **Total**, and then press ENTER.

Your worksheet should look similar to the following illustration.

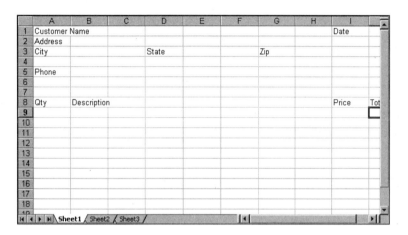

Enter labels for the subtotal and total area

In this exercise, you enter labels for the subtotal/total area.

1 In cell I23, type **Subtotal**, and then press ENTER.

2 In cell I24, type **Shipping & Handling**, and then press ENTER.

3 In cell I25, type **Tax**, and then press ENTER.

4 In cell I26, type **Total**, and then press ENTER.

Enter a farewell note at the bottom of the invoice

In this exercise, you enter a cheerful closing sentence.

➤ In cell A29, type **Thanks for your business!**, and then press ENTER.

Your worksheet should look similar to the following illustration.

33

Arranging the Labels

In the following exercises, you will align the labels and set column widths so that the invoice layout makes the best use of the printed page space.

Align text entries for effective use of available space

By default, Microsoft Excel aligns text entries on the left side of the cell. However, you can modify the alignment. In this exercise, you change label alignment to create a better page layout.

Align Right

1 Select cells A1 through A5, and then click the Align Right button on the Formatting toolbar.

The entries in cells A1 through A5 are aligned to the right.

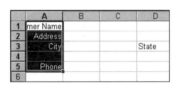

2 Select cells I23 through I26, and then click the Align Right button on the Formatting toolbar.

The entries in cells I23 through I26 are aligned to the right.

3 Select cell D3, hold down CTRL and select cells G3 and I1, and then click the Align Right button on the Formatting toolbar.

The entries in cells D3, G3, and I1 are aligned to the right.

4 Select cell A8, hold down CTRL and select cells I8 and J8, and then click the Center button on the Formatting toolbar.

The entries in cells A8, I8, and J8 are centered.

Center

Merge And Center

5 Select cells B8 through H8, and then click the Merge And Center button on the Formatting toolbar.

The entry in cell B8 is centered across all the selected cells.

34

TIP To indent text from the left without aligning it on the right of the cell, use the right mouse button to select the cell, and then click Format Cells. On the Alignment tab, under Horizontal, select Left (Indent). Under Indent, select a number of character widths to indent by, and then click OK.

Set column widths to space entries

In this exercise, you set column widths to make the best use of space on the invoice page.

1 Drag the right border of the column A header until the entry in cell A1 fits within the cell.

B8	Width: 14.57	=	Desc
	A	↔	B
1	mer Name		
2	Address		

As you drag, a tip appears indicating the column width.

2 Drag the right column border to manually change the column width based on the following table.

Column	Width
B	16
C	2
D	5
E	5
F	2
G	3
H	12

You can set multiple columns to the same width by selecting multiple columns before setting the column width. (Use CTRL to select non-adjacent columns.)

3 Use the right mouse button to click column I.

Column I is selected, and a shortcut menu appears.

4 Click Column Width.

The Column Width dialog box appears.

5 Type 12, and then click OK.

Column I width is set to a width of 12.

6 Repeat steps 3 through 5 to change the width for column J.

Your worksheet should look similar to the following illustration.

Column width is the number of characters (in the default font) that fit in a cell in the column.

35

	A	B	C	D	E	F	G	H	I	J
1	Customer Name								Date	
2	Address									
3	City			State			Zip			
4										
5	Phone									
6										
7										
8	Qty			Description					Price	Tota
9										
10										
11										

Save

7 On the Standard toolbar, click Save.

 NOTE If you want to delete a column or a row, use the right mouse button to click the column header, and then, on the shortcut menu, click Delete. If you want to insert a column or a row, use the right mouse button to click the column to the right of which you want to insert the new column or the row under which you want to insert the new row, and then, on the shortcut menu, click Insert.

Documenting the Template for Other Users

Your invoice will be used by several sales people at Island Tea & Coffee Company. You can ensure that it is used correctly by adding helpful instructions and data validation to the worksheet. Data validation can prevent the entry of inaccurate data (for example, entering text in a cell that should contain a number value), or allow the entry of any type of data but display an error message if an inappropriate data type is entered. This allows you to maintain control over the usefulness of the data.

Add an instruction in a comment

A simple way to insert the current date in a cell is to press CTRL+; and then press ENTER. You can help your co-workers by sharing this tip with them in a comment. In this exercise, you add a comment to the date cell.

1 Select cell J1.

2 On the Insert menu, click Comment.

A comment box, surrounded by a hatched border and containing your user name, appears on the worksheet.

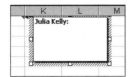

3 Type the instruction **Enter CTRL+; to insert the current date**, and then click outside the comment box.

The comment is entered in the cell. You can read the new comment by holding the mouse pointer over the cell.

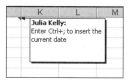

Control data entry with data validation

Sometimes it's critical that the correct type of data is entered in a cell. For example, at Island Tea & Coffee Company, products are sold by the pound, with a 10-pound minimum order per item. You can ensure that quantities in an invoice meet these requirements by adding data validation to the cells in the Qty column. In this exercise, you add data validation to the Qty cells.

1 Select cells A9 through A22.

2 On the Data menu, click Validation.

The Data Validation dialog box appears.

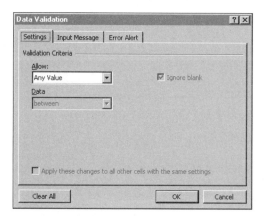

3 Click the Allow down arrow, and then click Whole Number.

4 Click the Data down arrow, and then select Greater Than Or Equal To.

5 In the Minimum box, type **10**

6 Click the Error Alert tab, and then verify that the Style box reads Stop.

7 In the Title box, type **Invalid Entry**, and then, in the Error Message box, type **You must enter a whole number greater than or equal to 10.**

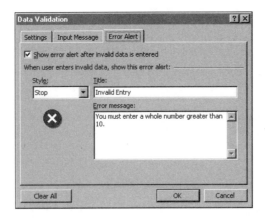

8 Click OK.

9 Select cell A16, type **9**, and then press ENTER.

An error message appears containing the text you entered in the Data Validation dialog box.

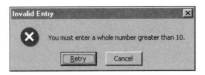

10 Click Retry, type **10**, and then press ENTER.

11 Select cell A16, and then press DELETE to delete the entry.

12 Save your work.

Printing a Copy Quickly

In the following exercises, you will preview your worksheet and print a single copy of it.

Preview the worksheet to see it before you print it

No matter how quickly you need to print a document, it is always a good idea to preview it before you print. Previewing saves time and paper by allowing you to find and fix small errors before sending the worksheet to the printer. It also gives you a clear view of the layout of the printed page.

IMPORTANT   You must have a printer set up and configured to work with Windows 95 before you can use Print Preview.

Print Preview

To print worksheet gridlines, click Page Setup on the File menu, and then select the Gridlines check box on the Sheet tab.

1 On the Standard toolbar, click the Print Preview button.

The Preview window appears, letting you see what the worksheet will look like when you print it. By default, worksheet gridlines are not printed.

2 Move the mouse pointer over the preview page so that the pointer takes the shape of a magnifying glass, and then click.

A close-up of the area you clicked appears.

3 Click the page again.

The full-page preview appears again.

4 Click Close.

Your worksheet reappears.

Print a quick copy

You can use the Print button to quickly print a single copy of the active worksheet, using the default print settings.

Print

➤ On the Standard toolbar, click the Print button.

Your worksheet is sent to the printer.

 NOTE If you'd like to build up on the skills you learned in this lesson, you can do the One Step Further. Otherwise, skip to Finish the Lesson.

One Step Further: Adding a Graphic to a Worksheet

Considering that the invoice will be sent to customers, it needs to look professional and attractive. One way to improve its appearance is to add the company logo to the invoice.

In this exercise, you first insert the logo picture, and then resize the row in which it was pasted to accommodate the picture.

1 Use the right mouse button to click the row 1 header.

Row 1 is selected and a shortcut menu appears.

2 On the shortcut menu, click Insert.

A new row is inserted at the top of the worksheet, above the selected row.

3 Select cell A1.

4 On the Insert menu, point to Picture, and then click From File.

The Insert Picture dialog box appears.

5 In the Look In box, locate the Excel SBS Practice folder, and then double-click the Logo file.

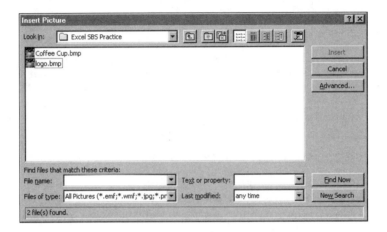

The Island Tea & Coffee Company logo is pasted into the worksheet, with the upper-left corner of the picture in the upper-left corner of the worksheet. The "handles" on the sides and corners of the picture indicate that the picture is selected, and that you can move or resize it.

6 Use the right mouse button to click the graphic, and then, on the short-cut menu, click Format Picture.

7 Click the Properties tab, select the Don't Move Or Size With Cells option button, and then click OK.

8 Move the pointer between the headers for rows 1 and 2 until the pointer becomes a two-headed arrow, and then drag the header border downward until it is taller than the picture (about 110).

Your worksheet should look similar to the following illustration.

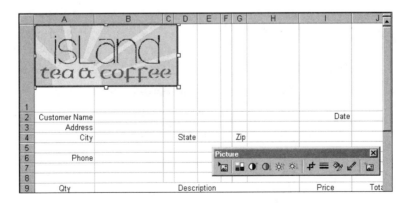

9 Save your work.

Finish the lesson

1 To continue to the next lesson, on the File menu, click Close.
2 If you are finished using Microsoft Excel for now, on the File menu, click Exit.

Lesson Summary

To	Do this	Button
Add a file property	On the File menu, click Properties. On the Summary tab, enter the properties you want, and then click OK.	
Name a worksheet	Double-click the sheet tab, type the new name, and then press ENTER.	
Delete a worksheet	Use the right mouse button to click the appropriate sheet tab, and then, on the shortcut menu, click Delete. Click OK in the message box to confirm the deletion.	
Align cell entries on the right	Select the cells, and then, on the Formatting toolbar, click the Right Align button.	
Center cell entries	Select the cells, and then, on the Formatting toolbar, click the Center button.	
Center a label across columns	Enter the label in the leftmost cell of the selection you want to center across. Select all the cells you want to center across, and then, on the Formatting toolbar, click the Merge And Center button.	
Set column width	Use the right mouse button to click the column header, and then click Column Width. Type a width, and then click OK.	
Add a comment to a cell	On the Insert menu, click Comment. Type your comment text, and then click outside the comment box.	

To	Do this	Button
Set data validation	Select the cells to be validated. On the Data menu, click Validation. Select the validation criteria, and then click OK.	
Preview a worksheet	On the Standard toolbar, click the Print Preview button.	
Print a worksheet	On the Standard toolbar, click the Print button.	

For online information about	On the Help menu, click Contents And Index, click the Index tab, and then type
Adding file properties	**files, properties**
Entering comments	**comments, adding**
Validating data	**data validation**
Printing	**printing**

Writing Formulas

Estimated time
30 min.

In this lesson you will learn how to:

- Find files using a keyword.
- Write formulas to calculate data.
- Name cells.
- Use names and labels in formulas.

As you work through lessons 2, 3, and 4, you are learning basic and important Microsoft Excel tasks while creating a template. In this lesson, you will learn to write formulas in Microsoft Excel by adding formulas to a partially built invoice that is going to become a template. The advantage of creating and using a template is that the time-consuming work of setting up the worksheet is done only once. To use a template, you open a copy of it, and then enter your current data. There is no need to write formulas to calculate totals because the formulas are already in place in the template worksheet.

If you completed Lesson 2 and the One Step Further exercise, you can continue working with the file you previously saved.

In the following exercises, you will add formulas to the invoice to calculate the item totals, subtotal, sales tax, and grand total automatically. You will also learn how to name cells, and then write formulas using names and labels.

To begin this lesson, you locate and open the 03Lesson.xls file in the Excel SBS Practice folder.

Finding Files Using File Properties

As time goes by and the number of Island Tea & Coffee Company invoice files increases, it becomes easier to have Microsoft Excel find the invoice files by searching for file properties that they have in common, rather than looking through folders to find them.

Whether you plan on using your own file or use the 03Lesson.xls file, you need to first locate the file.

Search for a file using a keyword

In this exercise, you search for the invoice keyword to find and open the ITC Invoice file.

Open

1 On the Standard toolbar, click the Open button.

2 Click the Look In down arrow, and then select the letter icon for your hard disk (usually C:).

Microsoft Excel will search the entire hard disk.

3 Click Advanced.

The Advanced Find dialog box appears.

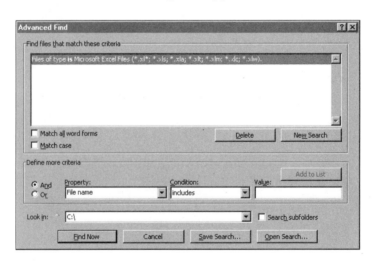

4 In the lower part of the Advanced Find dialog box, click the Property down arrow, and then scroll down and select Keywords.

5 Make sure that Includes Words appears in the Condition box, and then type **invoice** in the Value box.

6 Click Add To List.

The keyword is added to the Find Files That Match These Criteria list at the top of the dialog box.

7   Select the Search Subfolders check box.

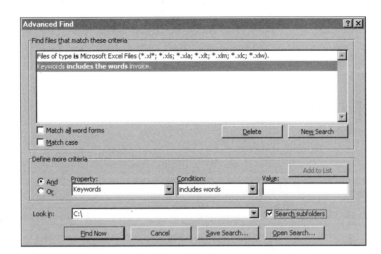

8   Click Find Now.

The results of the search appear in the Open dialog box.

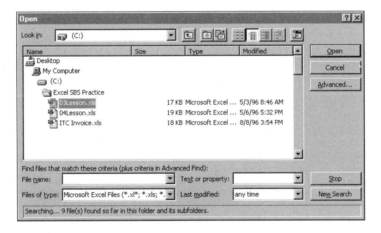

9   Double-click the 03Lesson file. (If you did Lesson 2, you can double-click the ITC Invoice file.)

The file opens.

Save the file with a new name

If you did not do Lesson 2, you need to save the 03Lesson file as ITC Invoice. If you opened the ITC Invoice file in the last exercise, you can skip this exercise.

1 On the File menu, click Save As.

The Save As dialog box opens. Be sure that the Excel SBS Practice folder appears in the Save In box.

2 Double-click in the File Name box, and then type **ITC Invoice**

3 Click Save, or press ENTER.

Adding Calculation Formulas

In the following exercises, you will write formulas to automate the calculations in your invoice. You will first create formulas that compute the total amount for each item in the order, and then add formulas that calculate the order subtotal, sales tax, and grand total.

Add mock data to test the formulas as you write them

When you write a formula, you can tell if it is written correctly by checking the accuracy of the result it displays. In this exercise, you enter a few items of mock data so that you can instantly verify that your formulas were written correctly by checking the results that are immediately displayed.

1 Select cell A10.

2 Type **20**, press TAB, type **Keemun Tea**, and then press ENTER.

When you press ENTER, AutoReturn returns the active cell to the beginning of the next row in your list.

3 Repeat step 2 to enter orders of 30 pounds of Darjeeling Tea and 100 pounds of Kona Coffee.

4 Select cell I10.

5 Type **4.85**, and then press ENTER.

6 Repeat step 5 to enter the price per pound of the Darjeeling Tea (10.15) and the Kona Coffee (5.25).

Your screen should look similar to the following illustration.

	A	B	C	D	E	F	G	H	I	J
2	Customer Name								Date	
3	Address									
4	City			State		Zip				
5										
6	Phone									
7										
8										
9	Qty				Description				Price	Tota
10	20	Keemun tea							4.85	
11	30	Darjeeling tea							10.15	
12	100	Kona coffee							5.25	
13										
14										

Write a formula to compute an item total

In this exercise, you write a formula that calculates an item total by multiplying the quantity ordered by the price.

1 Select cell J10.

2 Type =, click cell A10, type *, click cell I10, and then press ENTER.

J10	▼	= =A10*I10								
	B	C	D	E	F	G	H	I	J	K
8										
9		Description						Price	Total	
10	Keemun tea							4.85	97	
11	Darjeeling tea							10.15		
12	Kona coffee							5.25		

Copy the formula to other cells using AutoFill

All of the cells in the Total column need to use the formula you just wrote. Copying cells one by one can be tedious, but AutoFill provides an easy and quick alternative. It allows you to copy the formula into a range of adjacent cells and automatically adjust the cell references to new cells, so the results will be accurate in all the new formulas. In this exercise, you use AutoFill to quickly copy the formula you created in the previous exercise into additional cells.

1 Select cell J10.

2 Move the mouse pointer over the small black box, also called *fill handle*, located in the lower right corner of the active cell, until the pointer becomes a black cross shape.

In Lesson 4, you will apply formatting to hide the zeroes.

3 Drag the fill handle down to cell J23, and then release the mouse button.

The formula is copied into cells J11 through J23. Cells J13 through J23 display zeroes because Microsoft Excel will interpret the blank cells from A13 to A23 and I13 to I23 as having a value of zero.

Add a SUM formula to calculate the order total

In this exercise, you write a formula that adds up the total price of items ordered. You use AutoSum to write the formula quickly.

1 Select cell J24.

2 On the Standard toolbar, click the AutoSum button.

AutoSum inserts a formula that uses the SUM function, displays a moving border around the range Microsoft Excel anticipates you want to add up, and inserts the range reference in your formula. In this case, the range AutoSum has selected (J10 through J23) is correct.

Σ

AutoSum

If the AutoSum range isn't correct, simply drag the correct range before pressing ENTER.

Price	Total
4.85	97
10.15	304.5
5.25	525
	0
	0
	0
	0
	0
	0
	0
	0
	0
	0
	0
Subtotal	=SUM(J10:J23)
& Handling	
Tax	

3 Press ENTER.

The result of the SUM formula, 926.5, appears in the subtotal cell.

Calculate sales tax

The Island Tea & Coffee Company must charge 7% tax on all orders, and you want the invoice to calculate the tax automatically. In this exercise, you write a formula that calculates tax based on the subtotal cell.

1 Select cell J26.

2 Type =, click cell J24, type ***.07**, and then press ENTER.

The tax formula is entered.

In Lesson 4, you'll apply formatting to display the result as dollars and cents, with two decimal places.

=J24*0.07						
D	E	F	G	H	I	J
						0
					Subtotal	926.5
					Shipping & Handling	
					Tax	64.855
					Total	

3 Save your work.

Using Cell Names and Labels to Make Formulas Easier to Understand

All the formulas you've written so far are correct and functional, but when you read them, it's not immediately clear which values are being calculated. You can identify specific cells and ranges more clearly by giving them *names*, and then use those names instead of cell references when you write formulas. For example, the formula: =Price*Qty is instantly understandable, whereas =A16*I16 might not be so clear.

In the following exercises, you will name some of the cells in the invoice, and then write formulas using the new names.

Name cells to use in formulas

In this exercise, you name the Subtotal, Shipping & Handling, and Tax cells.

You can also use row and column labels in your formulas, without having to name the cells first.

1 Select the range I24 through J26.

This range contains the Subtotal, Shipping & Handling, and Tax labels and data cells. Be sure to select both the cells that include labels and the cells that include data.

2 On the Insert menu, point to Name, and then click Create.

The Create Names dialog box appears. The Left Column check box is selected because Microsoft Excel recognizes labels are located in the left column of the selected range.

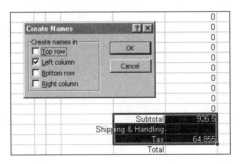

3 Click OK.

Cells J24 through J26 are named with the labels in cells I24 through I26.

4 On the formula bar, click the Name Box down arrow.

The names you created are listed.

5 Click Subtotal.

The cell named Subtotal is selected.

Write a formula using cell names

In this exercise, you write a formula in the Total cell that sums the named cells.

1 Select cell J27, and type =

The Functions list replaces the Name Box list.

2 On the Functions list, click SUM.

The Formula palette appears to help you write the SUM formula. The Number 1 box is highlighted.

3 Click cell J24, named Subtotal.

The cell name is inserted in the Number 1 box.

4 Press TAB, click cell J25 (named Shipping___Handling), press TAB, and then click cell J26 (named Tax).

The cell names are inserted in the Formula palette.

Spaces and ampersands (&) are not allowed in cell names, so Microsoft Excel changes Shipping & Handling to Shipping ___Handling when it creates the cell name.

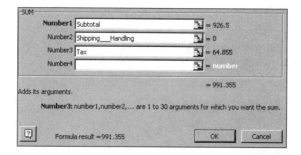

5 Click OK.

The SUM formula is entered in the Total cell. It is now easy to discern which cells are being calculated because you can read their names in the formula.

	B	C	D	E	F	G	H	I	J	K	
	J27			=	=SUM(Subtotal,Shipping___Handling,Tax)						
24								Subtotal	926.5		
25								Shipping & Handling			
26								Tax	64.855		
27								Total	991.355		
28											

Use labels in formulas

When cells have identifying labels nearby, you can often write clear formulas using those labels instead of cell references and instead of naming the cells. Using labels is quicker than using names because you don't have to perform the extra steps required to name cells. But there are instances in which using names is more efficient than using labels. For example, if you need to include the label of a range of cells in a formula, you must drag the whole range, but if the range is named you can simply insert its name. Also, you can name a non-contiguous range of cells, but you cannot label it; or, you might set up your worksheet so that the labels are too far away from the data to be recognizable to Microsoft Excel as labels.

In the ITC Invoice worksheet, Microsoft Excel automatically recognizes the labels for the Qty and Price columns. When you type a label into your formula, Microsoft Excel knows which cell to calculate. In this exercise, you rewrite your total price formula using labels.

1 In cell J10, type **=Qty*Price**, and press ENTER.

	J10		=	=Qty*Price						
	B	C	D	E	F	G	H	I	J	K
8										
9				Description				Price	Total	
10	Keemun tea							4.85	97	
11	Darjeeling tea							10.15	304.5	
12	Kona coffee							5.25	525	

Your new formula with labels is clearer than the old formula with cell references. In addition, if you change the label in the worksheet (for example, if you change Qty to Quantity in cell A10), the formula will change automatically to use the new label.

2 Use AutoFill to copy the new formula in cells J11 through J23.

3 Save your work.

 NOTE If you'd like to build up on the skills you learned in this lesson, you can do the One Step Further. Otherwise, skip to "Finish the Lesson."

One Step Further: Calculating a Specific Cost

You want to automate the calculation of the shipping charge for an order so that you do not have to look up the charge manually each time you fill out an invoice. In this section, you write a formula that sums the total weight of the order (in the Qty column), and then applies a lower shipping charge for orders under 50 pounds and a higher shipping charge for orders of 50 pounds or more.

In order to write your formula properly, you will have to use an IF function, a *logical* function that evaluates whether a mathematical statement is true or false. If the mathematical statement is true, the IF formula returns one value; if the statement is false, the IF formula returns another value.

An example of an IF formula is =IF(A3<5,100,350). This equation means that if A3 is less than 5, the value returned will be 100; if A3 is 5 or higher than 5, the value returned will be 350.

A function is a calculation tool that a formula can use; a formula is a mathematical equation that begins with an equal sign and returns a calculated value.

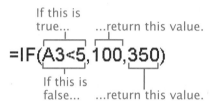

In the following exercises, you will write an IF formula that determines a shipping charge ($10 or $20) based on the order weight (less than 50 pounds, or 50 pounds and up). The IF formula will determine the order weight by using a *nested* SUM function. A nested function is a function within another function; in this case, the SUM function will be contained within the IF function. Microsoft Excel will calculate the SUM function first, and then the IF function will be calculated using the result of the SUM function.

Name the Qty range

In this exercise, you name the range of cells in the Qty column because a name is more efficient than a label when you're summing a range of cells.

1 Select the range A10 through A23.

2 On the formula bar, click in the Name Box.

The cell reference is highlighted.

3 Type **Pounds**, and then press ENTER.

The new name appears in the Name Box. Be sure you press ENTER before you click another cell.

Calculate the shipping cost using a named cell

In this exercise, you write the formula that determines the shipping charge.

1   On the formula bar, click the Name Box down arrow, and then click Shipping___Handling.

The cell named Shipping___Handling becomes the active cell.

2   Type =, and then click the Name Box down arrow, which is now called the Functions down arrow since you've begun to write a formula.

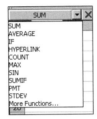

3   In the Functions list, click IF.

The Formula palette opens up to help you write the IF formula. The insertion point is in the Logical_Test box, which is the first of the three *arguments*, or components, required by the IF function.

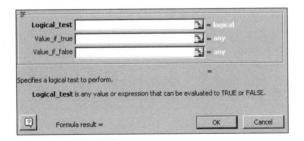

4   Type **sum(Pounds)<50**, and then press TAB.

The sum(Pounds)<50 statement is entered in the Formula palette as well as in the formula, and the insertion point moves to the Value_If_True box. The nested function, SUM(Pounds), has been inserted into the IF formula.

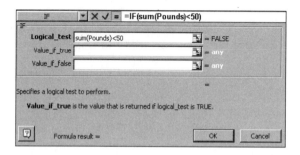

5 In the Value_If_True box, type **10**, and then press TAB.

6 In the Value_If_False box, type **20**, and then click OK.

The IF formula that calculates a shipping & handling charge based on the weight of the order is entered in the Shipping___Handling cell.

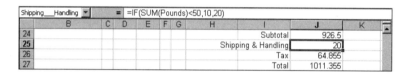

7 Save your work.

 TROUBLESHOOTING When you type a function name, such as SUM, be sure to type it in lowercase. This is a good way to check whether you've typed the function name correctly; if you have spelled it correctly, it will be converted to uppercase when you enter the formula. If you get an error message and the function name is still lowercase, check the spelling.

Finish the lesson

1 To continue to the next lesson, on the File menu, click Close.

2 If you are finished using Microsoft Excel for now, on the File menu, click Exit.

Lesson Summary

To	Do this	Button
Search for a file based on a keyword	Click the Open button, then select your hard disk or a folder to search. Click the Advanced button, select Keywords in the Property box, and then type the keyword in the Value box. Click Add To List, and then select the Search Sub-folders check box. Click Find Now.	
Copy cells using AutoFill	Drag the fill handle down to the last cell you want to include, and then release the mouse button.	
Sum a range using AutoSum	Click the cell where you want to insert the SUM formula, and then click the AutoSum button. Define the range you want to sum by dragging, and then press ENTER.	Σ
Create cell names using labels in adjacent cells	Select a range that includes the cells to be named and the cells containing the name labels. On the Insert menu, point to Name, then click Create. Be sure the correct label location is checked, and then click OK.	
Use names in formulas	Click the named cell to insert in the formula.	
Use labels in formulas	Type the data label in the formula.	
Write a formula using the Formula palette	Type =, then select a function name from the Functions list. Click cells to paste them into the Formula palette boxes, and then click OK when you are finished.	

For online information about	On the Help menu, click Contents And Index, click the Index tab, and then type
Searching files	**searching**
AutoFill	**autofill**
Naming cells	**naming, cells**
Cell labels (in formulas)	**labels in formulas**
IF function	**IF worksheet function**

Formatting Your Worksheet for a Professional Look

Estimated time
45 min.

In this lesson you will learn how to:

- Format cells.
- Create, apply, and change styles.
- Format numbers.
- Create a custom number format.
- Create custom headers and footers.
- Save a workbook as a template.

Now that you have automated the calculations in your invoice using formulas, you are ready to start formatting the invoice page to make it look professional. Formatting also allows you to make your worksheet easier to read and group data visually, for example. You can format fonts, cell borders, and cell shading, as well as the way numbers are displayed. You can create styles, which are packages of formatting attributes, to save you time in the future when you want to change the formatting of a group of cells. You can also create headers and footers that print on every page, and include codes that automatically print the current date or number of pages in the printed document. After you finish formatting your invoice worksheet, you'll save it as a template so that Island Tea & Coffee Company employees can easily open a copy of the invoice and fill it out.

Open a file and save it with a new name

As you begin this lesson, one of your co-workers has partially formatted your invoice worksheet for you. But he has been called away on other business, and has asked you to complete the invoice formatting.

Open

1　On the Standard toolbar, click the Open button.

2　In the Open dialog box, click the Look In Favorites button.

3　In the file list, double-click the Excel SBS Practice folder, and then double-click the 04Lesson file.

The Open dialog box closes, and the 04Lesson file appears in the document window.

4　On the File menu, click Save As.

The Save As dialog box opens. Be sure that the Excel SBS Practice folder appears in the Save In box.

5　In the File Name box, type **ITC Invoice**

6　Click the Save button or press ENTER.

Save

If a dialog box appears asking you confirm that you want to replace the existing file, click Yes.

Formatting Cells

In the following exercises, you will practice formatting with fonts and learn how to use styles to save time when changing cell formatting. You will also practice formatting borders and cell shading, as well as setting page margins so that the invoice fits in the center of a single page.

Format fonts

A co-worker at Island Tea & Coffee Company has formatted part of the invoice worksheet for you, but didn't complete the job. You need to format the remaining labels to make the worksheet look professional enough to be sent out to customers. In this exercise, you change the font for one of the labels, and then apply the new formatting to other labels.

1　Select cell A9.

Font

2　On the Formatting toolbar, click the Font down arrow, and then select Times New Roman.

Font Size

3　On the Formatting toolbar, click the Font Size down arrow, and then select 12.

Bold

4 On the Formatting toolbar, click the Bold button.

Your screen should look similar to the following illustration.

A9		=	Qty					
A	B	C D	E F G	H	I	J
8						
9	**Qty**	Description		Price	Tot
10	20	Keemun tea		4.85	
11	30	Darjeeling tea		10.15	
12	100	Kona coffee		5.25	
13					

Format Painter

5 With cell A9 still selected, on the Standard toolbar, double-click the Format Painter button.

The mouse pointer takes the shape of the Format Painter button face. Until you click the Format Painter button again to turn it off, the formatting from cell A9 will be applied to every cell you click.

6 Click cell B9, then cell I9, and then cell J9.

The new formatting is applied to all the selected cells.

7 On the Standard toolbar, click the Format Painter button to turn it off.

Your screen should look similar to the following illustration.

A	B	C D	E F G	H	I	J
8						
9	**Qty**	**Description**		**Price**	**Tot**
10	20	Keemun tea		4.85	
11	30	Darjeeling tea		10.15	
12	100	Kona coffee		5.25	
13					

Create styles by example

Applying formatting is a simple procedure, but if you have to apply the same formatting to several worksheets it can become quite tedious. Suppose you have several worksheets in a workbook that all have the same types of labels (such as titles and subtitles), and you need to change the formatting of all the labels. You can save a lot of time by applying a *style* instead of reapplying the formatting: you can simply change the style definition instead of reformatting each individual cell.

A style is a collection of formatting attributes such as font, font size, bold, italic, cell shading, or color, and is simple to create, apply, and change. When you apply a style to a cell, all of the formatting attributes contained in the style are applied to the cell. When you change a formatting attribute in a style (for example, you might change the font from Times New Roman to Tahoma), the attribute is automatically changed in all cells to which the style has been applied.

All Island Tea & Coffee Company documentation that will be seen by customers has to be approved by the Marketing manager. Considering that the Marketing manager will most likely request formatting changes, you have decided to set up the invoice formatting using styles to speed up future modifications. If you need to change the formatting later, you can simply redefine the style and the changes will be reflected in all the cells to which that style has been applied. In this exercise, you create a style based on existing cell formatting, and then apply the style to several cells.

1 Select cell A9.

You can remove an attribute from a style definition by clearing the appropriate check box in the Style dialog box.

2 On the Format menu, click Style.

The Style dialog box appears, and the Style Name box is highlighted. The dialog box lists the attributes associated with the style shown in the Style Name box.

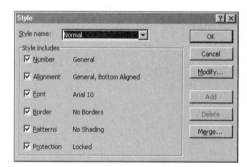

3 In the Style Name box, type **Label**, and then click OK.

The formatting applied to cell A9 is now available as a style named Label.

4 Click cell B9, and then hold down CTRL and click cells I9 and J9.

The three remaining information labels are selected.

5 On the Format menu, click Style. Click the Style Name down arrow, select Label, and then click OK.

The Label style is applied to all four information labels.

6 Select cells B9 through H9, and then click the Merge And Center button.

The Description text is centered, and the Label style continues to be applied.

Merge And Center

Change a style definition

You have just received the formatting changes requested by the Marketing manager. In this exercise, you change the font in the labels by simply modifying the Label style definition.

1 Click cell A9.

2 On the Format menu, click Style.

The Style dialog box appears.

3 On the Style dialog box, click Modify.

The Format Cells dialog box appears.

4 Click the Font tab, select Arial in the Font list, and then 10 in the Size list.

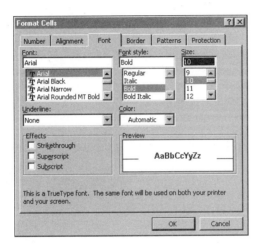

5 Click OK, and then click OK again.

All of the labels on the worksheet are reformatted. Your screen should look similar to the following illustration.

	A	B	C	D	E	F	G	H	I	J
8										
9	**Qty**				**Description**				**Price**	**Tot**
10	20	Keemun tea							4.85	
11	30	Darjeeling tea							10.15	
12	100	Kona coffee							5.25	
13										

Apply borders

Right now, your invoice is full of information that is not easily identifiable. In order to make the invoice more usable for the other employees of the Island Tea & Coffee Company and more readable for your customers, you decide to break the page into clearly defined areas. In this exercise, you apply borders to visually separate different areas of information.

TIP You can quickly select a range of cells by typing the range reference in the Name Box, and then pressing ENTER. For example, if you want to select the range A22 through A35, you can type **A22:A35** in the Name Box, and then press ENTER. The range will be selected.

1 Select cells A10 through A23, and then hold down CTRL and select cells B10 through H23, I10 through I23, and J10 through J23.

The ranges containing order information are selected. You can select each range individually and place a border around it, but you can also save time by selecting all of the individual ranges that you want to place borders around as if they were non-adjacent, using the CTRL key, and placing borders around each of the ranges all at once.

Borders

2 On the Formatting toolbar, click the Borders down arrow.

The Borders palette appears.

3 Click the top border of the Borders palette, and then drag it onto the worksheet.

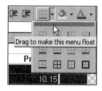

The Borders palette "floats" on the worksheet, which means it can be placed anywhere that is convenient, rather than being docked at one edge of the document window.

4 Click the Outline border button.

An Outline border is applied to each of the selected ranges.

5 Select cells J24 through J26, and then click the outline-and-inside border button.

6 On the Borders palette, click the Close button.

Your worksheet should look similar to the following illustration.

	B	C	D	E	F	G	H	I	J	K
13									0	
14									0	
15									0	
16									0	
17									0	
18									0	
19									0	
20									0	
21									0	
22									0	
23									0	
24								Subtotal	926.5	
25								Shipping & Handling	20	
26								Tax	64.855	
27								**Total**	**1011.355**	
28										

Apply shading

In order to ensure that your colleagues at the Island Tea & Coffee Company will not be entering information in cells that contain formulas, you decide to format them differently. Considering that one of the company's internal formatting conventions is that information is not entered into shaded cells, you elect to follow this convention. In this exercise, you apply shading to the cells that contain formulas as a visual reminder to users not to enter information in those cells.

1 Select cells J10 through J27.

Fill Color

You can also drag the Fill Color palette onto the worksheet.

2 On the Formatting toolbar, click the Fill Color down arrow, and then click the palest blue color.

Your screen should look similar to the following illustration.

	B	C	D	E	F	G	H	I	J	K
9					Description			Price	Total	
10	Keemun tea							4.85	97	
11	Darjeeling tea							10.15	304.5	
12	Kona coffee							5.25	525	
13									0	
14									0	
15									0	
16									0	
17									0	
18									0	
19									0	
20									0	
21									0	
22									0	
23									0	
24								Subtotal	926.5	
25								Shipping & Handling	20	
26								Tax	64.855	

63

Set page margins

Before printing your invoice, you preview it to make sure that it all fits on one page. In this exercise, you change the page margins so that the entire invoice fits on a single page, center the invoice on the printed page, and preview the invoice.

1 On the File menu, click Page Setup.

The Page Setup dialog box appears.

2 Click the Margins tab.

3 Double-click in the Left box, and then type **.5**

4 Double-click in the Right box, and then type **.5**

5 In the Center On Page area, select the Horizontally check box, and then click Print Preview.

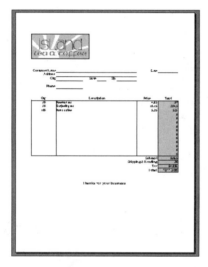

6 Click Close.

7 Save your work.

Your screen should look similar to the following illustration.

Formatting Numbers

Number formatting determines the display of number values, and such formatting takes effect only when a cell contains a number. By default, all the cells in a worksheet use the General number format, in which extra zeroes on the right of the decimal point are left out, all calculated decimal places are shown, and numbers are aligned on the right. For example, in column J, the formula results look like "general numbers" rather than dollars and cents.

You are now ready to finalize your invoice by formatting the numbers. In the following exercises, you will format the cells located in the Total column to display numbers as prices, remove the extra zeroes in the Total column, and format the Qty column to display numbers with the suffix "lbs," as in "100 lbs."

Format numbers to look like prices

In order to have the number formatting in the invoice look like product prices, you need to modify the formatting of the Total column. In this exercise, you format numbers in the Total column to have two decimal places and a thousands separator.

1 Select cells I10 through J26.

2 Use the right mouse button to click the selection, and then, on the shortcut menu, click Format Cells.

The Format Cells dialog box appears.

3 Click the Number tab.

4 In the Category list, select Number, verify that the number in the Decimal Places box is 2, and then select the Use 1000 Separator (,) check box.

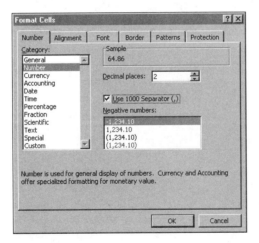

5 Click OK.

All the numbers in the Totals column are rounded to two decimal places, and extra zeroes are displayed to fill out the two decimal places on the right of the decimal point.

6 Select cell I10, and then hold down CTRL and click cells J10, J24, and J27.

7 Use the right mouse button to click any one of the selected cells, and then, on the shortcut menu, click Format Cells.

8 On the Number tab, select the category Currency, then click OK.

Your screen should look similar to the following illustration.

	B	C	D	E	F	G	H	I	J	K
9	Description							Price	Total	
10	Keemun tea							$4.85	$97.00	
11	Darjeeling tea							10.15	304.50	
12	Kona coffee							5.25	525.00	
13									0.00	
14									0.00	
15									0.00	
16									0.00	
17									0.00	
18									0.00	
19									0.00	
20									0.00	
21									0.00	
22									0.00	
23									0.00	
24								Subtotal	$926.50	
25								Shipping & Handling	20.00	
26								Tax	64.86	
27								Total	$1,011.36	
28										

Invoice

Format numbers using a custom number format

You need to include the suffix "lbs" after entries in the Qty column. This is to make sure that the employees of the Island Tea & Coffee Company using the invoice know to enter quantities in pounds in this column, and to make it clear to customers that the amount of each order is measured in pounds. In this exercise, you format the numbers in the Qty column to include the "lbs" text suffix.

1 Select cells A10 through A23, use the right mouse button to click the selection, and then, on the shortcut menu, click Format Cells.

2 In the Category list, click Custom.

3 In the Type box, select the entry, then type **0 "lbs"**

Be sure you type a zero, not the letter O.

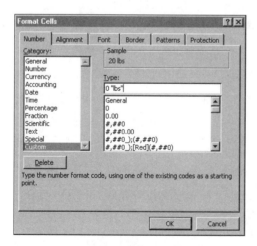

4 Click OK.

The Custom number format is applied, and saved as a Custom format that you can apply again later.

	A	B
9	**Qty**	
10	20 lbs	Keemun tea
11	30 lbs	Darjeeling tea
12	100 lbs	Kona coffee
13		
14		

 NOTE A custom format is similar to a style. A style encompasses many aspects of a cell's formatting, including the number format; a custom number format is like any other number format. In fact, you can create a style that includes your new custom number format.

Turn off zeroes

The formulas located in the Totals column that don't have data to calculate are displaying values of zero, and that might be confusing to future users and to customers. In this exercise, you turn off the zero values display.

1 On the Tools menu, click Options.

The Options dialog box appears.

2 Click the View tab, clear the Zero Values check box, and then click OK.

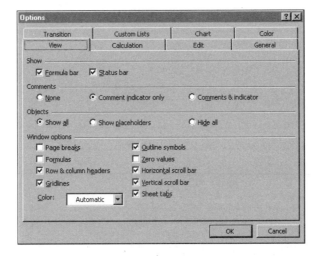

The extraneous zero values on the worksheet are hidden.

Creating Custom Headers and Footers

By default, Microsoft Excel creates no headers or footers, but you can easily create and customize the header and/or the footer, if you want.

Create a custom header

After looking at the ITC invoice in the Print Preview window, you decide that it needs a custom header. In this exercise, you create a custom header to match the rest of the invoice.

1   On the File menu, click Page Setup.

The Page Setup dialog box appears.

2   Click the Header/Footer tab.

3   Click Custom Header.

The Header dialog box appears.

Font button

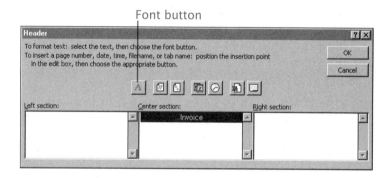

4   In the Center box, type **Invoice**, double-click the text to select it, and then click the Font button.

The Font dialog box appears

5   In the Font Style box, select Bold, and in the Size box, select 12, and then click OK.

The Font dialog box closes.

6   In the Header dialog box, click OK.

The Header dialog box closes. You can see the changes to your header in the Header/Footer tab.

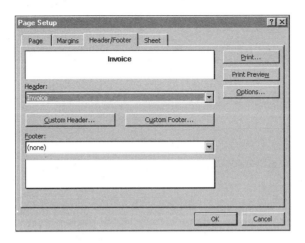

Create a custom footer

In order to track each invoice more easily, you decide to add useful information in the footer. In this exercise, you create a footer that will display the print date as well as the individual page number and number of pages on each invoice page.

1 On the Header/Footer tab, click Custom Footer.

2 In the Left Section box, type **printed**

3 Press SPACEBAR, and then click the Date button.

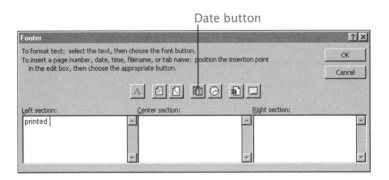

4 Select all the text in the Left Section box, and then click the Font button.

The Font dialog box appears.

5 Select 8 in the Size box, and then click OK.

The Font dialog box closes.

6 In the Center Section, type **Page**, and then press SPACEBAR.

7 Click the Page button, press SPACEBAR, type **of**, and then press SPACEBAR.

8 Click the Pages button, press SPACEBAR, and then type **Pages**

Page button

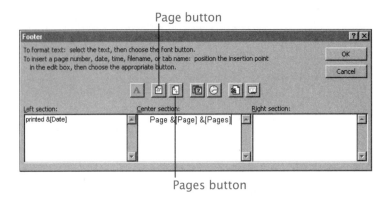

Pages button

The Page and Pages codes will automatically appear, and print the individual page number and the total number of pages in the invoice, for example, "Page 1 of 2."

9 Click OK to close the Footer dialog box, and then click OK to close the Page Setup dialog box.

Saving Your Workbook as a Template to Re-Use It Easily

Now that you are finished building the ITC invoice, you are ready to save it as a template. In the following exercises, you will delete the mock data you inserted during the creation of the invoice and save the workbook as a template.

Delete the mock data

➤ Select cells A10 through I12, and then press DELETE.

The mock data is deleted and the formula cells are cleared, but the important formatting work that you've done remains. The Shipping & Handling value remains because the cell contents are based on the result of the formula you created in Lesson 3, "Writing Formulas."

Save a workbook as a template

Your invoice is now ready to be saved as a template. In this exercise, you save the workbook as a template.

1 On the File menu, click Save As.

2 In the Save As Type box, select Template.

The filename automatically changes to ITC Invoice.xlt.

3 In the Save In box, locate the Spreadsheet Solutions folder.

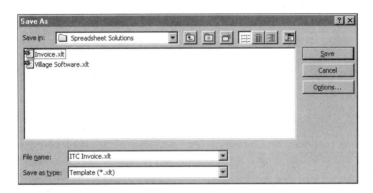

4 Click Save.

The workbook is saved as a template in the Spreadsheet Solutions folder.

5 On the File menu, click Close.

Open a copy of the template

The template is complete and available to any Island Tea & Coffee Company employee who has access to your templates folder. In this exercise, you verify that your invoice opens correctly and looks the way you want.

1 On the File menu, click New.

2 Click the Spreadsheet Solutions tab.

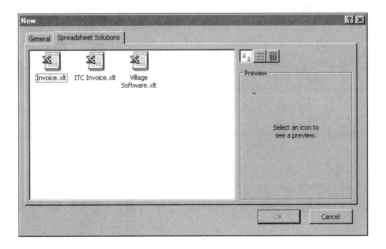

3 Double-click the ITC Invoice icon.

A copy of your invoice, temporarily named ITC Invoice1, opens and is ready to be filled out and saved with a permanent name.

4 Close the ITC Invoice File. If prompted to save, click No.

If You Have Microsoft FrontPage...

If you have Microsoft FrontPage, you can place a link to your template in a Web page on the company intranet. Then, the rest of the Island Tea & Coffee Company employees will be able to open your Web page, click the hotlink you created to the invoice template, and open copies of the template on their computers.

 NOTE If you'd like to build on the skills you learned in this lesson, you can do the One Step Further. Otherwise, skip to "Finish the Lesson."

One Step Further: Editing the Template

During the Marketing manager's final review of the invoice, she suggested that the shading added to the formula cells in column J should not appear on the customer copy. But you still want to keep the shaded cells on the ITC invoice template to help the Island Tea & Coffee Company employees fill out the invoice properly. Fortunately, Microsoft Excel allows you to prevent the shading from being printed.

Open the template

If you need to make changes to your template (for example, add more formulas or modify the formatting), you should open the template itself rather than a copy of the template. In this exercise, you open the template.

1 On the File menu, click Open, and then locate the Spreadsheet Solutions folder.

2 Double-click the ITC Invoice file.

The template opens, rather than a copy. The name in the title bar is ITC Invoice.

Select black and white printing

You don't want the shaded cells to be printed on the copies that you mail or fax to customers. In this exercise, you set the worksheet to print in black and white, with no shades of gray except in the graphic so that your customers will not see the cell shading.

Print Preview

1 On the File menu, click Page Setup.

The Page Setup dialog box appears.

2 Click the Sheet tab.

3 Select the Black And White check box, and then click OK.

4 On the Standard toolbar, click the Print Preview button.

Your worksheet should look similar to the following illustration.

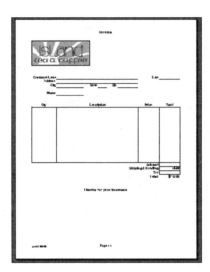

5 Click Close, and then save your work.

Finish the lesson

1 To continue to the Review and Practice, on the File menu, click Close.

2 If you are finished using Microsoft Excel for now, on the File menu, click Exit.

Lesson Summary

To	Do this	Button
Format font for typeface, size, or formatting (such as bold, italic or underline)	Select cells, and then click the appropriate buttons on the Formatting toolbar.	
Copy formatting	Select a cell that contains the formatting you want to apply to other cells, and then double-click the Format Painter button.	
Create a style by example	Select a cell that contains all the formatting attributes you want to include in the style, and then, on the Format menu, click Style. Type a new style name, and then click OK.	
Apply a style	Select cells you want to apply the style to, and then, on the Format menu, click Style. Select the style you want in the Style Name box, then click OK.	
Change a style definition	On the Format menu, click Style. Select the style to change in the Style Name box, and then click Modify. Change the style attributes as needed, and then click OK twice.	
Apply borders	Select cells to be formatted. On the Formatting toolbar, click the Borders down arrow, and then click the appropriate border button.	
Drag a palette away from the toolbar to make it float on the worksheet	Drag the palette by its top border onto the worksheet.	
Apply shading	Select cells to be formatted. On the Formatting toolbar, click the Fill Color down arrow, and then click a color.	
Set page margins	On the File menu, click Page Setup. Click the Margins tab, and then set the margins.	

To	Do this
Format numbers	Select the cells containing the numbers you want to format, and then use the right mouse button to click one of them. On the shortcut menu, click Format Cells, click the Number tab, select a Category, and then set the appropriate formatting options for the category.
Hide zero values on the worksheet	On the Tools menu, click Options. On the View tab, clear the Zero Values check box.
Create custom headers and footers	On the File menu, click Page Setup. Click the Header/Footer tab, and then click the Custom Header or Custom Footer button. Type and format headers and footers in the Header and Footer dialog boxes.
Save a workbook as a template	On the File menu, click Save As. In the Save As Type box, select Template, and then click Save.
Open a copy of a template	On the File menu, click New. Click the tab representing the folder where you stored your template, and then double-click the template icon.

For online information about	On the Help menu, click Contents And Index, click the Index tab, and then type
Formatting worksheets	**formatting cells**
Styles	**styles**
Headers and footers	**headers; footers**
Templates	**templates**

Review &
Practice

You will review and practice how to:

Estimated time
20 min.

- Name and delete worksheets.
- Enter labels and formulas.
- Format cells.
- Apply borders.
- Add comments.
- Save a workbook as a template.

Before you move on to Part 2, in which you will learn about and practice consolidation, subtotaling, and filtering, you can practice the skills you learned in Part 1 by working through the steps in this Review & Practice section.

Scenario

The State University Alumni Association (SUAA) is a non-profit organization that conducts fundraising activities. As the office manager, you've been asked to help standardize and streamline the accounting system by creating a time-sheet template for the Alumni Association's employees.

Step 1: *Open a File and Enter Labels*

You first need to set up your timesheet. In this step, you start a new workbook, delete any extra sheets, and then enter labels. You also add a keyword that will help users find the timesheet.

1   Open a new workbook, and then save it as SUAA Timesheet.

2   Delete all but one sheet.

3   Rename the remaining sheet with the place holder text **Your Name Here**

4   Enter **Monday** in cell B1, and then AutoFill the weekday names across to cell F1.

5   Enter the following labels into cells A2 through A9:

Dates
Tasks
Telephone contacts
Answer mail
Organize events
Update computer
Administrative tasks
Vacation

6   In cell A16, enter **Total hours**

7   Add the keyword **timesheet** to the workbook's file properties. (Hint: On the File menu, click Properties.)

For more information about	See
Opening a new file	Lesson 1
Saving files	Lesson 1
Deleting sheets	Lesson 2
Naming sheets	Lesson 2
Entering data	Lesson 1
Using AutoFill	Lesson 3
Adding keywords	Lesson 2

Step 2: *Format the Worksheet and Add Borders*

Now that you have entered the labels, you are ready to format your timesheet. In this step, you format the labels and apply borders to the cells where users will enter their daily hours for each task.

1   Format cells B1 through F1 as centered and bold, and format cells B2 through F2 as centered.

2 Format cell A2 ("Dates") and cell A16 ("Total hours") as bold and aligned right, and cell A3 ("Tasks") as bold and centered.

3 Apply inside-and-outside borders to cells B3 through F15.

For more information about	See
Formatting cells	Lesson 4
Applying borders	Lesson 4

Step 3: Write Formulas and Add Instructions

Now that your timesheet looks the way you want, you need to make it functional. In this step, you add formulas and helpful instructions to the timesheet, and then save the workbook as a template.

1 In cell B16, use AutoSum to write a SUM formula that adds up cells B3 through B15.

2 Use AutoFill to copy the SUM formula to cells C16 through F16.

3 In cell A1, add the comment **Be sure to replace the sheet name with your name.**

4 In cell B2, add the comment **To enter the current date, press CTRL+;**

5 In cell A10, add the comment **Enter other tasks as necessary.**

6 Adjust the width of each column so that its contents are displayed.

7 Save the workbook as a template in the Spreadsheet Solutions folder.

Your finished template should look similar to the following illustration.

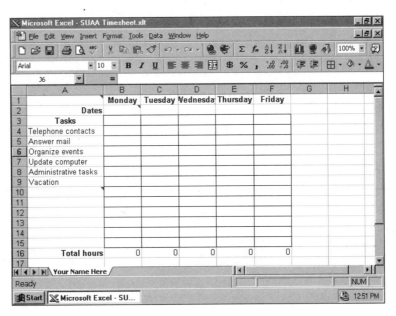

For more information about	See
AutoSum	Lesson 3
Adding comments	Lesson 2
Saving a workbook as a template	Lesson 4

Finish the Review & Practice

1 To continue to the next lesson, on the File menu, click Close.

2 If you are finished using Microsoft Excel for now, on the File menu, click Exit.

Organizing and Summarizing Your Data

Part 2

Consolidating Multiple Lists

In this lesson you will learn how to:

Estimated time
30 min.

- ■ Open multiple files at the same time.
- ■ Work with a group of files displayed in multiple windows.
- ■ Move worksheets between workbooks.
- ■ Consolidate detailed data into a summary.
- ■ Create a conditional number format to make specific values stand out.
- ■ Use a built-in Microsoft Excel template to automate the consolidation process.

In its most basic form, data consists of a series of detailed information (for example, lists of expenses, individual sales records, item quantities in an inventory, or results from scientific experiments). To make this information useful in a decision-making process, data must be organized and summarized. Microsoft Excel provides several ways to summarize details, including the Consolidate command, the Subtotals command, and PivotTables. Usually, one method is more appropriate than the others in specific situations.

At the Island Tea & Coffee Company, expenses are entered in a Microsoft Excel workbook as they are incurred. Due to personnel shifts at the beginning of the year, the January, February, and March expenses lists were recorded by various employees in three different workbooks. Each list consists of two columns: a column of text labels and a column of amounts. One of your tasks as office manager is to organize the three monthly expenses lists into a quarterly summary.

In this case, the best method of summarizing the quarterly expenses is to use the Consolidate command. Consolidation is the easiest method to learn and quickest to perform; it also works best on simple lists that contain a single column of text labels on the left side of the list (as your monthly expenses lists do). Consolidation combines all like items into a single totaled item; for example, all the Supplies entries will be combined into a single Supplies total. One of the advantages of using consolidation is that you can consolidate data stored in different worksheets and workbooks; one of the drawbacks is that the resulting consolidated summary will not provide any details. In the case of the quarterly expenses summary, the lack of details isn't an issue, so you will use the Consolidate command. You will learn about the Subtotals command in Lesson 7, and about creating PivotTables in Lesson 8.

Opening and Arranging a Group of Files

For a demonstration of how to open multiple files, double-click the Camcorder Files On The Internet shortcut on your Desktop or connect to the Internet address listed on page xxvii.

The Island Tea & Coffee Company employees who kept the expenses lists during the first quarter of 1997 have saved those files with the keyword "expenses." You can use the keyword to locate the files quickly, and then open all three at once.

In the following exercises, you will practice opening a group of expenses files by searching for a common keyword, and then opening all of them at once. You will also practice arranging the files in multiple windows so that you can see all the files and work with them more easily.

Open a group of files that share a keyword

The monthly expenses data has been entered in three different worksheets by various employees. In this exercise, you locate and open the three monthly expenses files.

Open

1   On the Standard toolbar, click the Open button.
2   In the Open dialog box, click the Look In Favorites button.
3   In the file list, double-click the Excel SBS Practice folder.
4   Click Advanced.
5   Click the Property down arrow, and then scroll down and select Keywords.
6   Be sure that Includes Words appears in the Condition box, and then type **expenses** in the Value box.
7   Click Add To List, and then click Find Now.

    The results of the search appear in the Open dialog box.

8 Click Expenses Feb 97, then hold down CTRL and click Expenses Jan 97 and Expenses Mar 97, and finally click Open.

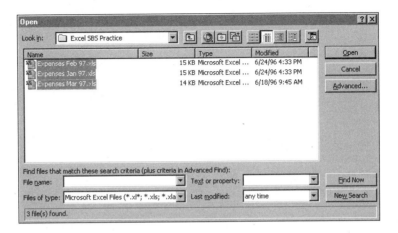

The three expenses files are opened.

Arrange windows to get a better view of your workbooks

The name of any open Microsoft Excel workbook is listed at the bottom of the Window menu; each workbook can be displayed by selecting its name from the list. But, if you need to move rapidly between workbooks, or drag and drop sheets between workbooks, it's more efficient to display all of the workbooks at the same time. You can put each workbook in its own window, and arrange the windows in a convenient manner.

For a demonstration of how to arrange files displayed in multiple windows, double-click the Camcorder Files On The Internet shortcut on your Desktop or connect to the Internet address listed on page xxvii.

In this exercise, you arrange the windows containing the expenses files, add a new workbook, and then rearrange the windows to display it.

1 Click the Window menu.

The three open workbooks are listed at the bottom of the menu.

2 On the Window menu, click Arrange.

The Arrange Windows dialog box appears.

3 Under Arrange, click the Horizontal option button, and then click OK.

The workbooks are arranged in horizontal windows, and you can see the sheet tabs for each workbook.

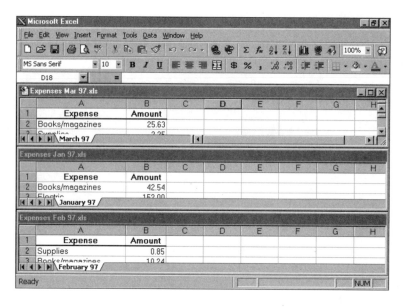

New

4 On the Standard toolbar, click the New button.

A new workbook appears on top of the arranged windows.

5 On the Window menu, click Arrange.

6 Under Arrange, click the Tiled option button, and then click OK.

The four open workbooks are arranged in windows in a tiled configuration. You can use any configuration option you wish, as long as you can easily see the sheet tabs.

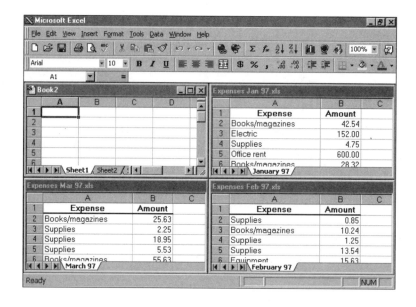

Consolidating Data from Several Worksheets

Now that you have the three expenses files open, you can drag copies of these worksheets into the new workbook where you will perform the consolidation.

 NOTE   Even though you can consolidate ranges that are located in different workbooks, it will be easier to learn about consolidation if all the partial lists are in the same workbook. When you consolidate ranges from different workbooks, you must either add the ranges from each separate workbook (if the workbooks are open) or remember the filenames and references so you can type them into the Consolidate dialog box (if the workbooks are closed).

In the following exercises, you will copy sheets from three files into a new workbook, and then consolidate them in a single worksheet.

Copy sheets into a single workbook

Now that you have created the workbook in which the consolidation will take place and arranged the windows so that they are all visible, you are ready to compile the worksheets in your newly created workbook. In this exercise, you copy the three expenses worksheets in the new workbook in preparation for the consolidation.

1   Click in the Expenses Jan 97 workbook window to make it active.

To move a worksheet to another workbook rather than copying it, drag the sheet tab without holding down CTRL.

2   Hold down CTRL and drag the January sheet tab from the Expenses Jan 97 workbook to the new workbook, placing the sheet tab to the right of the last sheet in the workbook.

The January worksheet is copied into the new workbook.

3   Repeat steps 1 and 2 to drag the February and March sheet tabs from the expenses workbooks to the new workbook, placing each to the right of the previous sheet tab.

All three worksheets have been copied into the new workbook. Your screen should look similar to the following illustration.

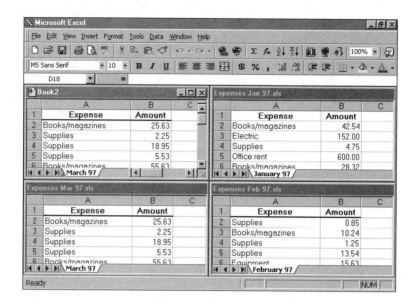

4 Close the Expenses Jan 97, Expenses Feb 97, and Expenses Mar 97 workbooks.

5 Double-click the title bar of the new workbook.

The new workbook is maximized.

6 Save the new workbook as **Quarterly Expenses**

Consolidate data into a single list

You're ready to consolidate the three monthly expenses lists into one quarterly summary. In this exercise, you consolidate the partial lists into a single summary list.

1 In the Quarterly Expenses workbook, change the name of the Sheet1 sheet to **First Qtr 1997**

2 On the First Qtr 1997 sheet, click cell A1, and then, on the Data menu, click Consolidate.

3 In the Consolidate dialog box, be sure that the Function box contains Sum, and then click in the Reference box, if necessary.

4 Select the January 97 sheet, and then drag to select the entire table (cells A1 through B20).

The selected reference appears in the Reference box.

5 In the Consolidate dialog box, click Add.

The range reference is added to the All References box.

6 Repeat steps 4 and 5 to add the February 97 and March 97 sheets (cells A1 through B17).

Your dialog box should look similar to the following illustration.

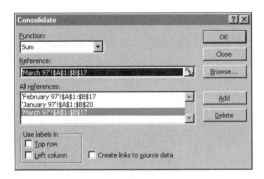

7   Under Use Labels In, select the Top Row and Left Column check boxes, and then click OK.

The three monthly lists are consolidated in the First Qtr 1997 sheet. Your consolidated list should look similar to the following illustration.

Creating a Conditional Number Format

One of the managerial concerns at the Island Tea & Coffee Company is to keep an eye on quarterly expenses that exceed $2000. When you present the expenses summary, management likes to have any quarterly expense that exceeds $2000 pointed out or highlighted in some way.

Instead of picking out the excessive expenses manually (and running the risk of missing some), you can easily format numbers that are above a specific value to be displayed in a different color, font, or other format, so they stand out and can be easily located.

Create a number format that depends on the value in the cell

In preparation for the quarterly management meeting, you have to format the quarterly expenses summary. In this exercise, you apply a *conditional format* (a format that appears only if the cell value meets certain conditions) to the Amount column so that any entries above 2000 appear in red.

1 In the First Qtr 1997 sheet, select column B by clicking the column letter.

2 On the Format menu, click Conditional Formatting.

The Conditional Formatting dialog box appears.

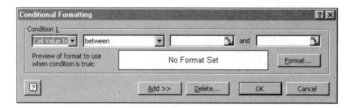

3 Under Condition 1, verify that Cell Value Is appears in the first drop-down list box.

4 In the second drop-down list box, select Greater Than.

The two right-most boxes become a single box.

5 In the right-most box, type **2000**

You have entered a *condition*, or qualifying value, which tells Microsoft Excel to apply a special format to cells that contain a number that is more than 2000.

6 Click Format.

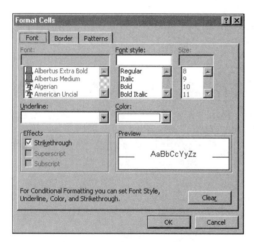

7 In the Format Cells dialog box, be sure that the Font tab is selected, and then, in the Font Style list, select Bold.

8 In the Color list, select red, and then click OK.

The Conditional Formatting dialog box appears again, and should look similar to the following illustration.

9 Click OK.

Your worksheet should look similar to the following illustration.

	A	B	C	D	E	F	G	H	I
1		**Amount**							
2	Supplies	166.71							
3	Profession	378.00							
4	Books/mag	268.70							
5	Equipment	**2367.15**							
6	Advertising	599.75							
7	Online ser	59.85							
8	Electric	456.00							
9	Office rent	1800.00							
10	Warehouse	**3000.00**							
11	Basic telep	108.00							
12	Long dista	367.73							
13									

10 Save and close the workbook.

TIP You might want to add a comment to the worksheet that explains what the formatting means.

Using a Built-in Template to Automate Data Collection

As you learned in the previous series of exercises, you can manually consolidate data in separate lists. You can also automate the collection of data in a single list by using one of the built-in templates that come with Microsoft Excel.

One of the templates that Microsoft Excel provides is an Expense Statement template. All of the automation work is already done for you, and all that remains to be done is to customize the template for the Island Tea & Coffee Company. When you or your co-workers create and save workbooks based on the Expense Statement template, the data entered in each workbook is automatically copied to a *linked*, or attached, *database*. The term database in Microsoft Excel is just another term for list; it's simply a worksheet with data organized into *records*, or rows, and *fields*, or columns. A list has column labels, and no blank rows or columns within it. For example, each expenses list you consolidated in the previous exercise is a database.

91

When you need to see the collected list of expenses from all the Expense Statement workbooks, you simply open the database workbook, where the data from each Expense Statement has been copied. The linking and automation is carried out by the Template Wizard.

 IMPORTANT You must have the Template Wizard With Data Tracking add-in installed to perform the following exercises. If you do not see the Template Wizard command on your Data menu, click Add-ins on the Tools menu. If you do not see Template Wizard With Data Tracking in the list of available add-ins, you will need to install it from the disk by using Custom Installation. To do this, click Start, point to Settings, and then click Control Panel. Click the Add/Remove Programs icon, select Microsoft Office 97, and then click Add/Remove. Insert the Microsoft Office 97 CD-ROM, and then click Add/Remove in the Microsoft Office 97 Setup dialog box. Select Microsoft Excel and click Change Option. Select the Spreadsheet Templates and Add-Ins, click Change Options, and be sure that Expense Statement Template and Template Wizard With Data Tracking are selected, respectively. Click OK, and then follow the prompts to install the two components.

Create an expenses template that collects data automatically

After having consolidated three expenses lists into one, you decide to automate the data collection process to save time in the future. In this exercise, you open the built-in Expense Statement template and modify it.

1   On the File menu, click New.

2   In the New dialog box, click the Spreadsheet Solutions tab, and then double-click the Expense Statement icon.

A copy of the Expense Statement, named Expense Statement1, opens and contains a special toolbar and a worksheet.

3   Click the Customize Your Statement sheet tab.

4   Click in the Type Company Information Here section, and fill in the company information as follows:

Company Name	**Island Tea & Coffee Company**
Address	**123 Any Street**
City	**Bigtown**
State	**WA**
Zip Code	**99999**
Phone Number	**800-555-6666**
Fax Number	**800-555-7777**

For more infor-mation about the Template Wizard Data-base, click Tem-plate Help on the Expense toolbar.

Print Preview

5 In the section titled Specify Default Expense Statement Information Here, look at the entries in the Common Database box and in the Template Wizard Database box—these boxes tell you that the Microsoft Excel Li-brary folder is where you will find the database of expenses later, and that the name of the database is expdb.xls.

To use a database other than the default expdb.xls, you will need to cre-ate it using the Template Wizard.

6 Click the Expense Statement sheet tab.

7 On the Standard toolbar, click the Print Preview button.

The Select Employee and Customize buttons won't print, nor will the shading in the total cells. Your screen should look similar to the follow-ing illustration.

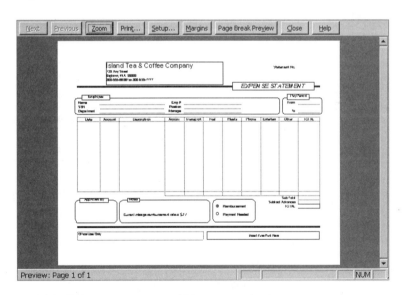

8 Close the Print Preview window, and then click the Customize button in the upper right corner of the expense statement.

The Customize Your Statement sheet appears.

Save the new template

Now that your new company template is customized, you can save it in the Spreadsheet Solutions folder so that it will always be available to you, along with all the other built-in Microsoft Excel templates.

 TIP To make the template available to all of your co-workers, be sure to save it in a folder that is accessible to every computer on the company intranet. You might want to store the template in a network location that is accessible by all users in your group. Then, you can have them create a shortcut icon to the folder or template in their Templates folder.

1 At the top of the worksheet, click the Lock/Save Sheet button to protect and then save the template you created.

The Lock And Save Sheet button becomes the Unlock This Sheet button after you click it, and vice versa.

2 In the Lock/Save Sheet dialog box, be sure that the Lock And Save Template option button is selected, and then click OK.

3 In the Save Template dialog box, double-click the Spreadsheet Solutions folder.

4 Select the current filename, type **ITC Expenses**, and then click Save.

5 Read the informational dialog box that appears, and then click OK.

6 On the File menu, click Close.

The template is saved and closed.

 NOTE If you want to further customize your template at a later time, you can click the Open command on the File menu, then navigate to the Spreadsheet Solutions folder (in the Templates folder, in the Microsoft Office folder) and open the template file. Click the Customize button in the upper right corner of the statement to show the Customize Your Statement sheet. Then, click the Unlock This Sheet button, make your changes, and when you're done, click the Lock/Save Sheet button to save your changes.

Test the new expenses template

Before you make the template available to your co-workers, you decide to test it. In this exercise, you try the new template and capture the information in the database.

1 On the File menu, click New.

2 In the New dialog box, double-click the ITC Expenses icon.

A copy of the ITC Expenses template, named ITC Expenses1, opens.

3 Enter the required information (such as your name) in the appropriate locations, and then enter the following expense information:

Date	Description	Accom	Transport	Meals
5/12/97	meeting in Boston	129.00	78.00	36.85
5/13/97	meeting in Boston	129.00	78.00	42.94

The formulas that are built into the shaded cells calculate your totals automatically. Your expense statement should look similar to the following illustration.

Date	Account	Description	Accom	Transport	Fuel	Meals	Phone	Entertain	Other
5/12/97		meeting in Boston	$129.00	$78.00		$36.85			
5/13/97		meeting in Boston	$129.00	$78.00		$42.94			

*Capture Data
In A Database*

4 On the Expense toolbar, click the Capture Data In A Database button.

5 In the Create And Interact With Database dialog box, be sure that the Update Existing Database option button is selected, and then click OK.

6 In the Template File–Save To Database dialog box, be sure that the Create A New Record option button is selected, and then click OK.

7 On the File menu, click Save, and then in the Template File–Save To Database dialog box, be sure that the Continue Without Updating option is selected, and finally click OK.

The Save As dialog box appears.

8 Be sure that the Excel SBS Practice folder is in the Save In box, name the file Expenses 5-14-97, and then click Save.

9 Close the workbook.

Look at the expenses database

Now you can check the new expenses database to be sure that your template is saving entries properly. The databases that are created automatically are saved by default in the Microsoft Excel Library folder.

NOTE The template and database that are created by the Template Wizard will only collect a single record of data from each expense statement that you create and save. If you need to compile a list of details instead of a list of totals, a better approach would be to use a *shared workbook*, a workbook that you make available on the company intranet so that all employees can enter details about their expenses into the same list. You'll learn about shared lists in Lesson 12, "Sharing Your Workbooks with Others."

1   On the File menu, click Open.

2   In the Open dialog box, locate your Microsoft Office folder, double-click your Excel folder, and then double-click the Library folder.

The Template Wizard has given your expenses database the default name of expdb, which is the default database for the built-in Expense Statement template.

3   Double-click the expdb file to open it.

The expenses total from your expense statement has been entered in the expdb database. Every time you create and save a copy of the expenses statement, a new record will be created in the database.

4   Close the database.

NOTE If you'd like to build up on the skills you learned in this lesson, you can do the One Step Further. Otherwise, skip to "Finish the Lesson."

One Step Further: Adding Employee Names to the Expense Statement Template

You might have noticed the Select Employee button in the Employee information area of the Expense Statement template. You can modify the list that appears when you click the Select Employee button so that the Island Tea & Coffee Company employee information appears instead of sample information. Then, each employee can click his or her own name in the list and all the information is automatically filled in.

IMPORTANT Be sure that no templates or copies of templates are open when you start this exercise.

1   On the File menu, click Open, locate the Microsoft Office folder, double-click the Excel folder, double-click the Library folder, and then double-click the Common file.

2   In the Common file, click the Employee Info sheet tab.

    The Employee Info worksheet contains employee information provided as an example by Microsoft Excel.

3   Delete the sample data and add the following records to the Employee Info worksheet:

	Paul Garnier	**Mark Davis**
SSN	222-22-2222	333-33-3333
Emp #	5	6
Position	Shipping	Clerical
Region	US	US
Department	Warehouse	Management
Manager	Barbara Lang	Barbara Lang

4   Save and close the Common file.

5   Open a copy of the ITC Expenses template.

6   On the Expense Statement worksheet, click the Select Employee button.

    The Select An Employee dialog box appears, with the names you added to the Common file.

7   Select Mark Davis, and then click OK.

    All of Mark Davis' employee information is entered in the expense statement automatically.

Finish the lesson

1   To continue to the next lesson, on the File menu, click Close (do not save the workbook).

2   If you are finished using Microsoft Excel for now, on the File menu, click Exit.

Lesson Summary

To	Do this
Open a group of files	In the Open dialog box, hold down CTRL and click multiple files. Click Open.

To	Do this
Arrange multiple windows	On the Window menu, click Arrange, select a type of arrangement, and then click OK.
Copy a sheet between workbooks	Hold down CTRL and drag a sheet tab from one workbook to another.
Consolidate lists into a single list	On the Data menu, click Consolidate. Click in the Reference box, select a worksheet containing a list, select the list by dragging, and then click Add. Repeat these steps for each list you want to include in the consolidation. Select the Use Labels In Top Row and Left Column check boxes, and then click OK.
Create a conditional number format	Select the cells to be formatted, and then, on the Format menu, click Conditional Formatting. Select cell value conditions, select the desired formatting, and then click OK.
Customize a built-in template	On the File menu, click New. In the New dialog box, click the Spreadsheet Solutions tab, and then double-click the template you want. Click the Customize sheet, customize the template, click the Lock/Save Sheet button, and then save the template in the Spreadsheet Solutions folder.
Open a database created using the Template Wizard	On the File menu, click Open. Locate the Library folder (in the Excel folder in the Microsoft Office folder), and then double-click the database that is linked to your template.

For online information about	On the Help menu, click Contents And Index, click the Index tab, and then type
Arranging multiple windows	**arranging windows**
Moving and copying sheets	**moving sheets in workbook** *or* **copying, sheets**
Consolidating data	**consolidating data**
Using templates and databases	**templates**

Filtering to Find Specific Information

Estimated time
30 min.

In this lesson you will learn how to:

- Filter a list to find specific information.
- Find totals and averages quickly using AutoCalculate.
- Calculate sets of filtered records using the SUBTOTAL function.

As the office manager for the Island Tea & Coffee Company, one of your responsibilities is to keep the inventory updated. For that reason, your co-workers often call you when they want to know what's in stock. You can easily answer their questions by using a few simple filtering techniques on your inventory list. Filtering allows you to quickly find and bring up information matching the criteria you set.

Your list is composed of records, or rows, and fields, or columns. All of the records in a list have the same information fields (for example, each record has a Product Name field, a Source Country field, a Warehouse Location field, and so on). Each field in a list provides a specific type of information (for example, the Source Country field contains the source country information for each record).

When you filter a list, you define conditions known as *criteria* that are shared by the subset of records you want to locate. For example, all of the records for products that come from Mexico share the criterion Source Country = Mexico, and all of the records for products that have a per pound price less than $10 share the criterion Price $/lb < 10. You can also filter your list using multiple criteria, such as all products from Mexico with prices less than $10 per pound.

Open an existing file

You have been asked to find out if some specific items are in stock. In order to perform the most accurate search possible, you need to open the current inventory list. In this exercise, you open the most up-to-date inventory file.

Open

1   On the Standard toolbar, click the Open button.

2   In the Open dialog box, click the Look In Favorites button.

3   In the file list, double-click the Excel SBS Practice folder.

4   Double-click the Lesson 6 Inventory file.

If you have Microsoft Outlook, you can open the file this way

If you have Microsoft Outlook, you can open Microsoft Excel and the Lesson 6 Inventory file by using the following procedure.

1   In the Microsoft Outlook Open dialog box, in the Folders list, click the Other Folders button.

2   In the Other Folders list, click the Favorites icon.

3   In the Favorites list, double-click the Excel SBS Practice folder.

4   Double-click the Lesson 6 Inventory file.

Filtering to Display a Set of Related Records

Filtering allows you to display only the records that share specific *criteria*, or field values. With Microsoft Excel, the easiest way to filter records in a list is to use AutoFilter. When you turn on AutoFilter, *filter arrows*, which look like down arrows, will appear next to the column headings in your list. You click an arrow to display a list of the values in that field, and then select a value to use as a criterion or condition for filtering the list. After you have selected a criterion, the filter arrow for that field and the row numbers for the filtered records appear in blue to provide a quick reminder of which field you filtered on.

Find a subset of items quickly using an AutoFilter

One of your co-workers needs to find out if the Island Tea & Coffee Company offers any coffees from Mexico. In this exercise, you filter the inventory list to locate coffees imported from Mexico, and then you remove the filter.

1   Select cell C7.

     You could select any cell in your list. Microsoft Excel will then select the entire contiguous range of cells.

2 On the Data menu, point to Filter, and then click AutoFilter.

Filter arrows appear next to your column headers.

Filter arrows

	A	B	C	D	E	F	
1	Product Name	Categor	Source Country	Cost $/l	Price $/l	Qty In Stock	War
2	Antigua	Coffee	Guatemala	5.25	10.50	500	
3	Blue Mountain	Coffee	Jamaica	28.00	36.00	400	
4	Bourbon Santos	Coffee	Brazil	4.75	9.50	200	
5	Celebes	Coffee	Indonesia	4.75	9.50	800	
6	Chanchamayo	Coffee	Peru	5.25	10.50	600	
7	Coatepec	Coffee	Mexico	5.25	10.50	900	
8	Coban	Coffee	Guatemala	4.75	9.50	800	
9	Costa Rica	Coffee	Costa Rica	5.25	10.50	1000	
10	Ecuador	Coffee	Ecuador	5.25	10.50	500	
11	Haiti	Coffee	Haiti	4.75	9.50	400	

3 Click the Source Country filter arrow column heading (in cell C1).

An alphabetical list of all the source countries appears.

	A	B	C	D	E	F	
1	Product Name	Categor	Source Country	Cost $/l	Price $/l	Qty In Stock	War
2	Antigua	Coffee	(All)	5.25	10.50	500	
3	Blue Mountain	Coffee	(Top 10...)	28.00	36.00	400	
4	Bourbon Santos	Coffee	(Custom...) Brazil	4.75	9.50	200	
5	Celebes	Coffee	China	4.75	9.50	800	
6	Chanchamayo	Coffee	Columbia	5.25	10.50	600	
7	Coatepec	Coffee	Costa Rica Dominican Republic	5.25	10.50	900	
8	Coban	Coffee	Ecuador	4.75	9.50	800	
9	Costa Rica	Coffee	Ethiopia	5.25	10.50	1000	
10	Ecuador	Coffee	Guatemala Haiti	5.25	10.50	500	
11	Haiti	Coffee	Hawaii	4.75	9.50	400	
12	Harrar	Coffee	India	4.95	9.90	800	
13	India	Coffee	Indonesia Jamaica	4.75	9.50	700	
14	Java	Coffee	Japan	5.25	10.50	800	
15	Kenya	Coffee	Kenya	5.40	10.80	900	
16	Kona	Coffee	Mexico Peru	5.25	10.50	1000	
17	Medellin	Coffee	Columbia	4.75	9.50	1100	

You can copy and paste the filtered records into another worksheet for further reference or manipulation, or into an e-mail message to your co-worker.

4 Click Mexico.

All the records for products from Mexico remain in view, and all other records are hidden.

5 To remove the filter, click the Source Country filter arrow (in cell C1), and then scroll to the top of the list and click All.

The filter is removed and all the records are displayed.

You can remove filtering from a list either by removing the specific criterion that you set, or by turning off the AutoFilter.

Find the seven lowest-priced coffees

One of the sales representatives of the Island Tea & Coffee Company wants to know what the seven lowest-priced coffees are, and what quantities of each are available. In this exercise, you filter your inventory list to find the seven lowest-priced coffees.

AutoFilter's Top 10 feature only works in numeric fields.

1 Click the Category filter arrow (in cell B1), and then click Coffee.

All the teas are hidden and only the coffees appear.

2 Click the Price $/lb filter arrow (in cell E1), and then click Top 10.

The Top 10 AutoFilter dialog box appears.

3 In the leftmost list box, select Bottom.

4 In the center list box, select 7, and then click OK.

The seven lowest-priced coffees are filtered. In fact, the filtered list contains nine entries because the nine lowest-priced coffees have the same price.

5 Click the Price $/lb filter arrow, and then click All.

6 Click the Category filter arrow, and then click All.

The filter is removed and all the records are displayed.

Filter data using multiple criteria with a custom AutoFilter

One of your co-workers in the Marketing department is creating a new ad campaign, and he wants to know which products are priced between $10 and $15 per pound. In this exercise, you create and then use a custom filter to quickly bring up the list requested by your colleague.

1 Click the Price $/lb filter arrow (in cell E1), and then click Custom.

The Custom AutoFilter dialog box appears.

2 In the upper-left list box, click Is Greater Than.

3 In the upper-right list box, type **10**

4 Be sure that the And option button is selected.

5 In the lower-left list box, click Is Less Than.

6 In the lower-right list box, type **15**

The dialog box should look similar to the following illustration.

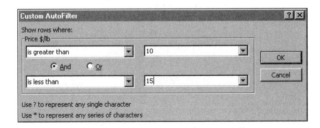

7 Click OK.

Products with prices higher than $10 per lb but lower than $15 per lb are in view, and all other products (those with prices $10/lb or less and those with prices $15/lb or more) are hidden.

Calculating Filtered Sets of Records

After you have filtered the records you need, you might want to manipulate them further. For example, you might have several fields in a list that need to be summed or averaged, and you might need to perform the same calculations on several different filtered subsets of records; or, you might want to average both price and cost for products from different countries. There are specific functions, such as SUBTOTAL, that are very useful when trying to calculate filtered data quickly.

In the following exercises, you will also learn about AutoCalculate, a Microsoft Excel feature that performs calculations without written formulas.

Calculate a total using AutoCalculate

Your list is currently filtered to show the records for products priced between $10 and $15 per pound. Your colleague in Marketing also wants to know what the average price is. In this exercise, you find out what the average price of the coffees in the $10 to $15 range is.

1 Select cells E2 through E38, and then look at the AutoCalculate box on the status bar.

	A	B	C	D	E	F
9	Costa Rica	Coffee	Costa Rica	5.25	10.50	1000
10	Ecuador	Coffee	Ecuador	5.25	10.50	500
14	Java	Coffee	Indonesia	5.25	10.50	800
15	Kenya	Coffee	Kenya	5.40	10.80	900
16	Kona	Coffee	Hawaii	5.25	10.50	1000
18	Merida	Coffee	Venezuela	5.25	10.50	700
19	Mocha	Coffee	Yemen	5.75	11.50	800
21	Pluma	Coffee	Mexico	5.25	10.50	400
23	Sumatra	Coffee	Indonesia	5.75	11.50	600
26	Black Lychee	Tea	China	5.25	10.50	250
27	Ceylon	Tea	Sri Lanka	5.85	11.70	600
31	Lapsang Souchong	Tea	China	5.05	10.10	250
32	Oolong	Tea	Taiwan	10.00	14.40	150
35	Dragonwell	Tea	China	5.35	10.70	500
37	Gyokuru	Tea	Japan	5.60	11.20	150
38	Pi Lo Chun	Tea	China	5.55	11.10	500
39						

Inventory 1-15-97

19 of 37 records found   Sum=208.00   NUM

AutoCalculate box

Your AutoCalculate box might look different from the illustration if a different function was previously selected.

2 Use the right mouse button to click the AutoCalculate box, and then click Average.

The selected cells are averaged. Only the visible records (those not hidden by the filter) are averaged, and the hidden records are ignored.

Calculate filtered sets of records using the SUBTOTAL function

In preparation for an upcoming sales meeting, your manager asks you to compare the average costs and average prices of products from each different country. In this exercise, you filter your inventory to first locate the country of origin for each product, and then average their prices using the SUBTOTAL function.

1 Click the Price $/lb filter arrow (in cell E1), and then click All.

The previous filter is removed.

2 Click the Source Country filter arrow (in cell C1), and then click China.

Your list only shows products from China.

	A	B	C	D	E	F	
1	Product Name ▾	Catego ▾	Source Country ▾	Cost $/l ▾	Price $/l ▾	Qty In Stoc ▾	War
26	Black Lychee	Tea	China	5.25	10.50	250	
29	Jasmine	Tea	China	4.90	9.80	500	
30	Keemun	Tea	China	4.85	9.70	600	
31	Lapsang Souchong	Tea	China	5.05	10.10	250	
34	Chunmee	Tea	China	4.85	9.70	100	
35	Dragonwell	Tea	China	5.35	10.70	500	
36	Gunpowder	Tea	China	4.50	9.00	400	
38	Pi Lo Chun	Tea	China	5.55	11.10	500	
39							

3 Select cell D41.

4 On the Standard toolbar, click the AutoSum button, and then press ENTER.

AutoSum

The SUBTOTAL formula for a sum is entered. If a range is filtered, the AutoSum button enters a SUBTOTAL formula; if the range is not filtered, the AutoSum button enters a SUM formula.

5 Double-click the cell containing the formula.

The formula is ready for editing.

6 Select the first argument in the parentheses to the left of the first comma: the number 9 in this case.

Arguments provide the information that tells the function what data to calculate and what operations to perform. Arguments are contained within parentheses and separated by commas. The first argument in the SUBTOTAL function indicates which function should be used in the subtotal calculation. A "9" represents the SUM function, but you want to use the AVERAGE function, which is represented by a "1." Your formula should look similar to the following illustration.

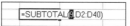

=SUBTOTAL(,D2:D40)

7 Type **1**, and then press ENTER.

Your SUBTOTAL formula calculates an average of the filtered cells in the Country Source field.

> **NOTE** For your easy reference, the SUBTOTAL function arguments are as follows: 1=AVERAGE, 2=COUNT, 3=COUNTA, 4=MAX, 5=MIN, 6=PRODUCT, 7=STDEV, 8=STDEVP, 9=SUM, 10=VAR, and 11=VARP. To learn more about these functions, you can ask the Office Assistant for help.

8 Select cell D41, and then drag its fill handle to cell E41.

The SUBTOTAL formula is copied to cell E41.

9 Change the filter criterion to India.

The average cost and price of products imported from India appear.

	A	B	C	D	E	F	
1	Product Name ▾	Categoi ▾	Source Country ▾	Cost $/l ▾	Price $/l ▾	Qty In Stocl ▾	Wan
13	India	Coffee	India	4.75	9.50	700	
25	Assam	Tea	India	4.85	9.70	550	
28	Darjeeling	Tea	India	10.15	20.30	550	
39							
40							
41				6.5833333	13.166667		
42							

10 On the Data menu, point to Filter, then click AutoFilter.

The AutoFilter is removed.

11 On the File menu, click Save.

> **NOTE** If you'd like to build on the skills you learned in this lesson, you can do the One Step Further. Otherwise, skip to "Finish the Lesson."

One Step Further: Summing Up a Set of Records Without Filtering

You can use the SUMIF function to calculate a sum of values for specific records. The SUMIF function sums cells that meet conditions you specify, without having to filter the list first.

Your manager wants to quickly find out the total quantity of tea that is in stock. In this exercise, you write a SUMIF formula to rapidly produce the answer.

Calculate the quantity of tea in stock

1 Select cell I2, and then click the equal sign in the formula bar.

The Formula palette appears, and the Name Box becomes a Formula list.

2 Click the Formula list down arrow, and then click SUMIF.

The Formula palette expands to help you write your SUMIF formula. You might need to drag it out of your way when you select cells on the worksheet.

3 Click in the Range box, and then click the column B header to select the entire column.

"B:B" appears in the Range box.

4 In the Criteria box, type **"tea"** (be sure you include the quotation marks).

5 Click in the Sum_Range box, and then click the column F header to select the entire column.

6 Click OK.

The sum of pounds of tea in stock, 5700, appears in cell I2.

7 Save your work.

Finish the lesson

1 To continue to the next lesson, on the File menu, click Close.

2 If you are finished using Microsoft Excel for now, on the File menu, click Exit.

Lesson Summary

To	Do this
Turn AutoFilter on and off	Select a cell in the table that you want to filter. On the Data menu, point to Filter, then click AutoFilter.
Select filter criteria	Use the filter arrows to select filtering criteria.
Remove a filter criterion	In the column header, click the filter arrow for the criterion you want to remove, and then click All.
Filter the ten highest or lowest values	In the column header, click Top 10, and then in the Top 10 AutoFilter dialog box, select Top or Bottom.
Filter using multiple criteria	Click any filter arrow, and then click Custom.
Select an AutoCalculate function	Use the right mouse button to click the AutoCalculate box, and then click the function you want.
Calculate filtered records using the SUBTOTAL function	Turn on AutoFilter, and then select a cell at least one row beneath the last cell in the field you want to calculate. On the Standard toolbar, click the AutoSum button, and then edit the first argument as appropriate. Σ

For online information about	On the Help menu, click Contents And Index, click the Index tab, and then type
Using AutoFilter	**autofilter**
Filtering records	**filters, overview** *or* **filters, in lists**
The SUBTOTAL function	**subtotal worksheet function**

Sorting and Subtotaling to Organize Your Data

Estimated time
30 min.

In this lesson you will learn how to:

■ Sort a list by several categories.

■ Subtotal an entire list of data at one time.

■ Use a subtotal outline to show only the level of detail you want.

As the office manager for the Island Tea & Coffee Company, one of your responsibilities is to present the current inventory to the management team for analysis. Management wants the data they see to be summarized in a logical way. For example, you might need to sort the inventory so that products are arranged by category, and then by source country within each category, and then by value within each source country. To make the inventory more useful to management, you need to add subtotals to the Cost, Price, and Value fields so that they can evaluate and compare meaningful data rather than details.

In this lesson, you'll learn how to quickly sort a list of data, add subtotals to the list, and modify worksheet outlines to summarize the details the way you want.

Open an existing file

One of your monthly tasks is to summarize the current inventory before it's presented to management. In this exercise, you open the current inventory file.

Open

1   On the Standard toolbar, click the Open button.

2 In the Open dialog box, click the Look In Favorites button.

3 In the file list, double-click the Excel SBS Practice folder.

4 Double-click the Lesson 7 Inventory file.

Save the file with a new name

1 On the File menu, click Save As.

The Save As dialog box opens. Be sure the Excel SBS Practice folder appears in the Save In box.

2 In the File Name box, type **Subtotaled Inventory**, and then click Save.

Sorting a List of Information

Before you can subtotal the details in your inventory, you have to sort the details into logical groups because the subtotaling only works with sorted data. You begin by selecting a cell within the list that you want to sort, and then use column labels to define how you want to sort your data. You can sort your inventory by any column in the list. The column that you sort by is called a *sort key*; you can sort by more than one key.

Management wants your final inventory report to show summaries of stock value by category (coffee or tea) and by country within each category. Furthermore, they want to see the value of stock on hand sorted from highest to lowest within each summary group. With the requirements for this final report in mind, you'll begin by sorting the data into groups.

Sort the inventory list

In this exercise, you sort your inventory list by category, then by country, and finally by value so that all of the coffees will be grouped together, followed by all of the teas.

1 Select any cell within the inventory list.

2 On the Data menu, click Sort.

3 Click the Sort By down arrow, and then click Category.

Your data will be sorted by Category, and the categories will be listed in alphabetical order.

4 Click the first Then By down arrow, and then click Source Country.

5 Click the second Then By down arrow, and click Value; then, click the Descending option button next to the second Then By box, and finally click OK.

Your worksheet should look similar to the following illustration.

	A	B	C	D	E	F
1	**Product Name**	**Category**	**Source Country**	**Cost $/lb**	**Price $/lb**	**Qty In Stock**
2	Bourbon Santos	Coffee	Brazil	4.75	9.50	200
3	Medellin	Coffee	Columbia	4.75	9.50	1100
4	Costa Rica	Coffee	Costa Rica	5.25	10.50	1000
5	Santo Domingo	Coffee	Dominican Republic	4.75	9.50	400
6	Ecuador	Coffee	Ecuador	5.25	10.50	500
7	Harrar	Coffee	Ethiopia	4.95	9.90	800
8	Coban	Coffee	Guatemala	4.75	9.50	800
9	Antigua	Coffee	Guatemala	5.25	10.50	500
10	Haiti	Coffee	Haiti	4.75	9.50	400
11	Kona	Coffee	Hawaii	5.25	10.50	1000
12	India	Coffee	India	4.75	9.50	700
13	Java	Coffee	Indonesia	5.25	10.50	800
14	Celebes	Coffee	Indonesia	4.75	9.50	800
15	Sumatra	Coffee	Indonesia	5.75	11.50	600
16	Blue Mountain	Coffee	Jamaica	28.00	36.00	400
17	Kenya	Coffee	Kenya	5.40	10.80	900

Inventory 1-15-97

Sorting on more than three keys

You may occasionally have a more complex list of data that you need to sort on more than three keys. For example, you might have an extensive company personnel list that you need to sort by division, then by department within each division, then by position within each department, and then by last name within each position. The Sort dialog box makes it easy to sort on up to three keys, but in order to sort on four keys, you will need to run the Sort command twice.

The trick to sorting on four keys is the order in which you run the sorts. The major sort key (which in this personnel list example would be the division) should be run in the second sort procedure; you sort the minor keys (by department, then by position, then by last name) first, and then you sort a second time by division only.

Summarizing Data with Subtotals

In Lesson 5, you summarized details by using the Consolidate command, which allowed you to consolidate detailed data from multiple lists but created a summary that contained no details. In this lesson, you will learn to summarize details by using the Subtotal command, which will summarize only a single list but will create a summary that includes details that you can show or hide.

When you want to summarize a list that has multiple columns (or fields) of text entries, such as the Island Tea & Coffee Company inventory, subtotaling is better than consolidation. Subtotaling will include all of the text fields and can create subtotals for groups within each text field; for example, you can create subtotals for each category and for each source country. In addition, the subtotaled summary will contain all of the detailed data as well as allow you to show any details that you choose. For example, you can show the details for all the teas but not the coffees, or for the products from China but not from other countries.

Now that your Island Tea & Coffee Company inventory list has been sorted into groups, you can subtotal those groups so that the management team can quickly find the summary information it needs. You can use the Subtotal command to add subtotals to the groups you choose, without having to manually insert rows for the subtotals or write formulas. The Subtotal command also adds outlining to your worksheet so that you can easily decide how much detail to show in your inventory report.

Calculate subtotals in a detailed list

Now that your inventory list has been sorted in preparation for subtotaling, you can organize the presentation of the information it contains. In this exercise, you create subtotals that sum the value of stock on hand for each source country.

1 Select any cell within the inventory list.

2 On the Data menu, click Subtotals.

The Subtotal dialog box appears.

3 Click the At Each Change In down arrow, and then click Source Country.

4 Click the Use Function down arrow, and then click Sum.

5 In the Add Subtotal To box, select the Value check box, and then scroll through the list to be sure that all the other check boxes are cleared.

6 Be sure that the Replace Current Subtotals and Summary Below Data check boxes are selected.

Your dialog box should look similar to the following illustration.

7   Click OK.

Subtotals are added to your worksheet in the Value field, and captions are added to the Source Country field. Your worksheet should look similar to the following illustration.

		A	B	C	D	E	F
	1	**Product Name**	**Category**	**Source Country**	**Cost $/lb**	**Price $/lb**	**Qty In Stock**
	2	Bourbon Santos	Coffee	Brazil	4.75	9.50	2(
	3			**Brazil Total**			
	4	Medellin	Coffee	Columbia	4.75	9.50	110
	5			**Columbia Total**			
	6	Costa Rica	Coffee	Costa Rica	5.25	10.50	100
	7			**Costa Rica Total**			
	8	Santo Domingo	Coffee	Dominican Republic	4.75	9.50	4(
	9			**Dominican Republic Total**			
	10	Ecuador	Coffee	Ecuador	5.25	10.50	5(
	11			**Ecuador Total**			
	12	Harrar	Coffee	Ethiopia	4.95	9.90	8(
	13			**Ethiopia Total**			
	14	Coban	Coffee	Guatemala	4.75	9.50	8(
	15	Antigua	Coffee	Guatemala	5.25	10.50	5(
	16			**Guatemala Total**			
	17	Haiti	Coffee	Haiti	4.75	9.50	4(

Inventory 1-15-97

Add a second level of subtotals

Management wants to see a summary of stock value by product as well as by country, so you need to create a second level of subtotals. The trick to creating multiple levels of subtotals is to create them in the proper order. In this case, you want the smaller subtotals (by Source Country) to be nested in the larger subtotals (by Category). To do this, you need to create the larger subtotals first, and then the nested subtotals. In this exercise, you first remove the subtotals you created in the previous exercise, and then create subtotals for each category, and then for each source country within each category.

1   On the Data menu, click Subtotals.

2   In the Subtotal dialog box, click Remove All.

The subtotals and outlining are removed.

3   On the Data menu, click Subtotals.

113

4 Click the At Each Change In down arrow, and then click Category.

5 Be sure that the Use Function box contains Sum and that the Value check box is the only check box selected under Add Subtotal To, and then click OK.

The Category field is subtotaled. Subtotals have been added for the Coffee and Tea categories, and a Grand Total field has been added to the bottom of the list.

6 On the Data menu, click Subtotals.

7 Click the At Each Change In down arrow, and then click Source Country.

8 Be sure that the Use Function box contains Sum, and that the Value check box is the only check box selected under Add Subtotal To.

9 Clear the Replace Current Subtotals check box, and then click OK.

Subtotals for the Category and Source Country groups are calculated and displayed on your worksheet in the Value field, and captions are added to the Source Country field. Grand totals have been added at the bottom of the list. Your worksheet should look similar to the following illustration.

		A	B	C	D	E	F
	1	Product Name	Category	Source Country	Cost $/lb	Price $/lb	Qty In Sto
	2	Bourbon Santos	Coffee	Brazil	4.75	9.50	
	3			Brazil Total			
	4	Medellin	Coffee	Columbia	4.75	9.50	1
	5			Columbia Total			
	6	Costa Rica	Coffee	Costa Rica	5.25	10.50	1
	7			Costa Rica Total			
	8	Santo Domingo	Coffee	Dominican Republic	4.75	9.50	
	9			Dominican Republic Total			
	10	Ecuador	Coffee	Ecuador	5.25	10.50	
	11			Ecuador Total			
	12	Harrar	Coffee	Ethiopia	4.95	9.90	
	13			Ethiopia Total			
	14	Coban	Coffee	Guatemala	4.75	9.50	
	15	Antigua	Coffee	Guatemala	5.25	10.50	
	16			Guatemala Total			
	17	Haiti	Coffee	Haiti	4.75	9.50	

Inventory 1-15-97

Show and hide levels of detail to display only the information you want

One of the advantages of using the Subtotal command is that it allows you to manipulate the level of detail showing in the summary by clicking the outline buttons that appear next to your worksheet.

The new column that appeared to the left of your worksheet contains the outline buttons that you can use to hide and show details. The outline level buttons across the top of the new column (the buttons that are numbered) allow you to show a specific level of summary details—for example, the Level 1 button changes the worksheet display so that only the grand total level is shown and all other details and subtotals are hidden. The buttons next to each subtotal row allow you to hide and show the details for each specific subtotal. By clicking the outline buttons, you can show only the details that you want; for example, you can show subtotals for each country, but show the details only for Guatemala.

Outline level buttons

		Product Name	Category	Source Country	Cost $/lb	Price $/l
	1	Product Name	Category	Source Country	Cost $/lb	Price $/l
	2	Bourbon Santos	Coffee	Brazil	4.75	9.5
	3			Brazil Total		
	4	Medellin	Coffee	Columbia	4.75	9.5
	5			Columbia Total		
	6	Costa Rica	Coffee	Costa Rica	5.25	10.5

Hide Detail button

The Island Tea & Coffee Company management team only wants to see summary-type information, so you can take advantage of the Microsoft Excel outlining feature to quickly hide or show different levels of detail. In this exercise, you practice hiding and showing details, and then set up the final detail for your inventory report.

1 Click the Level 2 outline button.

Your worksheet changes to show only the sum of stock value for each product category. Each category summary row has a Show Detail button to its left.

		Product Name	Category	Source Country	Cost $/lb	Price $/l
	1	Product Name	Category	Source Country	Cost $/lb	Price $/l
	43		Coffee Total			
	64		Tea Total			
	65			Grand Total		
	66		Grand Total			
	67					

Show Detail button

2 Click the Show Detail button for Tea Total.

The outline expands to show the totals for each source country in the Tea category.

		Product Name	Category	Source Country	Cost $/lb	Price $/l
	1	Product Name	Category	Source Country	Cost $/lb	Price $/l
	43		Coffee Total			
	44	Keemun	Tea	China	4.85	9.7
	45	Pi Lo Chun	Tea	China	5.55	11.1
	46	Dragonwell	Tea	China	5.35	10.7
	47	Jasmine	Tea	China	4.90	9.8
	48	Gunpowder	Tea	China	4.50	9.0
	49	Black Lychee	Tea	China	5.25	10.5
	50	Lapsang Souchong	Tea	China	5.05	10.1
	51	Chunmee	Tea	China	4.85	9.7
	52			China Total		
	53	Darjeeling	Tea	India	10.15	20.3
	54	Assam	Tea	India	4.85	9.7
	55			India Total		
	56	Gyokuru	Tea	Japan	5.60	11.2
	57			Japan Total		
	58	Russian Blend	Tea	Republic of Georgia	4.90	9.8

Inventory 1-15-97

Show Detail

115

3   Click the Level 3 outline button.

The worksheet shows both Category and Source Country totals. This is the level of detail you will include in your inventory report to management. Your worksheet should look similar to the following illustration.

1 2 3 4		B	C	D	E	F	G
+	30		Kenya Total				9720.00
+	34		Mexico Total				20300.00
+	36		Peru Total				6300.00
+	38		Tanzania Total				9500.00
+	40		Venezuela Total				7350.00
+	42		Yemen Total				9200.00
-	43	Coffee Total					173290.00
+	52		China Total				31340.00
+	55		India Total				16500.00
+	57		Japan Total				1680.00
+	59		Republic of Georgia Total				5880.00
+	61		Sri Lanka Total				7020.00
+	63		Taiwan Total				2160.00
-	64	Tea Total					64580.00
-	65		Grand Total				237870.00
	66	Grand Total					237870.00
	67						

Inventory 1-15-97

4   On the File menu, click Save.

If you want to apply outlining without using automatic subtotals

If you have data that already contains manual subtotals or that you don't want to apply subtotals to, you can still apply outlining. First, you need to determine which rows or columns should be grouped so that they can be hidden and shown together.

1   Select the rows or columns that you want to combine into one outline detail group. Do not include subtotals in the group, or they will be hidden when you hide the group details.

2   On the Data menu, point to Group And Outline, and then click Group.

The group is outlined and a Hide Detail symbol appears at the left side of the worksheet. To hide the group of details, click the Hide Detail symbol.

3   Repeat steps 1 and 2 for each group you want to outline.

4   To remove the outlining, select all the rows or columns in the group, and, on the Data menu, point to Group And Outline, and then click Ungroup.

Hide Detail

NOTE If you'd like to build on the skills you learned in this lesson, you can do the One Step Further. Otherwise, skip to "Finish the Lesson."

One Step Further: Pasting a Subtotaled Summary into a Microsoft Word Document

In order to facilitate the review of the information from the inventory list, you decide to paste it in the inventory report, which is a Microsoft Word document. This way, the management team will be able to open the Microsoft Word document and read the report without having to use Microsoft Excel.

IMPORTANT In order to perform the following exercise, you'll need to have Microsoft Word 97 installed on your computer.

1 Start Microsoft Word, and then open the Inventory Report file, located in the Excel SBS Practice folder.

You can switch between programs by clicking the buttons on the taskbar at the bottom of your screen.

2 Switch to Microsoft Excel, and on the inventory worksheet, select the range B1 through G66 (this range includes all the data contained in the Category through Value fields).

3 On the Edit menu, choose Copy.

4 Switch to Microsoft Word, and be sure that the insertion point is at the end of the document.

5 On the Edit menu, click Paste.

A picture of the selected range from the Subtotaled Inventory workbook is pasted into the Inventory Report document.

6 On the File menu, click Save.

7 Close Microsoft Word.

Finish the lesson

1 To continue to the Review & Practice, on the File menu, click Close.

2 If you are finished using Microsoft Excel for now, on the File menu, click Exit.

Lesson Summary

To	Do this
Sort data by up to three keys	Select a cell within the list you want to sort, and then, on the Data menu, click Sort. In the Sort By and Then By boxes, select the fields you want to sort by, and then click OK.
Sort data by more than three keys	Sort first by the keys you want to be nested, and then sort again by the major key.
Add subtotals	Select a cell within the list you want to subtotal, and then, on the Data menu, click Subtotals. In the At Each Change In box, select the field you want to create subtotals for. In the Use Function box, select the type of calculation you want the subtotal to perform. In the Add Subtotal To box, select the fields that you want calculated, and then click OK.
Remove subtotals	On the Data menu, click Subtotals. Click Remove All.
Create a second level of subtotals	Create the major level of subtotals first, and then create the second level of subtotals using the same procedure, but clear the Replace Current Subtotals check box before running the second level of subtotals.
Hide details in an outline	Click a Hide Detail button or a low number outline button.
Show details in an outline	Click a Show Detail button or a high number outline button.

For online information about	On the Help menu, click Contents And Index, click the Index tab, and then type
Sorting data	**sorting, lists**
Subtotaling data	**subtotals, automatic** *or* **automatically, calculating subtotals**

Review & Practice

Estimated time
20 min.

You will review and practice how to:

- Consolidate lists.
- Filter and sort a detail list.
- Subtotal a list and define the level of detail to present.

Before you move on to Part 3, which covers PivotTables, charting, and printing, you can practice the skills you learned in Part 2 by working through the steps in this Review & Practice section. You will practice consolidating, filtering, sorting, and subtotaling expenses lists.

Scenario

You have been asked to organize the lists of business-related expenses that are kept by the permanent and volunteer staff of the State University Alumni Association for tax purposes. Four lists have already been copied into a single workbook. You will create two summaries, which will each have a different purpose: one will be a consolidated list for a quick reference to item totals, and the other will be a subtotaled list containing specific details that can be used to track down over-expenditures. You will also filter the detailed list to take a look at specific information.

Microsoft Excel 97 Step by Step

Step 1: Consolidate expenses lists

A co-worker has previously copied four expenses lists into a file named SUAA Expenses. The expenses lists are on the worksheets named Katz, Loren, Tanner, and Edmund (the employees' names). In this step, you will consolidate the multiple expenses lists into one.

1 Locate and open the practice file named R&P 2, and then save it as **SUAA Expenses**

2 Select the Sheet1 worksheet and use the Consolidate command to consolidate the lists on the Katz, Loren, Tanner, and Edmund worksheets. (Hint: Because the Consolidate command looks for text labels in the leftmost column, consolidate only columns B through E in each list.)

3 Adjust the column widths in the consolidated table so that the entries are easy to read, and then save the workbook.

Your consolidated summary should look similar to the following illustration.

	A	B	C	D	E	F	G	H
1		Vendor	Purpose	Amount				
2	Office Supplies			$13.70				
3	Tax preparation			$59.46				
4	Telephone Charges			$203.73				
5	Office Equipment			$568.60				
6	Travel			$47.20				
7	Legal and Professional Services			$91.60				
8	Books/Publications			$322.19				
9								
10								

For more information about	See
Consolidating lists	Lesson 5

Step 2: Filter the detail list

In this step, you will filter the worksheet named Big List because one of your co-workers needs to quickly find out what the total books and publications expenses are to include that information in a presentation he is giving.

1 Select the Big List worksheet.

2 Turn on the AutoFilter.

3 In the Category field, select the Books/Publications criterion.

120

4 Select the cells in the Amount field, and then look at the AutoCalculate sum (Hint: Be sure that AutoCalculate is set to the SUM function).

Your AutoCalculate sum should be 322.19.

5 Turn off the AutoFilter.

For more information about	See
Filtering data	Lesson 6

Step 3: *Sort and subtotal the detail list by tax categories*

In this step, you will sort and subtotal the Big List worksheet list so that it is ready for the association's accountant.

1 In the Big List worksheet, select a cell within the list, and sort the list first by Category, then by Vendor, and finally by Date.

2 Subtotal the list by Category only.

3 Show the second-level details. (Hint: Only the Category subtotals and Grand Total should show.)

Your finished worksheet should look similar to the following illustration.

		A	B	C	D	E	F
	1	Date	Category	Vendor	Purpose	Amount	
+	10		Books/Publications Total			$322.19	
+	12		Legal and Professional Services Total			$91.60	
+	20		Office Equipment Total			$568.60	
+	26		Office Supplies Total			$13.70	
+	28		Tax preparation Total			$59.46	
+	40		Telephone Charges Total			$203.73	
+	45		Travel Total			$47.20	
-	46		Grand Total			$1,306.48	
	47						

For more information about	See
Sorting data	Lesson 7
Subtotaling data	Lesson 7

Finish the Review & Practice

1 To continue to the next lesson, on the File menu, click Close.

2 If you are finished using Microsoft Excel for now, on the File menu, click Exit.

Part

3

Presenting Your Data to Others

Creating PivotTables to Summarize Data

Estimated time
30 min.

In this lesson you will learn how to:

- Import a text file.
- Create a PivotTable.
- Modify a PivotTable.
- Update a PivotTable.

In Part 2, you learned how to summarize data by using consolidation and sub-totaling, and you saw the strengths and weaknesses of each method. In this lesson you will learn how to create and use PivotTables as a data presentation tool. A *PivotTable* combines the best of consolidation and subtotals, and goes well beyond both of those tools to give you greater flexibility of presentation. When you create a PivotTable, you can organize data stored in multiple worksheets or workbooks as well as show or hide any details you want. Additionally, you can modify the PivotTable presentation by changing the layout or the level of detail shown without having to recreate the PivotTable—you can change the presentation "on the fly" by simply dragging items to new locations on your worksheet.

At the Island Tea & Coffee Company, your manager has requested a summary of last year's sales data. She wants the data summarized in three ways: monthly sales totals by each employee, for a comparison of monthly performances over the past year; quarterly sales totals in each product category, coffee or tea, for each individual employee; and average quarterly sales of each product.

You can create all of these summaries by creating a single PivotTable, and then manipulating it to show what you want.

The sales data for 1996 was assembled by another employee using his laptop computer; to keep the size of the database to a minimum, he entered the data in a text file. A text file is the simplest type of data file and can be opened by most programs, including Microsoft Excel. You will begin the task of creating the 1996 sales presentation by importing the data from the text file into a workbook.

Open a new workbook

If you have just started Microsoft Excel, you will already have a new, unsaved workbook open. If not, follow this procedure to open a new workbook.

New

➤ On the Standard toolbar, click the New button.

A new workbook appears. You do not need to save it yet.

Getting External Data into a Workbook

To import a text file, you simply open it. Opening a text file in Microsoft Excel automatically starts the Text Import Wizard, which guides you through the process of selecting a *delimiter* and formatting the columns of data. A delimiter is a character, like a space, a tab, or a comma, that separates fields of data in a database. For example, to create a tab-delimited database of names and addresses, you would separate each field by a tab character. The tab characters *parse*, or separate, each field in a record (such as first name or last name) into its own column in the database.

The Text Import Wizard usually detects the delimiter automatically, and allows you to select the data format for each field in the database. The default data format is General, which works fine for most data—Microsoft Excel will recognize dates as dates, numbers as numbers that can be calculated, and text as text; however, if you have a field of numbers that are not supposed to be calculated, such as zip codes, you need to format that field as text, or Microsoft Excel will delete leading zeroes (for example, 07654 will become 7654), and you will lose the integrity of the data.

Import a text file

The text file database of 1996 sales was passed along to you with the information that it is a tab-delimited text file with a header row. In this exercise, you import the text file into a workbook, and then verify that the tab delimiters are set properly.

Open

1 On the Standard toolbar, click the Open button, and locate the Excel SBS Practice folder.

2   In the Open dialog box, click the Files Of Type down arrow, and then select Text Files.

The names of all the text files contained in the folder are listed.

3   Double-click the 1996 Orders.txt file.

The Text Import Wizard appears.

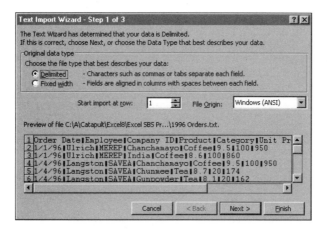

4   Since you have been told that the text file is tab-delimited and has a header row, be sure that the Delimited option button is selected and that the Start Import At Row box shows 1, and then click Next.

5   In the Step 2 dialog box, verify that the Tab Delimiters check box is selected.

By looking at the Data Preview box, you can tell that Tab is the correct delimiter, because the data is parsed into columns.

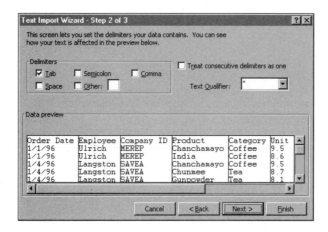

6 Click Next.

7 In the Step 3 dialog box, under Column Data Format, be sure that the General option button is selected, and that all of the column titles in the top row of the sample in the Data Preview box read "General."

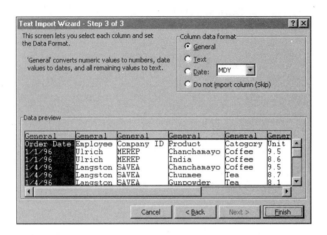

8 Click Finish.

The text file data is imported, and the worksheet name is automatically changed to the text file name. Your worksheet should look similar to the following illustration.

	A	B	C	D	E	F	G	H	I
1	Order Date	Employee	Company	Product	Category	Unit Price	Quantity	Total	
2	1/1/96	Ulrich	MEREP	Chancham	Coffee	9.5	100	950	
3	1/1/96	Ulrich	MEREP	India	Coffee	8.6	100	860	
4	1/4/96	Langston	SAVEA	Chancham	Coffee	9.5	100	950	
5	1/4/96	Langston	SAVEA	Chunmee	Tea	8.7	20	174	
6	1/4/96	Langston	SAVEA	Gunpowde	Tea	8.1	20	162	
7	1/5/96	Hankins	ERNST	Keemun	Tea	8.7	20	174	
8	1/5/96	Hankins	ERNST	Kenya	Coffee	9.7	100	970	
9	1/6/96	Hankins	BERGL	Ecuador	Coffee	9.5	100	950	
10	1/6/96	Hankins	BERGL	Harrar	Coffee	8.9	100	890	
11	1/6/96	Hankins	BERGL	Pi Lo Chur	Tea	10	20	200	
12	1/6/96	Hankins	BERGL	Tanzania	Coffee	8.6	100	860	
13	1/6/96	Garnier	REGGI	Keemun	Tea	8.7	20	174	
14	1/6/96	Garnier	REGGI	Medellin	Coffee	8.6	100	860	
15	1/7/96	Hankins	BERGL	Java	Coffee	9.5	100	950	
16	1/7/96	Hankins	BERGL	Kenya	Coffee	9.7	100	970	
17	1/8/96	Langston	RICAR	Black Lych	Tea	9.5	20	190	

1996 Orders

Save the new workbook

1 On the Standard toolbar, click the Save button.

Save

2 In the Save As Type box, select Microsoft Excel Workbook, and then save the workbook in the Excel SBS Practice folder as 1996 Sales Summary.

Creating a Dynamic Summary with a PivotTable

To quickly and efficiently review last year's sales, your manager has asked you to generate three summaries of the 1996 sales data. In the following exercises, you'll create the monthly sales totals summary for each employee in 1996, and then format the table.

Create a PivotTable to summarize data for easy analysis

The first step toward creating the summary report is to organize the records that are currently contained in the workbook. In this exercise, you create a PivotTable that includes Order Date and Employee data.

For a demonstration of how to create and use a PivotTable, double-click the Cam-corder Files On The Internet shortcut on your Desktop or connect to the Internet address listed on page xxvii.

1 Click any cell in the list, and then, on the Data menu, click PivotTable Report.

The PivotTable Wizard appears.

2 Be sure that the Microsoft Excel List Or Database option button is selected, and then click Next.

The Step 2 dialog box shows the range Microsoft Excel has selected as the data for the PivotTable.

3 Click Next.

The Step 3 dialog box appears.

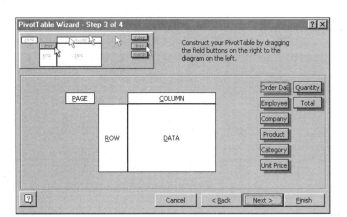

The white boxes in the middle of the dialog box form a PivotTable layout diagram. You drag the buttons located on the right side of the dialog box, which are labeled with the field names from the data list, to create your PivotTable.

4 Drag the Order Date field button to the Row box in the layout diagram.

5   Drag the Employee field button to the Column box in the layout diagram.

6   Drag the Total field button to the Data box in the layout diagram.

The Total field button becomes a Sum Of Total button when you drop it in the Data box. Your dialog box should look similar to the following illustration.

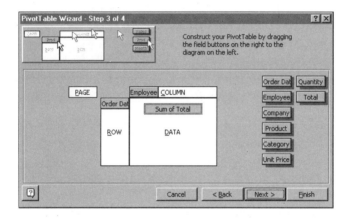

7   Click Next.

8   In the Step 4 dialog box, be sure that the New Worksheet option button is selected, and then click Finish.

Your worksheet should look similar to the following illustration.

	A	B	C	D	E	F	G	H	I
1	Sum of Total	Employee							
2	Order Date	Davis	Garnier	Gebhardt	Hankins	Katz	Langston	Newbert	Ulrich
3	1/1/96								1810
4	1/4/96						1286		
5	1/5/96				1144				
6	1/6/96		1034		2900				
7	1/7/96				1920				
8	1/8/96						1242		2580
9	1/11/96						1810		
10	1/12/96				1810				
11	1/13/96		1920				2292		
12	1/14/96		1036						
13	1/15/96	260					1316		
14	1/18/96		1316						
15	1/19/96		950	3240					
16	1/20/96								
17	1/21/96						1070		

Sheet1 / 1996 Orders /

Group PivotTable dates by month

The PivotTable Wizard has arranged the information in the layout you selected, but it shows every detail. Since your manager requested a summary report, you need to organize and condense the level of detail. In this exercise, you group dates by month for a more meaningful and easy-to-read summary.

1 Use the right mouse button to click any cell in the Order Date column.

2 On the shortcut menu, point to Group And Outline, and then click Group.

The Grouping dialog box appears.

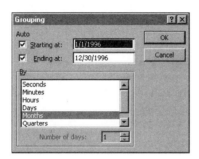

3 Be sure that Months is selected in the By list, and then click OK.

Your worksheet should look similar to the following illustration.

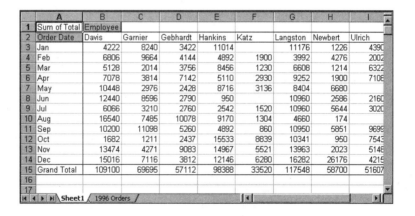

	A	B	C	D	E	F	G	H	I
1	Sum of Total	Employee							
2	Order Date	Davis	Garnier	Gebhardt	Hankins	Katz	Langston	Newbert	Ulrich
3	Jan	4222	8240	3422	11014		11176	1226	4390
4	Feb	6806	9664	4144	4892	1900	3992	4276	2002
5	Mar	5128	2014	3756	8456	1230	6608	1214	6322
6	Apr	7078	3814	7142	5110	2930	9252	1900	7108
7	May	10448	2976	2428	8716	3136	8404	6680	
8	Jun	12440	8596	2790	950		10960	2586	2160
9	Jul	6066	3210	2760	2542	1520	10960	5644	3020
10	Aug	16540	7485	10078	9170	1304	4660	174	
11	Sep	10200	11098	5260	4892	860	10950	5851	9699
12	Oct	1682	1211	2437	15533	8839	10341	950	7543
13	Nov	13474	4271	9083	14967	5521	13963	2023	5148
14	Dec	15016	7116	3812	12146	6280	16282	26176	4215
15	Grand Total	109100	69695	57112	98388	33520	117548	58700	51607
16									
17									

TROUBLESHOOTING If you are unable to group dates in a PivotTable, it is most likely because the dates are not formatted properly and Microsoft Excel does not recognize them as dates. To fix this, change the format of the Date field in the source data to a Date format, and then, on the Data menu, click Refresh PivotTable.

Apply an AutoFormat to the PivotTable

Your PivotTable is now a concise summary, so it is time to make it more appealing by formatting it. In this exercise, you apply an AutoFormat to the PivotTable for a professional look.

1 Select any cell within the PivotTable.

2 On the Format menu, click AutoFormat.

The AutoFormat dialog box appears.

3 In the Table Format list, scroll down and select List 1, and then click OK.

The List 1 AutoFormat is applied to your PivotTable. Your worksheet should look similar to the following illustration.

	A	B	C	D	E	F	G	H	
1	*Sum of Total*	Employee							
2	Order Date	*Davis*	*Garnier*	*Gebhardt*	*Hankins*	*Katz*	*Langston*	*Newbert*	U
3	Jan	4222	8240	3422	11014		11176	1226	
4	Feb	6806	9664	4144	4892	1900	3992	4276	
5	Mar	5128	2014	3756	8456	1230	6608	1214	
6	Apr	7078	3814	7142	5110	2930	9252	1900	
7	May	10448	2976	2428	8716	3136	8404	6680	
8	Jun	12440	8596	2790	950		10960	2586	
9	Jul	6066	3210	2760	2542	1520	10960	5644	
10	Aug	16540	7485	10078	9170	1304	4660	174	
11	Sep	10200	11098	5260	4892	860	10950	5851	
12	Oct	1682	1211	2437	15533	8839	10341	950	
13	Nov	13474	4271	9083	14967	5521	13963	2023	
14	Dec	15016	7116	3812	12146	6280	16282	26176	
15	**Grand Total**	109100	69695	57112	98388	33520	117548	58700	
16									
17									

Sheet1 / 1996 Orders /

Format the numbers in the PivotTable

The numbers in the data section of the PivotTable are not very intuitive. In this exercise, you apply formatting that shows that the numbers represent dollars.

1 Use the right mouse button to click any cell containing a number within the data portion of the table.

2 On the shortcut menu, click Field.

The PivotTable Field dialog box appears.

3 Click the Number button.

The Format Cells dialog box appears, but it contains only number formatting options.

4 In the Category list, click Currency.

5 In the Decimal Places box, change the value to 0.

For a demonstration of how to format numbers in a PivotTable, double-click the Camcorder Files On The Internet shortcut on your Desktop or connect to the Internet address listed on page xxvii.

132

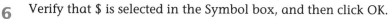

6   Verify that $ is selected in the Symbol box, and then click OK.

7   In the PivotTable Field dialog box, click OK.

The first summary your manager requested is complete, and ready to be printed. Your worksheet should look similar to the following illustration.

	A	B	C	D	E	F	G	H	
1	*Sum of Total*	Employee							
2	Order Date	*Davis*	*Garnier*	*Gebhardt*	*Hankins*	*Katz*	*Langston*	*Newbert*	*U*
3	Jan	$4,222	$8,240	$3,422	$11,014		$11,176	$1,226	
4	Feb	$6,806	$9,664	$4,144	$4,892	$1,900	$3,992	$4,276	
5	Mar	$5,128	$2,014	$3,756	$8,456	$1,230	$6,608	$1,214	
6	Apr	$7,078	$3,814	$7,142	$5,110	$2,930	$9,252	$1,900	
7	May	$10,448	$2,976	$2,428	$8,716	$3,136	$8,404	$6,680	
8	Jun	$12,440	$8,596	$2,790	$950		$10,960	$2,586	
9	Jul	$6,066	$3,210	$2,760	$2,542	$1,520	$10,960	$5,644	
10	Aug	$16,540	$7,485	$10,078	$9,170	$1,304	$4,660	$174	
11	Sep	$10,200	$11,098	$5,260	$4,892	$860	$10,950	$5,851	
12	Oct	$1,682	$1,211	$2,437	$15,533	$8,839	$10,341	$950	
13	Nov	$13,474	$4,271	$9,083	$14,967	$5,521	$13,963	$2,023	
14	Dec	$15,016	$7,116	$3,812	$12,146	$6,280	$16,282	$26,176	
15	**Grand Total**	$109,100	$69,695	$57,112	$98,388	$33,520	$117,548	$58,700	$!
16									
17									

Sheet1 / 1996 Orders /

Modifying the Data Displayed in a PivotTable

The second summary your manager asked for is a quarterly sales totals summary, sorted by category and individual employees. You need to add the Category field to the PivotTable, and change the date grouping from months to quarters. You will also create Page fields in the upper-left corner of the PivotTable for the Employee data so that individual summaries can be displayed.

Add another field to the PivotTable and change the date grouping

To create a quarterly sales summary by category, you need to add the Category field to the PivotTable and re-group the order dates into quarters. In this exercise, you add the Category field to the PivotTable and switch the Order Date data to a quarterly summary.

For a demonstration of how to group dates in a PivotTable, double-click the Camcorder Files On The Internet shortcut on your Desktop or connect to the Internet address listed on page xxvii.

1   Use the right mouse button to click any cell within the PivotTable.

2   On the shortcut menu, click Wizard.

Step 3 of the PivotTable Wizard appears.

3   Drag the Category field button to the Row box of the layout diagram.

Your Step 3 dialog box should look similar to the following illustration.

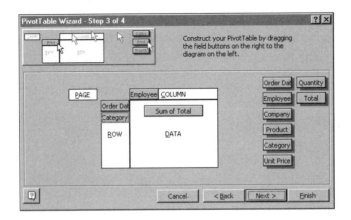

4 Click Finish.

Your worksheet should look similar to the following illustration.

	A	B	C	D	E	F	G	H	I
1	*Sum of Total*		Employee						
2	Order Date	Category	*Davis*	*Garnier*	*Gebhardt*	*Hankins*	*Katz*	*Langston*	*Newl*
3	Jan	Coffee	$3,800	$7,350	$3,240	$7,400		$9,140	
4		Tea	$422	$890	$182	$3,614		$2,036	
5	**Jan Total**		$4,222	$8,240	$3,422	$11,014		$11,176	$1
6	Feb	Coffee	$4,282	$7,318	$3,194	$3,374	$1,900	$2,580	$3
7		Tea	$2,524	$2,346	$950	$1,518		$1,412	
8	**Feb Total**		$6,806	$9,664	$4,144	$4,892	$1,900	$3,992	$4
9	Mar	Coffee	$4,770	$1,840	$2,850	$7,630	$970	$5,340	$1
10		Tea	$358	$174	$906	$826	$260	$1,268	
11	**Mar Total**		$5,128	$2,014	$3,756	$8,456	$1,230	$6,608	$1
12	Apr	Coffee	$6,520	$3,640	$6,410	$4,570	$2,670	$8,700	$1
13		Tea	$558	$174	$732	$540	$260	$552	
14	**Apr Total**		$7,078	$3,814	$7,142	$5,110	$2,930	$9,252	$1
15	May	Coffee	$9,670	$2,610	$1,900	$8,190	$2,760	$7,270	$6
16		Tea	$778	$366	$528	$526	$376	$1,134	
17	**May Total**		$10,448	$2,976	$2,428	$8,716	$3,136	$8,404	$6

Sheet1 / 1996 Orders

5 In the Order Date column, use the right mouse button to click any month cell.

Both of the rows for the month cell you click will be automatically selected; for example, if you click March (cell A9), rows 9 and 10 will both be selected.

6 On the shortcut menu, point to Group And Outline, and then click Group.

7 In the By list, click Months to clear it, click Quarters to select it, and then click OK.

Your screen should look similar to the following illustration.

	A	B	C	D	E	F	G	H	I
1	*Sum of Total*		Employee						
2	Order Date	Category	*Davis*	*Garnier*	*Gebhardt*	*Hankins*	*Katz*	*Langston*	*Newl*
3	Qtr1	Coffee	$12,852	$16,508	$9,284	$18,404	$2,870	$17,060	$5
4		Tea	$3,304	$3,410	$2,038	$5,958	$260	$4,716	$1
5	**Qtr1 Total**		$16,156	$19,918	$11,322	$24,362	$3,130	$21,776	$8
6	Qtr2	Coffee	$27,620	$14,470	$11,100	$13,710	$5,430	$25,610	$10
7		Tea	$2,346	$916	$1,260	$1,066	$636	$3,006	
8	**Qtr2 Total**		$29,966	$15,386	$12,360	$14,776	$6,066	$28,616	$11
9	Qtr3	Coffee	$30,950	$18,910	$16,000	$13,580	$2,760	$22,890	$9
10		Tea	$1,856	$2,883	$2,098	$3,024	$924	$3,680	$1
11	**Qtr3 Total**		$32,806	$21,793	$18,098	$16,604	$3,684	$26,570	$11
12	Qtr4	Coffee	$23,920	$9,550	$10,220	$38,230	$18,300	$35,990	$26
13		Tea	$6,252	$3,048	$5,112	$4,416	$2,340	$4,596	$3
14	**Qtr4 Total**		$30,172	$12,598	$15,332	$42,646	$20,640	$40,586	$29
15	**Grand Total**		$109,100	$69,695	$57,112	$98,388	$33,520	$117,548	$58
16									
17									

Sheet1 / 1996 Orders /

Create page fields

One of the goals of this summary is to show the sales totals for each employee. In this exercise, you create Page fields for individual employees so that the PivotTable can show data for one employee at a time.

For a demonstration of how to show data on separate pages in a PivotTable, double-click the Camcorder Files On The Internet shortcut on your Desktop or connect to the Internet address listed on page xxvii.

1 Use the right mouse button to click any cell within the PivotTable.

2 On the shortcut menu, click Wizard.

The Step 3 dialog box appears.

3 In the layout diagram, drag the Employee button from the Column box to the Page box, and then click Finish.

Your worksheet should look similar to the following illustration.

	A	B	C	D	E	F	G	H	I
1	Employee	(All) ▼							
2									
3	*Sum of Total*								
4	Order Date	Category	*Total*						
5	Qtr1	Coffee	$110,500						
6		Tea	$25,172						
7	**Qtr1 Total**		$135,672						
8	Qtr2	Coffee	$125,370						
9		Tea	$12,026						
10	**Qtr2 Total**		$137,396						
11	Qtr3	Coffee	$137,060						
12		Tea	$18,435						
13	**Qtr3 Total**		$155,495						
14	Qtr4	Coffee	$185,870						
15		Tea	$31,839						
16	**Qtr4 Total**		$217,709						
17	**Grand Total**		$646,272						

Sheet1 / 1996 Orders /

To the right of the Employee button in the PivotTable is a list that shows All, and the data shown in the PivotTable is the summary data for all employees. You can show the data for an individual employee by selecting his or her name from the drop-down list.

135

4   Click the Employee down arrow, and then click Davis.

Davis' sales data for 1996 appears in the PivotTable. Your worksheet should look similar to the following illustration.

	A	B	C	D	E	F	G	H	I
1	Employee	Davis							
2									
3	*Sum of Total*								
4	Order Date	Category	*Total*						
5	Qtr1	Coffee	$12,852						
6		Tea	$3,304						
7	Qtr1 Total		$16,156						
8	Qtr2	Coffee	$27,620						
9		Tea	$2,346						
10	Qtr2 Total		$29,966						
11	Qtr3	Coffee	$30,950						
12		Tea	$1,856						
13	Qtr3 Total		$32,806						
14	Qtr4	Coffee	$23,920						
15		Tea	$6,252						
16	Qtr4 Total		$30,172						
17	Grand Total		$109,100						

Sheet1 / 1996 Orders /

Change the PivotTable view

For a demonstration of how to change a PivotTable's presentation, double-click the Camcorder Files On The Internet shortcut on your Desktop or connect to the Internet address listed on page xxvii.

In your PivotTable, the Order Date data is displayed in rows; this presentation is called a *row orientation*. The data contained in the Category column is also displayed in a row orientation, but the Employee names appear in a *page orientation*, since the data for each employee is summarized individually (as if it were on its own page).

Having both the Order Date and the Categories data presented in a row orientation is cumbersome to read. In this exercise, you change the presentation of the Order Date data from row to *column orientation* so that the data for each quarter is displayed in a separate column.

1   Drag the Order Date button up and to the right of the Sum Of Total label (so it's over cell B3).

As you drag the button to different areas of the worksheet, the mouse pointer icon will change to indicate what will happen to the data orientation when you drop the button. The following icon shapes appear depending on where the mouse pointer is.

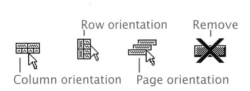

Row orientation   Remove

Column orientation   Page orientation

136

2 When the mouse pointer looks like the Column Orientation icon, release the mouse button.

The second summary your manager requested is complete and ready to be printed. Your worksheet should look similar to the following illustration.

	A	B	C	D	E	F	G	H
1	Employee	Davis						
2								
3	Sum of Total	Order Date						
4	Category	Qtr1	Qtr2	Qtr3	Qtr4	Grand Total		
5	Coffee	$12,852	$27,620	$30,950	$23,920	$95,342		
6	Tea	$3,304	$2,346	$1,856	$6,252	$13,758		
7	Grand Total	$16,156	$29,966	$32,806	$30,172	$109,100		
8								
9								

3 Save the workbook.

Showing Average Sales by Product

The third summary your manager requested was a presentation of the average sales of each product by quarter. You can quickly and easily create this summary in the existing PivotTable by removing the Category and Employee fields, adding the Product field, and changing the summary function from Sum to Average.

Remove data from the PivotTable

In this exercise, you remove the Category and Employee fields from the PivotTable.

1 On the worksheet, drag the Category button away from the PivotTable until the mouse pointer looks like the Remove icon, and then release the mouse button.

The Category data is removed from the PivotTable.

For a demon-stration of how to change a PivotTable's presentation, double-click the Camcorder Files On The Internet shortcut on your Desktop or connect to the Internet address listed on page xxvii.

2 Repeat step 1 to remove the Employee data from the PivotTable.

Add a new field to the PivotTable and change the summary function

To create a summary of average sales by product by quarter, you need to add a new field. In this exercise, you add the Product field to the PivotTable, and change the summary function from Sum to Average.

1 Use the right mouse button to click any cell in the PivotTable, and then click Wizard.

137

2 In the Step 3 dialog box, drag the Product field button to the Row box in the layout diagram.

3 Double-click the Sum Of Total button.

The PivotTable Field dialog box appears.

4 In the Summarize By list, select Average, and then click OK.

In the Step 3 dialog box, the Sum Of Total button becomes the Average Of Total.

5 Click Finish.

The PivotTable has been changed to show a summary of average quarterly sales by Product. The Grand Total column shows the average for the year. Your worksheet should look similar to the following illustration.

	A	B	C	D	E	F	G
1							
2							
3	Average of Total	Order Date					
4	Product	Qtr1	Qtr2	Qtr3	Qtr4	Grand Total	
5	Antigua	$950	$950	$950	$1,017	$967	
6	Assam	$174	$174	$232	$274	$225	
7	Black Lychee	$190	$190	$222	$297	$228	
8	Bourbon Santos	$860	$860	$860	$885	$869	
9	Celebes	$871	$860	$860	$883	$871	
10	Ceylon	$457	$210	$263	$333	$321	
11	Chanchamayo	$696	$950	$950	$990	$892	
12	Chunmee	$375	$174	$226	$277	$274	
13	Coatepec	$678	$950	$950	$964	$900	
14	Coban	$777	$860	$860	$905	$838	
15	Costa Rica	$928	$950	$950	$979	$951	
16	Darjeeling	$347	$366	$366	$582	$420	
17	Dragonwell	$382	$192	$240	$299	$265	

Sheet1 / 1996 Orders /

Refreshing Data and Showing Details

Refresh the PivotTable data

One of the sales people, Mr. Langston, calls to tell you there is a mistake in the data that was sent out: he actually sold 400 lbs of Antigua coffee, worth $4200, in his 12/15/96 order. You need to first make the change in the underlying database, and then refresh the PivotTable to include the correction in the summary.

You can find this record rapidly by using AutoFilter and filtering on the employee name, the product name, or the date.

1 Select the 1996 Orders worksheet, and select cell G773 (Langston's Antigua order on 12/15/96).

2 Change the amount in cell G773 to 400, and the amount in cell H773 to 4200.

3 Select Sheet1 (the PivotTable worksheet), and then use the right mouse button to click any cell in the PivotTable.

4 On the shortcut menu, click Refresh Data.

The PivotTable data is updated, and the average sale amount of Antigua coffee for the fourth quarter has increased to $1542. Your worksheet should look similar to the following illustration.

	A	B	C	D	E	F	G
1							
2							
3	Average of Total	Order Date					
4	Product	Qtr1	Qtr2	Qtr3	Qtr4	Grand Total	
5	Antigua	$950	$950	$950	$1,542	$1,098	
6	Assam	$174	$174	$232	$274	$225	
7	Black Lychee	$190	$190	$222	$297	$228	
8	Bourbon Santos	$860	$860	$860	$885	$869	

Show the details underlying a specific calculation

After a quick review of the summary reports you compiled, your manager decides to take a closer look at the data for the Jamaican Blue Mountain coffee sales in the fourth quarter. She wants to see the specific details used to calculate the fourth quarter average. You can generate this information quickly by doing a *drilldown*. A drilldown creates a new worksheet that lists all the records used to calculate a PivotTable figure.

In this exercise, you do a drilldown to extract the requested information.

You can sort the Product column alphabetically by selecting a cell in the column, and then clicking the Sort Descending button on the Standard toolbar.

1 Double-click the Qtr4 figure for Jamaican Blue Mountain.

A new worksheet is added to the workbook, containing a list of detailed information on the sales of Jamaican Blue Mountain coffee for the fourth quarter. Your screen should look similar to the following illustration.

	A	B	C	D	E	F	G	H
1	Order Date	Employee	Company ID	Product	Category	Unit Price	Quantity	Tot
2	12/19/96	Newbert	RICAR	Jamaican Blue Mountain	Coffee	36	100	36
3	12/13/96	Newbert	SUPRE	Jamaican Blue Mountain	Coffee	36	100	36
4	12/8/96	Davis	ALFRE	Jamaican Blue Mountain	Coffee	36	100	36
5	12/2/96	Newbert	LILAS	Jamaican Blue Mountain	Coffee	36	100	36
6	11/22/96	Langston	WELLI	Jamaican Blue Mountain	Coffee	32.4	100	32
7	11/18/96	Katz	KONIG	Jamaican Blue Mountain	Coffee	32.4	100	32
8	11/2/96	Hankins	LEHMA	Jamaican Blue Mountain	Coffee	32.4	100	32
9	10/14/96	Katz	WARTI	Jamaican Blue Mountain	Coffee	32.4	100	32
10	10/13/96	Langston	ISLAN	Jamaican Blue Mountain	Coffee	32.4	100	32
11	10/11/96	Katz	QUICK	Jamaican Blue Mountain	Coffee	32.4	100	32
12								
13								
14								
15								
16								
17								

Sheet2 / Sheet1 / 1996 Orders /

2 Save the workbook.

> **NOTE** If you'd like to build on the skills you learned in this lesson, you can do the One Step Further. Otherwise, skip to "Finish the Lesson."

One Step Further: Creating Page Reports for Distribution to Individuals

In preparation for performance reviews, your manager asks you to compile a report of average quarterly sales by employee, broken down by product. You can do this by using the current PivotTable and adding Employee data in a page orientation, and then creating separate worksheets for each employee's average quarterly sales by product.

In this exercise, you create printable page reports for each employee.

1   On the worksheet containing the PivotTable, use the right mouse button to click any cell in the PivotTable.

2   On the shortcut menu, click Wizard.

3   In the Step 3 dialog box, drag the Employee field button to the Page box, and then click Finish.

The Employee button appears in a page orientation in the PivotTable.

4   Use the right mouse button to click any cell in the PivotTable.

5   On the shortcut menu, click Show Pages.

6   In the Show Pages dialog box, click OK.

A new worksheet for each employee is added to the workbook. Each new worksheet contains a PivotTable that summarizes the employee's quarterly sales by product.

7   Save your workbook.

Finish the Lesson

1   To continue to the next lesson, on the File menu, click Close.

2   If you are finished using Microsoft Excel for now, on the File menu, click Exit.

Lesson Summary

To	Do this	Button
Import a text file	On the Standard toolbar, click the Open button. In the List Files Of Type box, select Text Files, and then open the text file. Using the Text Import Wizard, select a delimiter, select the column formatting you want, and then click Finish.	
Create a PivotTable	Select any cell in the data list. On the Data menu, click PivotTable Report. Follow the steps in the Wizard, and arrange the data by dragging the field buttons and placing them appropriately in the layout diagram.	
Group dates	Use the right mouse button to click a date cell, and then, on the shortcut menu, point to Group And Outline and click Group. Select the date grouping that you want, and then click OK.	
Apply an AutoFormat	Select any cell in the PivotTable. On the Format menu, click AutoFormat. Select a Table Format, and then click OK.	
Format PivotTable numbers	Use the right mouse button to click any cell in the data portion of the table. On the shortcut menu, click Field. In the PivotTable Field dialog box, click Number, and then select a number format for the data. Click OK twice.	
Add a new field	Use the right mouse button to click any cell in the PivotTable. On the shortcut menu, click Wizard, and then in the dialog box, drag the field button for the data you want to add into the layout diagram. Click Finish.	

To	Do this	Button
Create page fields	Use the right mouse button to click any cell in the PivotTable. On the shortcut menu, click Wizard. Drag the field button for the data you want in the Page field into the Page box in the layout diagram, and then click Finish.	
Change data orientation	In the PivotTable, drag a field button to a new orientation position. Drop the field button when the mouse pointer icon changes to the correct shape for the data orientation you want.	
Remove data	In the PivotTable, drag a field button away from the PivotTable. Drop the field button when the mouse pointer takes the shape of the Remove icon.	✖
Change the summary function	Use the right mouse button to click any cell in the PivotTable. On the shortcut menu, click Wizard. Double-click the button in the Data box in the layout diagram. In the PivotTable Field dialog box, select a new summary function in the Summarize By list, click OK, and then click Finish.	
Refresh data	Use the right mouse button to click any cell in the PivotTable. On the shortcut menu, click Refresh Data.	
Show underlying details	In the PivotTable, double-click the data cell for which you want to find additional information.	

For online information about	On the Help menu, click Contents And Index, click the Index tab, and then type
Importing data	**importing data**
Creating PivotTables	**pivottables, creating**
Modifying PivotTables	**pivottables, adding and removing fields**
Updating PivotTables	**pivottables, updating**

Charting to Assess Trends and Relationships

**Estimated time
30 min.**

In this lesson you will learn how to:

- Create a chart.
- Customize a chart.
- Make a chart format re-usable.
- Create a trendline.

A worksheet can help you calculate precise numbers, trends, and changes over time, but it can be difficult to grasp the overall meaning of numbers and trends just by looking at figures. A chart, on the other hand, creates a visual presentation of data and its relationship to other data so that the overall meaning can be grasped very quickly.

You can easily create and customize charts in Microsoft Excel by using the Chart Wizard. You can also save the formatting of the chart you create, and then re-use it in other charts. Charts can be *embedded* on the worksheet next to your data; they can also appear on a *chart sheet*. A chart sheet is a sheet in a workbook that contains only a chart. You can easily make an embedded chart into a chart sheet, or a chart sheet into an embedded chart, depending on what you prefer at any point in time.

Other features, such as trendlines and secondary axes, make charted data even more useful. A trend in a series of data, such as monthly sales for a year, can be calculated and used to forecast sales; you can show that trend and forecast in the chart by using a trendline. Data series that are related but are on different number scales, for example volume sold (in thousands of pounds) and price per pound (in dollars per pound), can be displayed on the same chart by using a secondary axis for the second number scale. This enables you to relate sales volume to sales price in a direct and meaningful manner.

At the Island Tea & Coffee Company, your manager has asked you to generate two documents based on the current sales orders for 1997, which run through June: monthly sales performances for the entire company and for each employee, and a sales forecast for the next six months based on sales since January 1997. The data needed to produce these documents is currently stored in a PivotTable and in multiple worksheets.

Open an existing file

You keep the current orders data in a workbook named Current Orders. In this exercise, you open the Current Orders file.

Open

1   On the Standard toolbar, click the Open button.

2   In the Open dialog box, click the Look In Favorites button.

3   In the file list, double-click the Excel SBS Practice folder.

4   Double-click the Current Orders file.

Save the file with a new name

1   On the File menu, click Save As.

The Save As dialog box opens. Be sure the Excel SBS Practice folder appears in the Save In box.

2   In the File Name box, type **Charting Lesson**, and then click Save.

Presenting Data Graphically with Charts

Your manager at the Island Tea & Coffee Company has asked for a chart of the company's sales by category for each month this year. A PivotTable has been created on the PivotTable sheet (based on the 1997 Orders worksheet) to show this data. After you create the chart, you'll customize it by changing the color of the Tea series to a two-color fade, and changing the column markers in the coffee series into picture markers of stacked coffee cups.

Create a chart

Now that you have opened your current orders list, you are ready to start chart-ing it. In this exercise, you create an embedded column chart based on the data in the PivotTable.

For a demon-stration of how to create an em-bedded chart based on a PivotTable, double-click the Camcorder Files On The Internet shortcut on your Desktop or connect to the Internet address listed on page xxvii.

1 Select the PivotTable sheet.

2 Use the right mouse button to click a cell within the PivotTable, point to Select, and if the Enable Selection command looks pushed in, click it.

3 Select cells C10 through A4 by dragging from cell C10 up and left to cell A4 so that the Order Date button stays in the PivotTable.

4 On the Standard toolbar, click the Chart Wizard button.

The Chart Wizard appears.

5 In the Step 1 dialog box, be sure that Column is selected in the Chart Type list, and then click Next.

6 In the Step 2 dialog box, be sure that the Columns option button is se-lected, and then click Next.

7 In the Step 3 dialog box, on the Titles tab, click in the Chart Title box, type **Current Orders by Category**, and then click Next.

8 In the Step 4 dialog box, be sure that the As Object In option button is selected and that the list reads PivotTable, and then click Finish.

The new chart is created in the middle of the worksheet. Your worksheet should look similar to the following illustration.

Chart Wizard

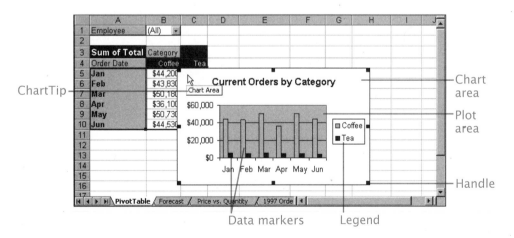

For a demonstration of how to customize charts, double-click the Camcorder Files On The Internet shortcut on your Desktop or connect to the Internet address listed on page xxvii.

Customize a chart to match specific requirements

Now that you have created your embedded chart, you need to format it according to the Island Tea & Coffee Company standard. In this exercise, you customize the formatting of your chart.

1　If you do not see handles around the edges of your chart, point to an empty area of the chart background, and then, when the ChartTip shows Chart Area, click the chart.

　　Handles appear around the edges of the chart showing that it is selected, and the Name box shows Chart Area.

2　Drag the corner handles of the chart until cells B3 through I16 are covered by the chart to make it larger and easier to see.

3　Point to the gray area behind the data markers (the plot area), and when the ChartTip shows Plot Area, double-click.

　　The Format Plot Area dialog box appears.

4　Under Area, click the None option button, and then click OK.

　　The plot area background color disappears.

If you have trouble selecting a chart element, select any element, and then press an arrow key to cycle through all the elements in the chart.

5　Double-click one of the data markers in the Tea series.

　　The Format Data Series dialog box appears.

6　On the Patterns tab, click the Fill Effects button.

　　The Fill Effects dialog box appears.

7　On the Gradient tab, under Colors, click the Preset option button; under Preset Colors, select Daybreak; under Shading Styles, be sure that Horizontal is selected; and under Variants, select the upper-right box.

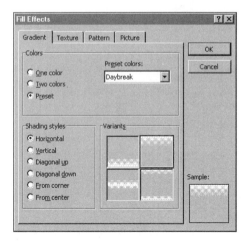

8 Click OK to close the Fill Effects dialog box, and then click OK again to close the Format Data Series dialog box.

Your chart should look similar to the following illustration.

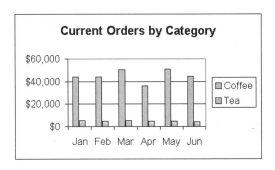

Add picture markers to a series

Before printing your chart, you need to finish bringing it up to the Island Tea & Coffee Company formatting standard. In this exercise, you make the data markers for the coffee series look like stacked coffee cups.

1 Double-click one of the data markers in the Coffee series.

The Format Data Series dialog box appears.

2 On the Patterns tab, click the Fill Effects button.

3 In the Fill Effects dialog box, click the Picture tab, and then click Select Picture.

The Select Picture dialog box appears.

4 In the Excel SBS Practice folder, double-click the Coffee Cup file.

The clipart picture appears in the Fill Effects dialog box.

147

5 Under Format, click the Stack option button, and then click OK.

6 In the Format Data Series dialog box, click OK.

Your completed chart should look similar to the following illustration.

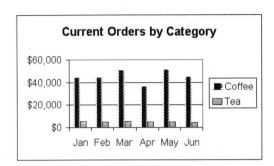

Draw your own markers

Another way to customize a chart is to draw your own markers using Microsoft Excel's drawing tools.

Using the drawing tools, you can draw objects of any shape in both worksheets and charts. You can replace markers in a chart with an object you draw—you can replace an entire series, or just a single marker to make it stand out. You can even draw an object and give it a shadow or a 3-D effect.

Before you print the chart, you decide to experiment with its look—you want to replace the Tea series markers with a drawn object of your own.

1 Use the right mouse button to click a toolbar, and then click Drawing.

The Drawing toolbar appears.

2 On the Drawing toolbar, click the Oval button.

The mouse pointer becomes a crosshair.

Oval

3 Drag the crosshair pointer diagonally on the chart or the worksheet to draw a circular object.

The object can be either circular or oblong.

4 Make the object approximately 1 inch in diameter.

When you release the mouse button, the object is selected and has handles around it.

5 While the object is selected, on the Formatting toolbar, select a red color from the Fill Color button palette.

Fill Color

The drawn object is colored red.

3-D

6 On the Drawing toolbar, click the 3-D button.

A shortcut menu of 3-D shapes appears.

148

7   Click the shape in the lower right corner (3-D Style 20).

The drawn object takes on a 3-D shape.

8   While the object is still selected, on the Standard toolbar, click the Copy button.

Copy

9   In the chart, click a Tea series marker.

The entire Tea series is selected.

10   On the Standard toolbar, click the Paste button.

The Tea series markers take on the shape of your drawn, 3-D object.

Paste

11   Click the object you drew, and then press DELETE.

The drawn object is deleted, and your chart has custom-drawn markers in it.

To replace a single marker, click the marker twice (do not double-click), and then paste the drawn object.

12   Close the Drawing toolbar.

Undo the changes

You decide that you don't like the drawn-object markers in this particular chart, so you undo the changes you made.

Undo

➤   On the Standard toolbar, click the down arrow next to the Undo button, and undo actions until the Tea series markers are in their original form.

Print the chart

 IMPORTANT   In order to complete this exercise, you'll need to be connected to a printer.

Before distributing the chart for further review, you decide to show it to your manager. In this exercise, you print a copy of the chart.

Print

➤   Click the chart to select it, and then, on the Standard toolbar, click the Print button.

Create and print different charts by changing the PivotTable

Your manager also wants to see monthly sales by category for each employee. In this exercise, you create the new charts, and then print one of them. But first, you have to be able to identify whose data is in each chart. The simplest way is to extend the range of data included in the chart so that the cell containing the employee name is included.

Chart Wizard

1   Click in the chart, and then click the Chart Wizard button.

2 Click Next, and in the Step 2 dialog box, in the Data Range box, change A4 to A1, and then click Finish.

The chart is updated, but the legend is too large at the current font size.

Font Size

3 In the chart, click the legend, and then on the Formatting toolbar, in the Font Size box, select 9.

The legend fits neatly into the chart area.

4 Click the PivotTable Page down arrow (cell B1), and then select Davis.

Davis' data appears in the PivotTable, and the chart is automatically updated to display the PivotTable data.

Print

5 On the Standard toolbar, click the Print button.

Make an embedded chart into a chart sheet (and vice versa)

The embedded chart is convenient because it streamlines the process of generating charts for each employee. But, since the PivotTable you want to experiment with is large, the embedded chart is in your way. In this exercise, you convert the embedded chart into a chart sheet so that it remains functional but is off the worksheet.

1 Use the right mouse button to click in the chart area.

2 On the shortcut menu, click Location.

The Chart Location dialog box appears.

3 Click the As New Sheet option button, and then click OK.

The embedded chart is moved onto a separate chart sheet.

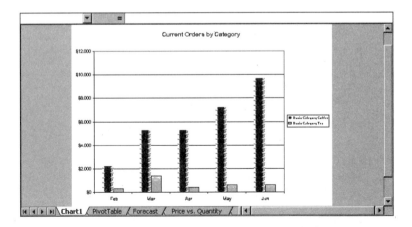

You can rename, move, copy, and delete a chart sheet in the same way that you would a worksheet.

Making a Chart Format Re-Usable

Even though customizing your chart was easy, it would be even easier in the future if you could reapply the Island Tea & Coffee Company custom formatting to any chart without having to perform the individual formatting steps. You can save your chart formatting by making it into a custom chart type, and then simply reapply it whenever you create a new chart.

Create a custom chart type

Because you formatted your chart based on the Island Tea & Coffee Company guidelines, you decide to save the settings for future use. In this exercise, you create a custom chart type and remove the chart title so that it doesn't become part of the custom chart type formatting.

1 Click the chart title, and then press DELETE.

2 On the Chart menu, click Chart Type.

3 Click the Custom Types tab.

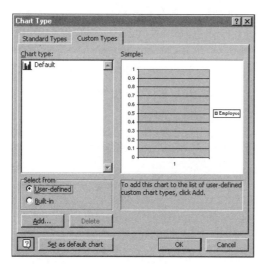

4 Under Select From, click User-Defined, and then click Add.

5 In the Name box, type **ITC Standard**, and in the Description box, type **Company standard chart format**, and then click OK.

The new chart type is added to the Chart Type list. The next time you run the Chart Wizard, you can click the User-Defined option button, and then select your custom chart type on the Custom Types tab in the Step 2 dialog box.

6 Click OK.

Forecasting Trends

One of the charts your manager requested is a six-month sales forecast based on the sales data for the first five months. By using one of several mathematical line equations, Microsoft Excel can create a *trendline* for a data series that shows the trend of the existing data. You can extend that trendline into a forecast for as many periods as you want.

Forecast future sales based on current data trends

In preparation for a company-wide sales meeting, your manager asks you to create a chart that will help her forecast the projected company sales for the next six months. In this exercise, you create a chart with a trendline and six-month forecast for total company sales.

Chart Wizard

1 Select the Forecast worksheet.

2 Select cells A1 through B6, and then click the Chart Wizard button.

3 In the Chart Wizard Step 1 dialog box, click Finish.

A default column chart is created.

4 Use the right mouse button to click any data marker in the chart.

The entire data series is selected.

5 On the shortcut menu, click Add Trendline.

The Add Trendline dialog box appears.

6 On the Type tab, click Linear.

7 On the Options tab, under Forecast, in the Forward box, click the up arrow until it shows 6, and then click OK.

A trendline with a six-month forecast is inserted in the chart. You might want to try different trendlines to decide which type best displays a logical forecast based on your data.

8 Save your work.

NOTE If you'd like to build on the skills you learned in this lesson, you can do the One Step Further. Otherwise, skip to "Finish the Lesson."

One Step Further: Creating a Chart with a Secondary Axis

After reviewing the six-month forecast you created in the previous exercise, your manager requests a chart of sales volume vs. average price, to see if changing prices affect the volume sold. The two series in your chart, sales volume and price per pound, have very different number scales: the volume will be in thousands, and the average price will be less than 15. This means that when both series are displayed in the same chart using the same value axis, only the volume series will be visible. The solution is to show each series on a different value axis. This way you can see how the volume and price change relative to each other over time, and then estimate how changing the price affects the volume sold.

Use a secondary axis to display data series that have different value scales

To make the chart as useful as possible, you decide to add a second axis to display each data series at the appropriate scale. In this exercise, you create a chart of sales volume vs. average price, and then add a secondary axis so that the average price series can be seen in the chart.

1   Select the Price Vs. Quantity sheet.

2   Select cells A1 through C7, click the Chart Wizard button, and then, in the Step 1 dialog box, click Finish.

   A default chart is created on the worksheet.

If the Chart toolbar is not displayed, use the right mouse button to click any toolbar, and then click Chart.

3   On the Chart toolbar, click the Chart Objects down arrow, and then select Series "price."

4   On the Format menu, click Selected Data Series.

   The Format Data Series dialog box appears.

5   On the Axis tab, under Plot Series On, click the Secondary Axis option button, and then click OK.

   A secondary axis is added to the right side of the chart. The Price data markers are visible because they have an axis that is scaled to their values.

6   Use the right mouse button to click the Price series, and then click Chart Type.

7   In the Chart Type dialog box, click the Standard Types tab, verify that the Apply To Selection check box is selected, click the Line icon, and then click OK.

   The Price data is displayed by line markers instead of by column markers, which makes it easier to distinguish.

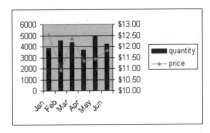

8   Save the workbook.

Finish the lesson

1   To continue to the next lesson, on the File menu, click Close.

2   If you are finished using Microsoft Excel for now, on the File menu, click Exit.

Lesson Summary

To	Do this	Button
Create a chart	Select the data you want to chart, and then click the Chart Wizard button. Follow the steps in the Chart Wizard to create the chart.	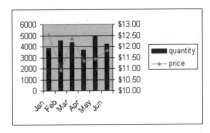
Customize a chart	Double-click the chart element you want to customize, and then select the desired colors, patterns, and effects in the Format dialog box.	
Add picture markers to a series	Double-click a marker in the series you want to add picture markers to, and then, in the Format Data Series dialog box, click Fill Effects. Click the Picture tab, click Select Picture, and then locate a picture you want. Double-click the picture you want, click OK to close the Fill Effects dialog box, and then click OK to close the Format Data Series dialog box.	

To	Do this	Button
Replace series markers with a drawn object	Use the right mouse button to click a toolbar, and then select Drawing. In the Drawing toolbar, click a shape button and draw an object in the worksheet or chart. Select the object, and then, on the Standard toolbar, click the Copy button. Click a marker in the series you want to replace. On the Standard toolbar, click the Paste button. Select the object you drew, and then press DELETE.	
Make a drawn object a 3-D object	Select the drawn object. On the Drawing toolbar, click 3-D, and then select a 3-D shape from the shortcut menu.	
Make an embedded chart into a chart sheet	Use the right mouse button to click in the chart area, and then, on the shortcut menu, click Location. In the Chart Location dialog box, select the As New Sheet option button, and then click OK.	
Create a custom chart type	On the Chart menu, click Chart Type, and then click the Custom Types tab. Click User Defined, and then click Add. Type a name and description for the new custom chart type, and then click OK.	
Create a trendline	Use the right mouse button to select the series you want a trendline for, and then, on the shortcut menu, click Add Trendline. On the Type tab, select a trendline type. If you want a forecast, on the Options tab, select a number of forecast periods, and then click OK.	

For online information about	On the Help menu, click Contents And Index, click the Index tab, and then type
Creating charts	**chart creation**
Customizing charts	**chart editing; chart formatting**
Trendlines	**trendlines**

Printing Reports to Distribute Information Offline

Estimated time

30 min.

In this lesson you will learn how to:

- Print a multiple-page worksheet.
- Set print titles to easily identify data on all pages.
- Change the page printing order.
- Print only selected data from a worksheet.
- Define print areas to print the same data repeatedly.
- Fit information onto a specific number of printed pages.
- Print charts with or without a worksheet.

As the office manager for the Island Tea & Coffee Company, you keep a current list of the company's orders. Different members of the sales staff often ask you for a printed copy of this data—sometimes the entire list, sometimes just portions of it.

In this lesson, you will learn a variety of methods for printing worksheet data depending on the requirements.

 IMPORTANT   In order to perform the exercises in this lesson, your computer will need to be connected to a printer.

Open an existing file

You keep the current orders in a workbook named 1997 Orders. In this exercise, you open the 1997 Orders workbook.

Open

1 On the Standard toolbar, click the Open button.
2 In the Open dialog box, click the Look In Favorites button.
3 In the file list, double-click the Excel SBS Practice folder.
4 Double-click the 1997 Orders file.

Save the file with a new name

In this exercise, you save the 1997 Orders file as Printing Lesson.

1 On the File menu, click Save As.

   The Save As dialog box opens. Be sure the Excel SBS Practice folder appears in the Save In box.

2 In the File Name box, type **Printing Lesson**, and then click Save.

Printing an Entire Worksheet

The 1997 Orders list is a very large worksheet that will extend over several pages when printed. A common problem encountered while printing large worksheets is that each identifying column or row label is printed only on the first page. Another common problem relates to the default layout of the printed pages. For example, the default layout may print six columns on one page and a single column on the next page; or it may print the left side of a long worksheet followed by the right side, when you would rather print the top of the worksheet followed by the bottom. You can remedy these problems easily by changing some print settings for the worksheet.

First, you will preview the worksheet using two different preview methods, and then you will change print settings so that the 1997 Orders list prints out the way you want it to.

Preview the worksheet

You usually preview a worksheet before printing it so that you can determine the optimal way to lay out the printed pages. In this exercise, you use two different methods of previewing: Print Preview and Page Break Preview. Print Preview shows you what the printed page will look like, page by page; Page Break Preview shows you how the worksheet is broken up into pages, and allows you to easily alter the page layout.

Print Preview

1 Be sure that the Orders worksheet is active, and then, on the Standard toolbar, click the Print Preview button.

Page 1 appears in Print Preview mode. Only four columns are printed on page 1, and the status bar message tells you that there are 16 pages in the worksheet.

2 On the button bar, click Page Break Preview.

3 If you see a Welcome To Page Break Preview dialog box, select the Do Not Show This Dialog Again check box, and then click OK.

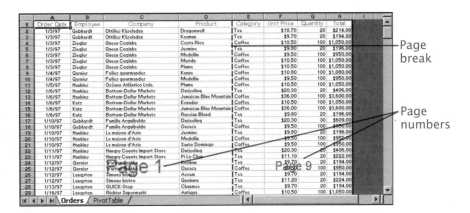

Page Break Preview shows you how the entire worksheet is broken into pages. The dotted lines show where the page breaks are, and the page numbers show the order in which the worksheet will be printed (in this case, the pages on the left side of the worksheet will be printed first, from the top down, and then the right side will be printed from the top down). This printing order is called *Down, Then Over*.

4 Point to the vertical page break line, and then, when the mouse pointer becomes a two-headed arrow, drag the line to the left by one column.

The vertical page break is reset so that only three columns print on the first eight pages. The page break line becomes a solid line after you move it to indicate that it is now a manual page break instead of an automatic page break.

5 On the Standard toolbar, click the Print Preview button.

6 On the button bar, click Next, and then click near the top of the page.

			Orders
1/27/97	Hankins	Split Rail Beer & Ale	
1/30/97	Hankins	Folk och fä HB	
1/30/97	Hankins	Folk och fä HB	
1/30/97	Hankins	Princesa Isabel Vinhos	
1/31/97	Garnier	Consolidated Holdings	
1/31/97	Garnier	Consolidated Holdings	

159

Page 2 is magnified, and there are no labels at the top of the page to identify the data in the columns. In the next exercise, you will fix this by adding *print titles*, labels that are automatically printed at the top of each page.

7 On the button bar, click Close.

Set print titles

While previewing the worksheet you saw that the identifying column labels appear only on pages 1 and 9, and the identifying order dates appear only on pages 1 through 8, so the data on every page except page 1 is not adequately identified. In this exercise, you set print titles so that no matter where the page breaks are, the order dates and column labels will be printed on each page.

1 On the File menu, click Page Setup.

2 In the Page Setup dialog box, click the Sheet tab.

3 Under Print Titles, click in the Rows To Repeat At Top box, and then click a cell in row 1. You might have drag the dialog box out of the way to click in row 1.

The row reference $1:$1 is entered in the Rows To Repeat At Top box.

4 Click in the Columns To Repeat At Left box, and then click a cell in column A.

The column reference $A:$A is entered in the Columns To Repeat At Left box.

5 Click OK.

6 On the Standard toolbar, click the Print Preview button, and then, on the button bar, click Next until you can see page 10.

Print Preview

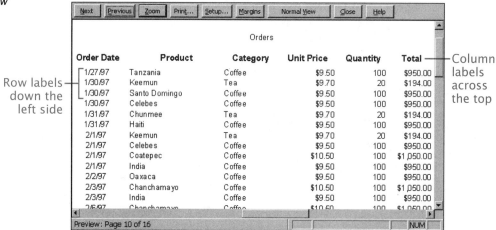

Column labels and order dates now appear on every page. Magnify the page to read the headings, if necessary.

7   On the button bar, click Close.

Change the page layout

Your list of current 1997 orders is wide as well as long, and you need to define whether to print the pages "Over, Then Down" or "Down, Then Over." In this exercise, you look at page printing order layouts to determine which is most effective.

1   If you are not in Page Break Preview, on the View menu, click Page Break Preview.

The default page layout is "Down, Then Over."

2   On the File menu, click Page Setup.

The Page Setup dialog box appears.

3   On the Sheet tab, click the "Over, Then Down" option button under Page Order, and then click OK.

	A	B	C	D	E	F	G	H
1	Order Date	Employee	Company	Product	Category	Unit Price	Quantity	Total
2	1/3/97	Gebhardt	Ottilies Käseladen	Dragonwell	Tea	$10.70	20	$214.00
3	1/3/97	Gebhardt	Ottilies Käseladen	Keemun	Tea	$9.70	20	$194.00
4	1/3/97	Ziegler	Queen Cozinha	Costa Rica	Coffee	$10.50	100	$1,050.00
5	1/3/97	Ziegler	Queen Cozinha	Jasmine	Tea	$9.80	20	$196.00
6	1/3/97	Ziegler	Queen Cozinha	Medellin	Coffee	$9.50	100	$950.00
7	1/3/97	Ziegler	Queen Cozinha	Merida	Coffee	$10.50	100	$1,050.00
8	1/3/97	Ziegler	Queen Cozinha	Pluma	Coffee	$10.50	100	$1,050.00
9	1/4/97	Garnier	Folies gourmandes	Kenya	Coffee	$10.80	100	$1,080.00
10	1/4/97	Garnier	Folies gourmandes	Medellin	Coffee	$9.50	100	$950.00
11	1/5/97	Hankins	Océano Atlántico Ltda.	Pluma	Coffee	$10.50	100	$1,050.00
12	1/6/97	Hankins	Bottom-Dollar Markets	Darjeeling	Tea	$20.30	20	$406.00
13	1/6/97	Hankins	Bottom-Dollar Markets	Jamaican Blue Mountain	Coffee	$36.00	100	$3,600.00
14	1/6/97	Katz	Bottom-Dollar Markets	Ecuador	Coffee	$10.50	100	$1,050.00
15	1/6/97	Katz	Bottom-Dollar Markets	Jamaican Blue Mountain	Coffee	$36.00	100	$3,600.00
16	1/6/97	Katz	Bottom-Dollar Markets	Russian Blend	Tea	$9.80	20	$196.00
17	1/10/97	Gebhardt	Familia Arquibaldo	Darjeeling	Tea	$20.30	30	$609.00
18	1/10/97	Gebhardt	Familia Arquibaldo	Oaxaca	Coffee	$9.50	100	$950.00
19	1/10/97	Hankins	La maison d'Asie	Jasmine	Tea	$9.80	20	$196.00
20	1/10/97	Hankins	La maison d'Asie	Medellin	Coffee	$9.50	100	$950.00
21	1/10/97	Hankins	La maison d'Asie	Santo Domingo	Coffee	$9.50	100	$950.00
22	1/11/97	Hankins	Hungry Coyote Import Store	Darjeeling	Tea	$20.30	20	$406.00
23	1/11/97	Hankins	Hungry Coyote Import Store	Pi Lo Chun	Tea	$11.10	20	$222.00
24	1/12/97	Garnier	Wartian Herkku	Keemun	Tea	$9.70	20	$194.00
25	1/12/97	Garnier	Wartian Herkku	Oaxaca	Coffee	$9.50	100	$950.00
26	1/12/97	Langston	Simons bistro	Assam	Tea	$9.70	20	$194.00
27	1/12/97	Langston	Simons bistro	Gyokuro	Tea	$11.20	20	$224.00
28	1/13/97	Langston	QUICK-Stop	Chunmee	Tea	$9.70	20	$194.00
29	1/16/97	Langston	Richter Supermarkt	Antigua	Coffee	$10.50	100	$1,050.00

Orders / PivotTable

Page 2 now appears on the right of page 1, which means that the pages will print from left to right instead of top to bottom.

4   On the View menu, click Normal.

Page Break Preview is replaced by the worksheet view.

Print

5   On the Standard toolbar, click the Print button.

Printing Selected Areas on a Worksheet

As keeper of the Island Tea & Coffee Company list of current orders, you receive many requests for printouts of different kinds: selected data for a specific month; a segment of data that needs to fit on a single page; or a summary report for a management meeting.

Print only selected data

In addition to a printout of the entire list of 1997 orders, your manager would like a printout of the orders data for March 1997. Because you have already set print titles, all you have to do is select the month's data; the column labels will be included automatically. In this exercise, you print the March orders data.

1   Select cells A121 through H182 (the March data).

2   On the File menu, click Print.

3   In the Print dialog box, under Print What, click the Selection option button.

4   In the Print dialog box, click Preview.

> The pages for your selected data are previewed. Because of the settings you defined in earlier exercises, the pages will print "Over, Then Down," and correct column and row labels will print on every page.

5   On the button bar, click Print.

> The worksheet is printed and Microsoft Excel returns to the worksheet view.

Define a print area

Co-workers regularly ask you for printouts of the list of orders for previous completed months, not including the orders for the current month. Since you do this several times each month, you can save time by defining a *print area*, an area of the worksheet that will be printed automatically when you click the Print button on the Standard toolbar. In this exercise, you define a print area that includes data for completed months only.

To set a print area from the worksheet view, select the print range, and then, on the File menu, point to Print Area and click Set Print Area.

1   On the View menu, click Page Break Preview.

2   In Page Break Preview, select the cells A1 through H356 (the records for January through June).

3   Use the right mouse button to click the selected range, and then click Set Print Area.

4   On the View menu, click Normal to return to worksheet view.

> Now that you have set a print area, only that area of the worksheet will be printed when you click the Print button on the Standard toolbar.

Print a worksheet on a specific number of pages

In preparation for a meeting, your manager has asked you if you can reduce the size of the completed months' data so that it will fit on a single page width and won't be longer than 5 pages. In this exercise, you make the print area 1 page in width by 5 pages in length.

1   On the File menu, click Page Setup.

2   On the Page tab, under Scaling, click the Fit To option button, and set the spinner boxes to show 1 Page(s) Wide By 5 Tall.

3   Click Print Preview.

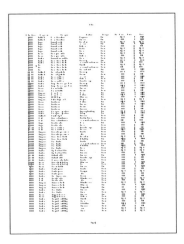

The status bar message indicates that the data fits on 5 pages, and you can see that it has been reduced in width so that all columns fit on a single page.

4   On the button bar, click Print.

The Print dialog box appears.

5   Click OK.

Center data on the printed page

The data on the printed page is left-aligned, but your manager wants it centered on the page. In this exercise, you center the data horizontally on the pages.

Print Preview

You can drag margin lines and column breaks to change margins and column widths.

1   On the Standard toolbar, click the Print Preview button, and then click the page to zoom out if you need to so that you can see the whole page.

2   On the button bar, click Margins.

Margin lines appear around the edges of the page, and column breaks appear across the top of the page. The margin lines help you see whether the data looks centered.

3   On the button bar, click Setup.

4   In the Page Setup dialog box, click the Margins tab.

5   Under Center On Page, select the Horizontally check box, and then click OK.

The data on every page is centered horizontally.

6   On the button bar, click Print.

The Print dialog box appears.

7   Click OK.

8   Save your workbook.

Printing Charts

As the office manager, you keep the Island Tea & Coffee Company workbooks arranged so that you can get to any type of data you want as quickly and efficiently as possible. This usually means that the worksheets and charts aren't arranged for instant printing. For example, you keep your charts embedded in worksheets because it's often more convenient to use an embedded chart than to flip back and forth between a worksheet and a chart; however, you sometimes need to print the worksheet without its embedded chart, or the chart without its source worksheet. You can easily do both without changing your workbook setup.

When you print a chart separately from its worksheet, you might notice that the chart's proportions are changed so that the printed chart is not in *scale* (not the same relative height and width) with the chart you created on the worksheet. If this presents a problem, you can easily re-scale the printed chart so that it retains the same relative proportions as the embedded chart.

Print a worksheet without printing the embedded chart

You can use the procedure in this exercise to prevent any graphical object on a worksheet from being printed with the worksheet.

Sometimes a chart covers up the data it is based on—for example, a large PivotTable might be covered by its embedded chart—and you need to print the data but don't want to print the chart. In this exercise, you print a worksheet without printing its embedded chart.

1   On the PivotTable sheet, point to an empty part of the chart background so that the ChartTip reads Chart Area, and then click with the right mouse button.

2   On the shortcut menu, click Format Chart Area.

3   In the Format Chart Area dialog box, click the Properties tab.

4   Clear the Print Object check box, and then click OK.

5   Click a cell in the worksheet, and then click Print Preview.

The Print Preview window appears showing you that the worksheet will be printed without the embedded chart.

Print Preview

6   On the button bar, click Close.

Print an embedded chart without printing the worksheet

Your manager has asked you to present your charted data at a company meeting. In order to create a clear overhead slide, you want to print the chart without the extra clutter of the worksheet data. In this exercise, you print an embedded chart without printing its source worksheet.

1 Click anywhere on the chart, and then click the Print Preview button.

The Print Preview window opens, showing you that the chart will be printed separately.

2 On the button bar, click Print.

The Print dialog box appears.

3 Click OK.

Re-scale a printed chart

When you print a chart on its own page, by default the chart is scaled (its proportions are changed) to fill up the entire page. Your PivotTable chart is a short, wide rectangle, but when you print it, its scale changes so that it is taller and narrower. In this exercise, you re-scale the chart to print it with its original proportions.

1 Click anywhere on the chart.

2 On the File menu, click Page Setup, and then click the Chart tab.

3 On the Chart tab, click the Scale To Fit Page option button, and then click Print Preview.

The Print Preview window appears showing you that the chart will be printed with the proportions it has in the worksheet.

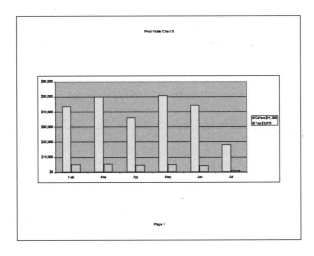

4   On the button bar, click Print.

The Print dialog box appears.

5   Click OK.

6   On the File menu, click Save.

NOTE   This lesson has covered various ways to print data in a single worksheet, but you can also print all the worksheets in a workbook with one step. Be sure that a worksheet cell (not a chart) is selected, and then on the File menu, click Print; under Print What, click the Entire Workbook option button, and then click OK.

NOTE   If you'd like to build on the skills you learned in this lesson, you can do the One Step Further. Otherwise, skip to "Finish the Lesson."

One Step Further: Setting Multiple Print Areas in a Worksheet

One of the Island Tea & Coffee Company's sales people has asked for printouts of March and June data. In this exercise, you set two print areas in one worksheet.

1   Select the Orders sheet, and then, on the View menu, click Page Break Preview.

2   Select cells A121 through H182 (the March records), and then hold down CTRL and select cells A302 through H356 (the June records).

3   Use the right mouse button to click in one of the selected ranges, and then, on the shortcut menu, click Set Print Area.

Two print areas are set.

Print Preview

4   On the Standard toolbar, click the Print Preview button.

Each print area prints on its own page, and since your settings from previous exercises are still in place, each print area is centered on a single page.

5   On the button bar, click Print.

The Print dialog box appears.

6   Click OK.

7   On the File menu, click Save.

Finish the lesson

1 To continue to the Review & Practice section, on the File menu, click Close.
2 If you are finished using Microsoft Excel for now, on the File menu, click Exit.

Lesson Summary

To	Do this	Button
See a preview of printed pages	On the Standard toolbar, click the Print Preview button.	
See a preview of the page layout	On the View menu, click Page Break Preview.	
Change page breaks	On the View menu, click Page Break Preview. Drag page break lines to reposition page breaks.	
Set print titles	On the File menu, click Page Setup, and then click the Sheet tab. Click in the Rows To Repeat At Top box, and then click a cell in the row you want to appear at the top of each page. Click in the Columns To Repeat At Left box, and then click a cell in the column you want to appear down the left side of each page. Click OK.	
Change the page printing order	On the File menu, click Page Setup, and then click the Sheet tab. Under Page Order, click the "Over, Then Down" option button or the "Down, Then Over" option button, and then click OK.	
Print only selected data on a worksheet	Select the range to print, and then, on the File menu, click Print. Under Print What, click the Selection option button, and then click OK.	
Define a print area	On the View menu, click Page Break Preview. Select the range you want to set as a print area, and then use the right mouse button to click the selection. On the shortcut menu, click Set Print Area.	

167

To	Do this	Button
Print a worksheet on a specific number of pages	On the File menu, click Page Setup, and then click the Page tab. Under Scaling, click the Fit To option button, and set the number of pages wide by number of pages tall, and then click OK.	
Center data on a printed page	On the File menu, click Page Setup, and then click the Margins tab. Under Center On Page, select the Horizontally or Vertically check box, or both, and then click OK.	
Print a worksheet with an embedded chart	On the Standard toolbar, click the Print button.	🖨
Print a worksheet without its embedded chart	Use the right mouse button to click an empty part of the chart, and then, on the shortcut menu, click Format Chart Area. Click the Properties tab, clear the Print Object check box, and then click OK. Click a cell in the worksheet, and then, on the Standard toolbar, click the Print button.	🖨
Print an embedded chart without its worksheet	Select any part of the chart, and then, on the Standard toolbar, click the Print button.	🖨
Print a chart sheet	Select the chart sheet, and then, on the Standard toolbar, click the Print button.	🖨
Re-scale a printed chart	Select the chart, and then, on the File menu, click Page Setup. Click the Chart tab, select the Scale To Fit Page option button, and then click OK.	

For online information about	On the Help menu, click Contents And Index, click the Index tab, and then type
Printing worksheets	**printing, page setup**

Review & Practice

You will review and practice how to:

- Import a text file.
- Create a PivotTable and group dates in the PivotTable by quarter.
- Create a chart.
- Format a chart.
- Print a PivotTable and a chart.

Estimated time
20 min.

Before you move on to Part 4, in which you will learn techniques for finding answers and sharing your workbooks with co-workers, you can practice the skills you learned in Part 3 by working through the steps in this Review & Practice section. You will import a text file, create a PivotTable, create a chart from the PivotTable, and then print the PivotTable and the chart.

Scenario

The State University Alumni Association (SUAA) is planning a meeting to discuss ways to reduce expenses. One of the items on the agenda is a discussion of last year's expenses and how they might be reduced and managed more efficiently. You've been asked to create a summary of last year's expenses and print copies for everybody. The expense records for last year are stored in a text file that you will need to import into Microsoft Excel.

Step 1:   Import a text file

You've been asked to create a PivotTable and a chart of last year's expense records. In this step, you start the process by importing the text file, in which the records are contained, into a Microsoft Excel worksheet.

1   Open the text file 1996exp.txt from the Excel SBS Practice folder.

2   In the Text Import Wizard, select the Tab Delimiter and use the default General format for each column.

3   After you import the data, apply the Currency format, with 2 decimal places, to column C (Amount).

4   Save the new file as a Microsoft Excel workbook, and name it 1996 SUAA Expenses.

For more information about	See
Importing data	Lesson 8

Step 2:   Create a PivotTable

Now that you have imported the expenses data, you are ready to display it in the form of a summary. In this step, you create a PivotTable that shows expenses by category and by quarter.

1   Create a PivotTable from the list of data.

2   Place the Category field in a row orientation, the Date field in a column orientation, and the Amount field in the data area. (Hint: The field button should say Sum of Amount.) Create the PivotTable in a new worksheet.

3   Group the dates by quarter.

4   Apply the Currency format, with 2 decimal places, to the numbers in the data area.

If a warning message appears, click Cancel. Use the right mouse button to click the selection, point to Enable Selection, and then repeat step 4.

5   Name the new PivotTable sheet Data Summary.

Your PivotTable should look similar to the following illustration.

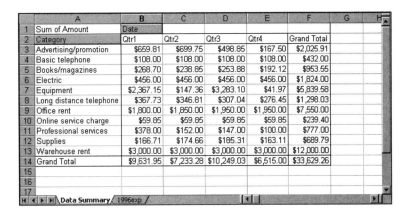

	A	B	C	D	E	F	G	H
1	Sum of Amount	Date						
2	Category	Qtr1	Qtr2	Qtr3	Qtr4	Grand Total		
3	Advertising/promotion	$659.81	$699.75	$498.85	$167.50	$2,025.91		
4	Basic telephone	$108.00	$108.00	$108.00	$108.00	$432.00		
5	Books/magazines	$268.70	$238.85	$253.88	$192.12	$953.55		
6	Electric	$456.00	$456.00	$456.00	$456.00	$1,824.00		
7	Equipment	$2,367.15	$147.36	$3,283.10	$41.97	$5,839.58		
8	Long distance telephone	$367.73	$346.81	$307.04	$276.45	$1,298.03		
9	Office rent	$1,800.00	$1,850.00	$1,950.00	$1,950.00	$7,550.00		
10	Online service charge	$59.85	$59.85	$59.85	$59.85	$239.40		
11	Professional services	$378.00	$152.00	$147.00	$100.00	$777.00		
12	Supplies	$166.71	$174.66	$185.31	$163.11	$689.79		
13	Warehouse rent	$3,000.00	$3,000.00	$3,000.00	$3,000.00	$12,000.00		
14	Grand Total	$9,631.95	$7,233.28	$10,249.03	$6,515.00	$33,629.26		
15								
16								
17								

Data Summary / 1996exp /

For more information about	See
Creating PivotTables	Lesson 8
Grouping dates	Lesson 8
Formatting PivotTable numbers	Lesson 8

Step 3: *Create a chart of the PivotTable*

Now that you have a summary of the data, you need to present it graphically. In this step, you create a chart to display the data visually.

1 Select cells E13 through A2 without including the grand totals in the chart. (Hint: Type **E13:A2** in the Name box.)

2 Create an embedded chart using the Chart Wizard.

3 Plot the data series in rows so that the legend lists categories and the horizontal axis shows quarters.

4 Add the text "1996 SUAA Expenses" to the chart as a title, and then complete the chart by formatting the chart so that it looks similar to the following illustration.

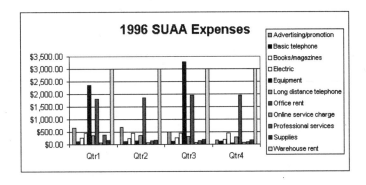

5   Save the workbook.

For more information about	See
Creating a chart	Lesson 9
Formatting a chart	Lesson 9
Adding a chart title	Lesson 9

Step 4:   *Print the chart and the PivotTable*

To complete your presentation for the meeting, you need to print the two documents you created. In this step, you print the PivotTable and the chart separately.

1   Move the chart down on the worksheet so that it does not cover the PivotTable.

2   Set a print area that consists only of the PivotTable.

3   Apply the AutoFormat named Classic 3 to the PivotTable.

4   Center the PivotTable horizontally on the printed page.

5   Print the worksheet.

6   Select the chart and scale it to fit the page with its original proportions. (Hint: Open the chart in Print Preview mode, and then click the Setup button on the button bar.)

7   Print the chart.

8   On the File menu, click Save.

For more information about	See
Setting a print area	Lesson 10
Applying an AutoFormat	Lesson 8
Centering on the printed page	Lesson 10
Scaling a chart for the printed page	Lesson 10
Printing an embedded chart without the worksheet	Lesson 10

Finish the Review & Practice

1   To continue to the next lesson, on the File menu, click Close.

2   If you are finished using Microsoft Excel for now, on the File menu, click Exit.

Analyzing and Sharing Your Data

Part 4

Comparing Alternatives for Better Decisions

Estimated time
30 min.

In this lesson you will learn how to:

- Use Goal Seek to find a mathematical answer.
- Create scenarios to compare alternative situations.

In this lesson, you will learn how to analyze data efficiently by using Goal Seek and Scenario Manager. Suppose you want to know by how much sales would have to increase to reach a specific operating income goal. When you know the answer (in this case, the desired operating income), Goal Seek can help you determine what the other side of the equation (sales) needs to be.

Goal Seek can give you a specific answer to a specific question, but often you need to determine which of several different scenarios is the best. Scenario Manager can help you set up a number of scenarios, each slightly different, to see how changing different figures in a situation can affect the outcome. By using Scenario Manager, you can make more informed business decisions.

At the Island Tea & Coffee Company, the management team is attempting to determine how much monthly sales need to increase to reach a monthly operating income of $10,000. A question of this nature can be complicated by the fact that other numbers in the budget also change when the sales volume changes. For example, each sales person gets a 50% commission; so, when sales go up, so do commissions, which affect the operating income.

You can also use Scenario Manager to set up various Island Tea & Coffee Company budget scenarios and compare the outcomes. Scenario Manager creates sets of values to use in different scenarios. Each scenario represents a set of "what-if" assumptions that you can use to view the outcome of a worksheet model. For example, you can ask "What if I change the COGs value?" or "What if I reduce the advertising expense?" With Scenario Manager, you can make these changes, and then view the results side-by-side for easy comparison and sound decision-making.

Open an existing file

You keep the current budget in a workbook named 1997 Budget. In this exercise, you open the 1997 Budget file.

Open

1 On the Standard toolbar, click the Open button.
2 In the Open dialog box, click the Look In Favorites button.
3 In the file list, double-click the Excel SBS Practice folder.
4 Double-click the 1997 Budget file.

Save the file with a new name

In this exercise, you save the 1997 Budget file as Analysis.

1 On the File menu, click Save As.

   The Save As dialog box opens. Be sure the Excel SBS Practice folder appears in the Save In box.

2 In the File Name box, type **Analysis**, and then click Save.

Using Goal Seek to Determine the Best Price

At the beginning of the new fiscal year, the Island Tea & Coffee Company management is reviewing the projected operating budget, and looking for a way to increase monthly operating income to $10,000 a month. For example, based on the current budget model, sales need to increase by $2,358 in order to increase the operating income to $10,000 for the month of July. However, the question is more complex than that, since the sales staff commission needs also to be taken into account.

This type of problem can be resolved efficiently by using Goal Seek. Goal Seek substitutes different values into the *changing cell* (in this case, the sales cell) until the value in the *goal cell* (operating income) is equal to the value you want ($10,000).

Use Goal Seek to determine the optimal sales level

With the July data at hand, you need to start the analysis process by determining by how much the July sales need to increase in order for the Island Tea & Coffee Company to reach a monthly operating income of $10,000. In this exercise, you use Goal Seek to answer this question.

1   Click cell B26 (Operating Income).

2   On the Tools menu, click Goal Seek.

3   Verify that the Set Cell box reads B26, and then, in the To Value box, type **10000**

4   Press TAB to place the insertion point in the By Changing Cell box, and then click cell B6 (Sales).

5   Click OK.

    The Goal Seek Status dialog box appears containing the answer to the question you asked. To reach a monthly operating income of $10,000, the Island Tea & Coffee Company will have to increase sales to $54,298, a difference of $4,717.

6   Click OK to keep the new values in your worksheet.

Return the worksheet to original values

You will use Scenario Manager in the next section to compare different budget possibilities, so you want to return your worksheet to the values it contained before you changed them with Goal Seek.

Undo

➤   On the Standard toolbar, click the Undo button.

    The Goal Seek changes are removed and the original values appear in the worksheet.

Creating Multiple Scenarios to Compare Alternatives

The management team believes that there are additional ways to increase the operating income, and they want to look at alternative changes to the budget. To provide a summary of alternatives, you can use Scenario Manager to create different budget scenarios. When you finish creating multiple scenarios, you can create a scenario summary that can then be presented to the management team members for their review and analysis.

Before you create any scenarios, you should name all the cells that you might use in each scenario; this way, when you generate a scenario summary, the cell names you defined are used and the readability is improved.

Name input cells

To generate the clearest scenarios and summary possible, you name the cells that you will be using. In this exercise, you name all possible input cells.

1   Select cells A6 through B26.

2   On the Insert menu, point to Name, and then click Create.

    The Create Names dialog box appears.

3 Verify that the Left Column check box is selected, and then click OK.

The cells are named using the labels in column A.

Create a scenario of changed costs

Before experimenting with different scenarios, you decide to create a scenario documenting the current budget so that you can refer back to it when you compare the alternatives. In this exercise, you create a first scenario based on your current budget.

1 On the Tools menu, click Scenarios.

The Scenario Manager dialog box appears.

2 Click the Add button.

The Add Scenario dialog box appears.

3 In the Scenario Name box, type **Current Budget**, and then press TAB to highlight the entry in the Changing Cells box.

4 Click cell B6, and then hold down CTRL and click cells B7, B10, B11, and B16.

The cell references are entered in the Changing Cells box and are separated by commas. These are the cells that you will change in different scenarios.

5 Click OK.

The Scenario Values dialog box appears containing the cell names.

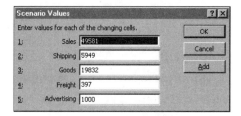

6 Click OK.

The Scenario Manager dialog box appears with your first scenario listed in the Scenarios list.

7 Click Close.

8 Save your workbook.

Create additional scenarios

Now that you have created a scenario based on your current budget, you're ready to start experimenting. In this exercise, you create different scenarios by changing the values in the Changing Cells box and saving each scenario.

1 On the Tools menu, click Scenarios.

The Scenario Manager dialog box appears.

2 Click Add.

3 In the Add Scenario dialog box, in the Scenario Name box, type **Low COGs**, and then click OK.

The Scenario Values dialog box appears.

4 Double-click in the Goods box to highlight the Goods value, type **15000**, and then press TAB.

5 In the Freight box, type **200**, and then click OK.

The Scenario Manager dialog box appears again. The new scenario, Low COGs, is added to the Scenarios list.

6 Click Add to add another scenario.

The Add Scenario dialog box appears.

7 In the Scenario Name box, type **High Shipping**, and then click OK.

8 Press TAB to highlight the Shipping box, type **8000**, and then click OK.

The Scenario Manager dialog box appears.

9 Click Add.

The Add Scenario dialog box appears.

10 In the Scenario Name box, type **Low Advertising**, and then click OK.

11 Double-click in the Advertising box, type **400**, and then click OK.

All the scenarios have been added.

View the scenarios

Now that you have created different scenarios, you're ready to take a closer a look at them. In this exercise, you view each scenario and the changes it creates in your worksheet.

1 In the Scenario Manager dialog box, click Low COGS in the Scenarios list, and then click Show.

The values in the worksheet change to reflect the changes produced by the Low COGS scenario, but because the Scenario Manager dialog box is still open, you cannot scroll down to see how the operating income has been affected.

2 In the Scenario Manager dialog box, click Close, and then scroll down to see the change in the operating income.

Create a scenario summary

It is difficult to assess the impact of different scenarios in your worksheet because you can only see one scenario at a time. A better way to compare the results of your scenarios is to create a summary that lays out all the scenarios side-by-side in a single worksheet. In this exercise, you make your budget scenarios more useful to the management team by creating a scenario summary.

1 On the Tools menu, click Scenarios.

2 In the Scenario Manager dialog box, click Summary.

The Scenario Summary dialog box appears.

3 Verify that the Scenario Summary option button is selected and that the Result Cells box reads B26, and then click OK.

A new worksheet named Scenario Summary is added to your workbook. It shows the changes and results for each scenario, and has outline symbols on the left and across the top that operate like outline symbols in a subtotaled worksheet.

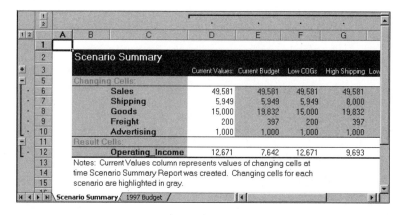

4 Save the Analysis workbook.

NOTE If you'd like to build on the skills you learned in this lesson, you can do the One Step Further. Otherwise, skip to "Finish the Lesson."

One Step Further: Editing a Scenario

While reviewing the scenarios before handing them off to the management team, you notice a mistake in the Low Advertising scenario: the advertising value should be $500 instead of $400. In this exercise, you edit the scenario appropriately, and then create a new Scenario Summary worksheet.

1 Delete the Scenario Summary worksheet. (Hint: Use the right mouse button to click the sheet tab, and then click Delete.)

2 On the Tools menu, click Scenarios.

3 Select the Low Advertising scenario, and then click Edit.

The Edit Scenario dialog box appears.

4 Under Protection, clear the Prevent Changes check box, and then click OK.

The Scenario Values dialog box appears.

5 Change the Advertising value to 500, and then click OK.

The Scenario Manager dialog box appears.

6 Click Summary.

The Scenario Summary dialog box appears.

7 Verify that the Scenario Summary option button is selected and that the Result Cells box reads B26, and then click OK.

A new Scenario Summary worksheet is added to your workbook.

8 Save your work.

Finish the lesson

1 To continue to the next lesson, on the File menu, click Close.

2 If you are finished using Microsoft Excel for now, on the File menu, click Exit.

Lesson Summary

To	Do this
Use Goal Seek to determine a specific value	Select the cell that contains the formula in which you want to produce a desired result, and then, on the Tools menu, click Goal Seek. In the To Value box, type a goal value, and then, in the By Changing Cell box, specify the cell containing the value you want to change to reach the goal. Click OK.
Create a scenario	On the Tools menu, click Scenarios. Click Add. In the Scenario Name box, type a name; in the Changing Cells box, click cells to specify the cells that will change; and then, click OK. In the Scenario Values dialog box, type the values that you want, click OK, and then click Close.
View a scenario using the Scenario Manager dialog box	On the Tools menu, click Scenarios. Select the scenario you want, and then click Show.
Create a scenario summary	On the Tools menu, click Scenarios. In the Scenario Manager dialog box, click Summary. In the Scenario Summary dialog box, verify that the Scenario Summary option button is selected and that the Result Cells box reads the appropriate result cell reference, and then click OK.

For online information about	On the Help menu, click Contents And Index, click the Index tab, and then type
Finding answers with Goal Seek	**goal seeking**
Creating scenarios	**scenario manager**

Sharing a Workbook with Others

Estimated time
30 min.

In this lesson you will learn how to:

- Allow others to share and edit a workbook simultaneously.
- See who is currently looking at or working on a workbook.
- Review workbook revisions made by others.
- Update a shared workbook, resolve conflicting changes, and accept or reject revisions.

In this lesson, you will learn how to share a workbook with other users on a network. A shared workbook can be edited simultaneously by multiple users. For example, you might enter formulas into a workbook at the same time as other users are entering data for those formulas into the same workbook. This saves time because users do not have to wait for a workbook to become available. Each user can see the changes that other users make in the workbook, and can resolve conflicts by choosing one entry.

To do this lesson, you will need to enlist the help of a co-worker on your network; you will also need to save the practice file in a shared folder on your network so that your co-worker can open it.

As the Island Tea & Coffee Company office manager and "keeper" of the inventory files, you have tried managing them using different techniques such as consolidation, subtotaling, and templates, but you have come to the conclusion that it would make more sense to keep the monthly inventories in a single workbook, and have everyone who works on the inventory enter their data directly into it. To make it an efficient process for everyone, you will make the inventory workbook a shared workbook; this will allow everyone involved to enter their part of the data when they are ready, without having to wait for other users to close the workbook.

In the following exercises, you will open the Shared Inventory List workbook and save it as a practice file with the name Shared Workbook Lesson.

Open an existing file

Open

1   On the Standard toolbar, click the Open button.

2   In the Open dialog box, click the Look In Favorites button.

3   In the file list, double-click the Excel SBS Practice folder.

4   Double-click the Shared Inventory List file.

Save the file with a new name

1   On the File menu, click Save As.

The Save As dialog box opens. If the Excel SBS Practice folder is not a shared folder on your network, locate a shared folder and be sure its name appears in the Save In box.

2   In the File Name box, type **Shared Workbook Lesson**, and then click Save.

Sharing a Workbook and Using it Simultaneously

You have decided to keep the Island Tea & Coffee Company inventory in a single workbook, and all of your co-workers who participate in the inventory count will enter their data in that workbook. When you *share* the workbook, each user can open it and enter data at any time, instead of having to wait for others to finish using the workbook. For example, one or several of your co-workers can enter monthly inventory data at the same time as you enter formulas to determine the average monthly inventory counts.

Before you and your co-workers can open and enter data in the Shared Workbook Lesson file, you need to make it a shared workbook.

Share a workbook so that multiple users can use it simultaneously

In this exercise, you make the Shared Workbook Lesson file a shared workbook.

1   On the Tools menu, click Share Workbook.

The Share Workbook dialog box appears.

2 On the Editing tab, select the Allow Changes By More Than One User At The Same Time check box, and then click OK.

3 When prompted to confirm that you want the workbook to be saved, click OK.

The workbook is shared and accessible to any other users on your network who have access to this folder.

 IMPORTANT In order to complete the following exercises, you will need to enlist the help of a partner. You must both open the Shared Workbook Lesson file on your respective computers.

Enter data—you

In this exercise, you enter monthly inventory data (while your partner is entering formulas).

1 On the Tools menu, click Share Workbook.

The Share Workbook dialog box appears. The Editing tab shows that both you and your partner have the shared workbook open.

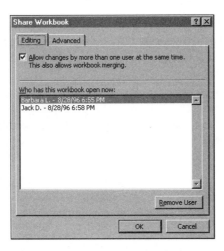

2 Click OK.

The Share Workbook dialog box closes.

3 Enter the following data in cells M12 through M25:

Cell	Entry
M12	200
M13	700
M14	600
M15	600
M16	1100
M17	800
M18	800
M19	600
M20	700
M21	600
M22	300
M23	300
M24	500
M25	800

Enter formulas—your partner

In this exercise, your partner enters formulas that average the monthly inventory data (while you are entering the remaining inventory data).

1 In cell N3, type **=average(g3:m3)**, and then press ENTER.

2 Drag the fill handle on cell N3 to copy the formula down to cell N39.

3 Use the right mouse button to click the column N header, click Format Cells, click the Number tab, and then select the Number format and 0 decimal places.

4 Click OK.

Bold

5 Enter the text **Average** in cell N2, click the Bold button on the Formatting toolbar, and then press ENTER.

Save the workbook—you and your partner

In this exercise, you and your partner save the file and see each other's entries. Each user should do this exercise on his or her own machine.

IMPORTANT Be sure that your partner has saved his or her changes before you save yours.

1 Save the Shared Workbook Lesson file.

If a message box appears, click OK. Each changed cell is highlighted with a colored border and a colored triangle in the upper-left corner. The highlighting color identifies the user who made the change.

2 Point to a highlighted cell.

A revision comment appears that indicates who made the change and what the change was.

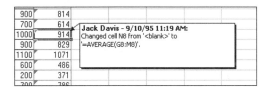

NOTE   You might both have to save again to guarantee that you can each see each other's changes.

Reviewing Changes in a Workbook

In a shared workbook, you can also make changes to the same data simultaneously with your co-workers, even if the changes conflict. The workbook maintains a change history so that you can see what changes have been made to the data and who made them. You can then resolve conflicting changes by choosing which changes to keep.

A co-worker helped perform the Island Tea & Coffee Company inventory count in July, and he wrote down an incorrect number for Haiti coffee: instead of 200, the entry should be 300. When he realized his error, he contacted both you and your partner with the change, but your partner misunderstood the message and changed the number from 200 to 100, while you entered the correct number, 300. In the following exercises, you will change the Haiti entry, and then resolve the conflict between the changes.

Make revisions in the workbook—your partner

In this exercise, your partner changes the Haiti count to 100.

1 Change the entry in cell M12 to 100.

2 Save the workbook.

Make revisions in the workbook—you

In this exercise, you change the Haiti count to 300.

1 Change the entry in cell M12 to 300.

2 Save the workbook.

The Resolve Conflicts dialog box appears.

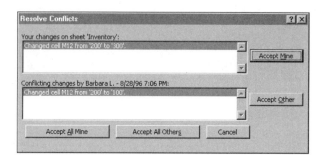

Resolve conflicts in a workbook

In this exercise, you resolve conflicting changes in the workbook.

1 In the Resolve Conflicts dialog box, click Accept Mine (which corresponds to the change from 200 to 300).

If a message box appears that says "Save Resulted In Some Changes From Other Users," click OK.

2 Your partner can save and close the shared workbook.

Accept or reject revisions in a shared workbook

1 On the Tools menu, point to Track Changes, and then click Accept or Reject Changes.

If a message box appears asking you to confirm that you want to save the workbook, click OK. The Select Changes To Accept Or Reject dialog box appears.

2 Be sure that the When check box is selected and that the When list box reads Not Yet Reviewed, and then click OK.

The Accept Or Reject Changes dialog box appears.

Undo

3 Click Accept All.

All of the changes in the worksheet are accepted, and the Undo button on the Standard toolbar is dimmed so that you cannot undo the changes that you accepted.

NOTE There are several things you cannot do in a shared workbook, such as delete worksheets; create or change the layout of PivotTables; and create conditional formats and data validation. In order to do any of these things, you will first need to remove the workbook from shared use. To do this, on the Tools menu, click Share Workbook, and then click the Editing tab. Clear the Allow Changes By More Than One User At The Same Time check box, and then click OK. When prompted to confirm your action, click Yes.

 NOTE If you'd like to build on the skills you learned in this lesson, you can do the One Step Further. Otherwise, skip to "Finish the Lesson."

One Step Further: Printing a Change History

Your manager wants to know when and by whom a specific change was made in the inventory count. In this exercise, you create and print a change history worksheet.

1 On the Tools menu, point to Track Changes, and then click Highlight Changes.

The History worksheet is temporary and is not saved when the workbook is saved. To generate a new History worksheet, repeat step 2.

2 Clear the When, Who, and Where check boxes if any are selected, select the List Changes On A New Sheet check box, and then click OK.

A new worksheet, named History, is inserted in the workbook. It lists the changes saved in the shared workbook and information about the changes.

The History sheet lists all saved changes, according to your When, Who and Where selections, whereas Change Highlighting highlights all unsaved changes.

Action Number	Date	Time	Who	Change	Sheet	Range	New Value
1	8/28/96	7:03 PM	Barbara L.	Cell Change	Inventory	N3	=AVERAGE(G3:M3)
2	8/28/96	7:03 PM	Barbara L.	Cell Change	Inventory	N4	=AVERAGE(G4:M4)
3	8/28/96	7:03 PM	Barbara L.	Cell Change	Inventory	N5	=AVERAGE(G5:M5)
4	8/28/96	7:03 PM	Barbara L.	Cell Change	Inventory	N6	=AVERAGE(G6:M6)
5	8/28/96	7:03 PM	Barbara L.	Cell Change	Inventory	N7	=AVERAGE(G7:M7)
6	8/28/96	7:03 PM	Barbara L.	Cell Change	Inventory	N8	=AVERAGE(G8:M8)
7	8/28/96	7:03 PM	Barbara L.	Cell Change	Inventory	N9	=AVERAGE(G9:M9)
8	8/28/96	7:03 PM	Barbara L.	Cell Change	Inventory	N10	=AVERAGE(G10:M10)
9	8/28/96	7:03 PM	Barbara L.	Cell Change	Inventory	N11	=AVERAGE(G11:M11)
10	8/28/96	7:03 PM	Barbara L.	Cell Change	Inventory	N12	=AVERAGE(G12:M12)
11	8/28/96	7:03 PM	Barbara L.	Cell Change	Inventory	N13	=AVERAGE(G13:M13)
12	8/28/96	7:03 PM	Barbara L.	Cell Change	Inventory	N14	=AVERAGE(G14:M14)
13	8/28/96	7:03 PM	Barbara L.	Cell Change	Inventory	N15	=AVERAGE(G15:M15)
14	8/28/96	7:03 PM	Barbara L.	Cell Change	Inventory	N16	=AVERAGE(G16:M16)
15	8/28/96	7:03 PM	Barbara L.	Cell Change	Inventory	N17	=AVERAGE(G17:M17)

Inventory \ **History**

3 Print the History sheet.

Finish the lesson

1   On the File menu, click Save.

2   To continue to the next lesson, on the File menu, click Close.

3   If you are finished using Microsoft Excel for now, on the File menu, click Exit.

Lesson Summary

To	Do this
Share a workbook	On the Tools menu, click Share Workbook. On the Editing tab, click the Allow Changes By More Than One User At The Same Time check box, and then click OK. When prompted, click OK to confirm your action.
See who is currently looking at or working on a workbook	On the Tools menu, click Share Workbook, and then look at the list of names on the Editing tab.
Enter data in a shared workbook	Enter the data you want, and then save the workbook.
Resolve conflicts between changes	In the Resolve Conflicts dialog box, click the button corresponding to the change you want to accept.
Accept or reject changes	On the Tools menu, point to Track Changes, and then click Accept or Reject Changes. In the Select Changes To Accept Or Reject dialog box, select the changes to review, and then click OK. In the Accept Or Reject Changes dialog box, click the Accept or Reject button to review changes one by one, or click the Accept All or Reject All buttons to accept or reject all changes.

For online information about	**On the Help menu, click Contents And Index, click the Index tab, and then type**
Sharing workbooks	**workbooks, shared**

Integrating Microsoft Excel with Other Programs

Estimated time
30 min.

In this lesson you will learn how to:

- Link information from another program.
- Edit linked information.
- Embed information from another program.
- Edit embedded information.
- Convert a Microsoft Excel worksheet into a Microsoft Access database.
- Connect documents with hyperlinks.

Reports usually consist of several different types of information; for example, numerical data and charts from Microsoft Excel might be presented along with an analysis of the data written in Microsoft Word. A report can be composed of a worksheet with part of a Microsoft Word document in it, or a Word document containing an Excel table or chart.

There are three ways to integrate information from different programs: pasting, linking, and embedding. *Pasting* means that you simply copy a picture of the information you want to include in a document, and then paste the picture into another program. The information in a pasted picture cannot be edited or formatted. *Linking* means that the information you copy into your worksheet is connected to the *source*, or original, document or worksheet that you copied it from. Linked information can be edited and formatted; when you edit or format linked information, you make changes to the source file from which the information came. *Embedding* means the information is connected to the program in which it was created (the source program), but not to the source file, so you can edit and format the information using the source program, but changes you make will not affect the source file.

In this lesson you will learn how to link and embed information between Microsoft Excel and Microsoft Word, and you will practice editing both embedded and linked information. You will also practice pasting a picture into a Microsoft PowerPoint slide. Finally, you will learn how to convert a Microsoft Excel worksheet into a Microsoft Access database.

As the Island Tea & Coffee Company office manager, you have been asked to generate two reports: an electronic report in which a sales analysis from a Microsoft Word document is included in a worksheet, and a printed report in which a Microsoft Excel chart is included in a Microsoft Word document.

In the following exercises, you will open and then save the two documents necessary to complete this lesson.

IMPORTANT You will need to have Microsoft Word 97 installed on your computer to perform the following exercises.

Open and save a Microsoft Excel file

Open

1 On the Standard toolbar, click the Open button.
2 In the Open dialog box, click the Look In Favorites button.
3 In the File list box, double-click the Excel SBS Practice folder.
4 Double-click the Sales Report file.
5 On the File menu, click Save As.

   The Save As dialog box appears. Be sure that the Excel SBS Practice folder appears in the Save In box.

6 In the File Name box, type **Integration Lesson**, and then click Save.

Open and save a Microsoft Word file

1 Click Start. Point to Programs, and then click Microsoft Word.
   Microsoft Word opens.

2 Open the Sales Analysis file located in your Excel SBS Practice folder, and then save it as **Integration Lesson**

Your window should look similar to the following illustration.

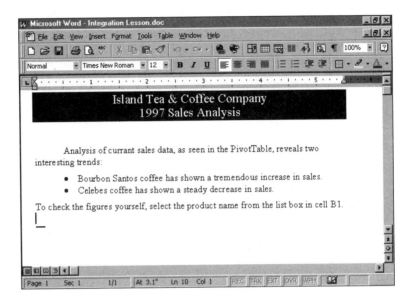

Linking Information Between Programs

The two files you have opened are related parts of an Island Tea & Coffee Company sales report for 1997: the workbook contains raw data and a PivotTable, and the document contains an analysis of the data. You've been asked to combine the two by pasting information from the Microsoft Word document into the Microsoft Excel worksheet that contains the PivotTable.

You will link the information from the Microsoft Word document so that any changes you might need to make to the analysis will also be made to the source Microsoft Word document. This way, any changes you make, such as correct spelling or grammar, will need to be made only once; all linked copies of the Microsoft Word document will be automatically updated when changes are made to the source document.

Paste a linked Microsoft Word document into a worksheet

In this exercise, you combine the Island Tea & Coffee Company's 1997 sales data and analysis into a complete report by copying and then pasting linked information from the Microsoft Word document into your Microsoft Excel worksheet.

1 In Microsoft Word, on the Edit menu, click Select All.

The entire document is selected.

2 On the Edit menu, click Copy.

3 On the taskbar, click the Microsoft Excel button.

The Microsoft Excel window appears.

4 On the Sales Report sheet, select cell D3.

5 On the Edit menu, click Paste Special.

The Paste Special dialog box appears.

6 Click the Paste Link option button.

7 Verify that Microsoft Word Document Object is selected in the As list, and then click OK.

A linked copy of the document is pasted into your worksheet, and when the linked object is selected, the path to the source file appears in the formula bar. Your worksheet should look similar to the following illustration.

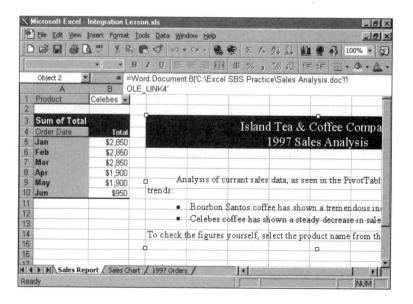

Edit a linked Microsoft Word document from within Microsoft Excel

When you double-click a linked object, the source program and file will open automatically.

While taking a quick look at the pasted Microsoft Word object, you noticed a misspelling in the first sentence. You need to correct the mistake in the source document as well as in the copy you pasted into your worksheet. In this exercise, you make the correction by editing the information from within Microsoft Excel.

1   Double-click the linked Microsoft Word object in your Microsoft Excel worksheet.

The source file opens in Microsoft Word.

2   Change the spelling of the word "currant" to "current."

3   Save the Microsoft Word document.

4   On the taskbar, click the Microsoft Excel button.

The object in your worksheet is updated to reflect the change in the Microsoft Word document.

5   Save the workbook.

Embedding Information Between Programs

You have been asked to create an Island Tea & Coffee Company sales report that contains an analysis report and a chart. You have elected to embed the chart into your Microsoft Word report because it will allow you to change the information and the formatting in the object using Microsoft Excel functionality without changing the pasted object. This is advantageous when you want to make changes to the object without changing the source, or when you need to be able to change the object but you don't have access to the source file (for instance, if the file you are working in is on your laptop computer and the source file is back at the office, on the Island Tea & Coffee Company network).

Embed a Microsoft Excel chart into a Microsoft Word document

Your Microsoft Excel file contains a chart sheet named Sales Chart. You will create an integrated report by embedding this chart into the Microsoft Word analysis document.

To go to the end of a document quickly, press CTRL+END.

1   Switch to Microsoft Word, and then place your pointer at the end of the document.

2   Switch to Microsoft Excel, and then select the Sales Chart sheet.

3 On the Edit menu, click Copy.

4 Switch to Microsoft Word, and then, on the Edit menu, click Paste Special.

5 Be sure that the Paste option button is selected and that Microsoft Excel Chart Object is selected in the As list, and then click OK.

The chart is embedded in the Microsoft Word document. You can resize the chart object by dragging the corner handles.

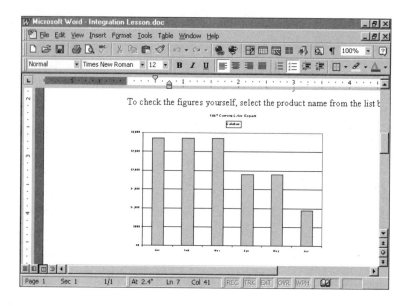

Edit an embedded chart from within Microsoft Word

Your manager has asked you to format the data markers in the report's chart with a pattern fill, without modifying the source chart. Because you embedded the chart rather than linking it, you can change the chart object in the document without affecting the source chart sheet. In this exercise, you edit the embedded object only.

1 In the Microsoft Word document, double-click the chart object.

The Microsoft Excel menu bar and toolbars appear. A hatched border appears around the chart object.

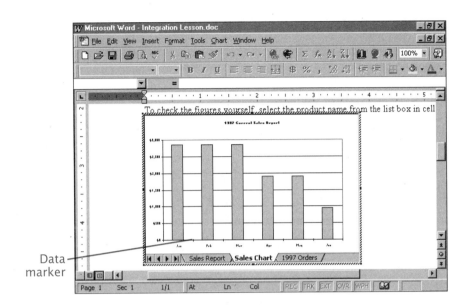

Data marker

2 In the chart object, double-click any data marker.

The Format Data Series dialog box appears.

3 On the Patterns tab, click the Fill Effects button.

The Fill Effects dialog box appears.

4 On the Texture tab, click Purple Mesh (the third texture down in the third column from the left—the name of the texture, "Purple mesh," appears in the box below the textures), click OK, and then click OK again.

The Format Data Series dialog box closes.

5 Click the Microsoft Word document (outside of the embedded chart) to return to Microsoft Word.

Your document should look similar to the following illustration. The source chart has not been changed.

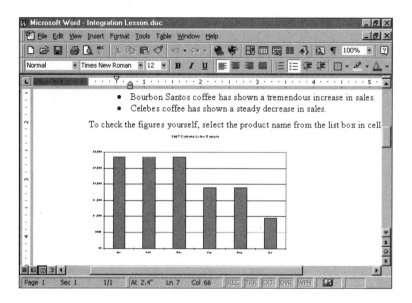

6   Save and then close the Integration Lesson document and Microsoft Word.

7   In Microsoft Excel, save the Integration Lesson workbook.

Pasting a Microsoft Excel Chart into a PowerPoint Slide

You have been asked to create a Microsoft PowerPoint slide containing a chart for a sales meeting. You will paste a picture of the chart into the slide, rather than linking or embedding it, because the slide will be presented from a laptop computer that only has Microsoft PowerPoint loaded.

IMPORTANT   You will need to have Microsoft PowerPoint 97 installed on your computer to complete this exercise.

Paste a chart into a slide

In this exercise, you paste a picture of the Microsoft Excel chart into a blank Microsoft PowerPoint slide.

1   In the Microsoft Excel Integration Lesson workbook, select the Sales Chart sheet.

2 Click Start. Point to Programs, and then click Microsoft PowerPoint. Microsoft PowerPoint starts, and the PowerPoint dialog box appears.

3 Click the Blank Presentation option button, and then click OK.

4 Click in the Click To Add First Slide box, and then click the Chart AutoLayout (the second layout down in the rightmost column).

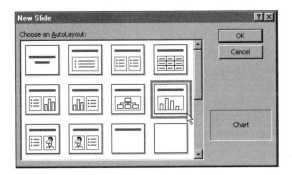

5 Click OK.

A blank slide appears that contains a text box at the top, and a picture box below the text box.

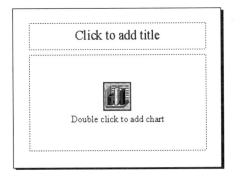

6 On the taskbar, click the Microsoft Excel button.

7 Be sure that the Sales Chart sheet is selected, and then, on the Edit menu, click Copy.

8 On the taskbar, click the Microsoft PowerPoint button.

9 Click in the picture box to select it, and then, on the Edit menu, click Paste Special.

10   Be sure that the Paste option button is selected, select Microsoft Excel Chart Object, and then click OK.

A picture of your Sales Chart is pasted into the slide. Your slide should look similar to the following illustration.

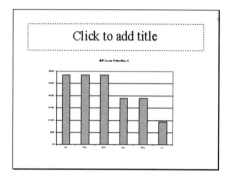

11   Save the presentation as Sales Chart, and then close the presentation and Microsoft PowerPoint.

12   Save the Integration Lesson workbook, but keep it open for a later exercise.

Converting a Worksheet into a Microsoft Access Table

For more information about Microsoft Access, see the Microsoft Access 97 Step by Step book.

The Island Tea & Coffee Company sales manager has decided to keep the customer list in Microsoft Access, where he can easily store large numbers of records and pull out, or extract, only those records that he needs. He has asked you to convert the customer list workbook into a Microsoft Access table.

IMPORTANT   You will need to have Microsoft Access 97 installed on your computer to complete this exercise. You will also need to have the AccessLink add-in installed in Microsoft Excel. To do so, on the Tools menu, click Add-Ins, select AccessLinks Add-In, and then click OK.

200

Convert a worksheet to a Microsoft Access table

In this exercise, you will open the Island Tea & Coffee Company customer list in Microsoft Excel and convert it to a Microsoft Access table. The Integration Lesson workbook is still open from previous exercises, and you will use it again in later exercises; it can remain open while you open the customer list for this exercise.

1 Open the Customer List file located in the Excel SBS Practice folder, and then select a cell in the worksheet list.

2 On the Data menu, click Convert To MS Access. (If you do not see the Convert To MS Access command on your Data menu, you need to install the AccessLinks add-in.)

The Convert to Microsoft Access dialog box opens.

3 Under Convert To, be sure that the New Database option button is selected, and then click OK.

The Microsoft Access Import Spreadsheet Wizard appears.

4 Follow the steps in the wizard to convert the customer list into a Microsoft Access table.

5 Close Microsoft Access, and then close the Customer List workbook.

Connecting Documents with Hyperlinks

When co-workers read your Sales Analysis workbook, they are often curious about the current prices for various Island Tea & Coffee Company products. You can make it easy for your co-workers to open and examine the current price list by creating a *hyperlink* (sometimes also called a jump) in the workbook that will open the price list file when clicked. Hyperlinks are another method of integrating the information contained in different Microsoft Office programs.

Create hyperlinks that open other documents

In this exercise, you create a hyperlink in the Integration Lesson workbook that opens the Price List file.

1 In the Integration Lesson workbook, click the Sales Report sheet, select cell A12, and then type **Price List**

2 Select cell A12, and then, on the Insert menu, click Hyperlink.

The Insert Hyperlink dialog box appears.

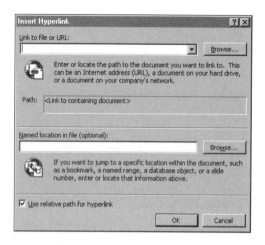

3   Click the first Browse button, locate your Excel SBS Practice folder, and then double-click the Price List workbook file.

The path to the Price List file is automatically entered in the Link To File Or URL box.

4   Click OK.

The text in cell A12 is colored blue and underlined, indicating that it is a hyperlink. When you point to the cell, the pointer becomes a pointing-hand icon, indicating that it is positioned over a hyperlink.

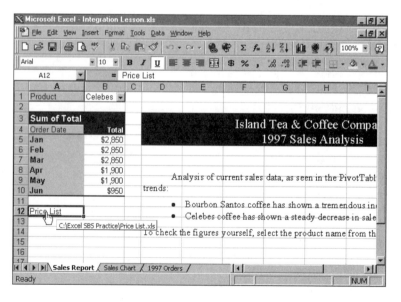

5   Save the workbook.

Test the hyperlink

In this exercise, you use the hyperlink you just created to open the Price List file.

1 Point to cell A12, and then click the hyperlink.

The Price List file opens.

2 Close the Price List file.

 NOTE If you'd like to build on the skills you learned in this lesson, you can do the One Step Further. Otherwise, skip to "Finish the Lesson."

One Step Further: Editing a Hyperlink to Open a Different File

You decide to change the hyperlink so it opens the inventory file instead of the price list.

1 Use the right mouse button to click the hyperlink.

A shortcut menu appears.

2 Point to Hyperlink, and then click Edit Hyperlink.

The Edit Hyperlink dialog box appears.

3 Delete the text in the Link To File Or URL box, click Browse, locate and double-click the Lesson 6 Inventory file in the Excel SBS Practice folder, and then click OK.

The hyperlink points to the inventory instead of the price list, but the hyperlink text still reads Price List.

4 Use the right mouse button to click the hyperlink.

A shortcut menu appears.

5 Point to Hyperlink, and then click Select Hyperlink.

6 Type **Inventory**, and then press ENTER.

The hyperlink text now correctly identifies the file it points to.

7 On the File menu, click Save.

Finish the lesson

1 To continue to the Review & Practice, on the File menu, click Close.

2 If you are finished using Microsoft Excel for now, on the File menu, click Exit.

Lesson Summary

To	Do this
Paste linked information from Microsoft Word into a Microsoft Excel worksheet	Copy the information in Microsoft Word, click in the worksheet where you want to paste it, and then, on the Edit menu, click Paste Special. Select the Paste Linked option button, select Microsoft Word Document Object, and then click OK.
Edit a linked Microsoft Word object from within Microsoft Excel	Double-click the linked object. The source file opens in Microsoft Word. Edit the document, save it, and then click the Microsoft Excel button on the taskbar to return to the Microsoft Excel workbook.
Paste an embedded chart from Microsoft Excel into Microsoft Word	Copy the chart in Microsoft Excel. Click in the Microsoft Word document where you want to paste the chart, and then, on the Edit menu, click Paste Special. Select the Paste option button, select Microsoft Excel Chart Object, and then click OK.
Edit a chart object embedded in a Microsoft Word document	Double-click the chart object. Microsoft Excel opens "within" Microsoft Word. Edit the chart object, and then click on the Microsoft Word document to return to Microsoft Word.

To	Do this
Paste a chart from Microsoft Excel into a Microsoft PowerPoint slide	Copy the chart in Microsoft Excel. In the Microsoft PowerPoint slide, select a picture box, and then, on the Edit menu, click Paste Special, select Microsoft Excel Chart Object, and then click OK.
Convert a worksheet into a Microsoft Access table	Select a cell in the worksheet. On the Data menu, click Convert To MS Access. In the Convert To Microsoft Access dialog box, select new Database or Browse to locate an existing database, and then click OK. Follow the steps in the Microsoft Access Import Spreadsheet Wizard.
Connect files with hyperlinks	Select the cell in which you want your hyperlink to appear, and then enter text to label the hyperlink. On the Insert menu, click Hyperlink. Browse to locate the file you want the hyperlink to open, double-click the filename, and then click OK.

For online information about	On the Help menu, click Contents And Index, click the Index tab, and then type
Linking	**linked objects**
Embedding	**embedded objects**
Microsoft PowerPoint slides	**Microsoft Powerpoint**
Microsoft Access database	**Microsoft Access Import Spreadsheet Wizard**
Hyperlinks	**hyperlinks**

Review & Practice

- Use scenarios to analyze data.
- Integrate documents created using different programs.
- Share a workbook.

**Estimated time
20 min.**

Now that you have finished Part 4, you can practice the skills you learned by working through the steps in this Review & Practice section. You will practice analyzing data using scenarios, integrating Microsoft Excel with Microsoft Word, and sharing a workbook.

Scenario

The State University Alumni Association quarterly expenses are entered in a list in a shared workbook so that all SUAA employees and volunteers have access to the workbook whenever they need to enter expenses; all the details in the list are then consolidated on another worksheet at the end of the quarter. The commentary is done in Microsoft Word and paste-linked into the consolidated worksheet so that an updated version is always ready to print for the newsletter. At the end of each quarter, you use scenarios to analyze the consolidated expenses list. When this process is complete, the workbook is shared again so that SUAA staff can continue to enter expenses.

Step 1: Analyze an expense list using scenarios

The shared status of the expense workbook has been removed and the detailed list has already been consolidated so that you can analyze the consolidated expenses using scenarios. In this step, you create three scenarios.

1 Open the practice file R&P 4, and then save it as Association Expenses.

2 On the Consolidated Expenses worksheet, create a scenario called 2nd Quarter Expenses that shows actual current expenses with no changes.

3 Create a scenario called Minimum Advertising that shows the advertising/promotion expense reduced to $200.00.

4 Create a scenario called Minimum Personal Expenses that shows the following expenses reduced to the specified amounts: basic telephone $75.00, books/magazines $0, and equipment $100.00.

5 Create a scenario summary so you can compare the scenarios easily. (Hint: Be sure the result cell is B14, the Total cell.)

For more information about	See
Creating scenarios	Lesson 11

Step 2: Paste a linked Microsoft Word document into the worksheet

One of the SUAA staff members has updated the Microsoft Word document that contains the expenses commentary, and it is ready to be paste-linked into the worksheet. In this step, you link the Microsoft Word document with the Microsoft Excel worksheet.

1 Open the Microsoft Word file named SUAA Newsletter Commentary, and then select and copy the entire text.

2 On the Microsoft Excel worksheet named Consolidated Expenses, paste a linked copy of the Microsoft Word text into cell A17.

3 Save the workbook.

For more information about	See
Pasting linked objects from other programs	Lesson 13

Step 3: *Share the workbook*

Now that you have set up the scenarios, you need to share the workbook again so that other staff members can add their expenses for the next quarter. In this step, you make the Association Expenses workbook a shared workbook.

1 Make the workbook a shared workbook.

2 Click OK when prompted to save the workbook.

For more information about	See
Sharing a workbook	Lesson 12

Finish the Review & Practice

1 On the File menu, click Close.

2 If you are finished using Microsoft Excel for now, on the File menu, click Exit.

Appendixes

If You're New to Windows 95, Windows NT, or Microsoft Excel

If you are new to Microsoft Windows 95, Microsoft Windows NT version 4.0, or Microsoft Excel 97, this appendix will show you all the basics you need to get started. You'll get an overview of Windows 95 and Windows NT features, and you'll learn how to use online Help to answer your questions and find out more about using these operating systems. You'll also get an introduction to Microsoft Excel.

If You're New to Windows 95 or Windows NT

Windows 95 and Windows NT are easy-to-use computer environments that help you handle the daily work that you perform with your computer. You can use either Windows 95 or Windows NT to run Microsoft Excel 97—the explanations in this appendix apply to both operating systems. The way you use Windows 95, Windows NT, and programs designed for these operating systems is similar. The programs have a common look, and you use the same kinds of controls to tell them what to do. In this section, you'll learn how to use the basic program controls. If you're already familiar with Windows 95 or Windows NT, skip to the section titled "What is Microsoft Excel?"

Start Windows 95 or Windows NT

Starting Windows 95 or Windows NT is as easy as turning on your computer.

1   If your computer isn't on, turn it on now.

In Windows 95, you will also be prompted for a username and password if your computer is configured for user profiles.

2 If you are using Windows NT, press CTRL+ALT+DEL to display a dialog box asking for your username and password. If you are using Windows 95, you will see this dialog box if your computer is connected to a network.

3 Type your username and password in the appropriate boxes, and then click OK.

If you don't know your username or password, contact your system administrator for assistance.

Close

4 If you see the Welcome dialog box, click the Close button.

Your screen should look similar to the following illustration.

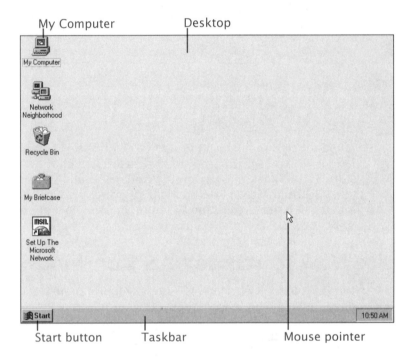

Using the Mouse

Although you can use the keyboard for most actions, many of these actions are easier to do by using a mouse. The mouse controls a pointer on the screen, as shown in the previous illustration. You move the pointer by sliding the mouse over a flat surface in the direction you want the pointer to move. If you run out of room to move the mouse, lift it up and then put it down in a more comfortable location.

214

NOTE In this book we assume that your mouse is set up so that the left button is the primary button and the right button is the secondary button. If your mouse is configured the opposite way, for left-handed use, use the right button when we tell you to use the left, and vice versa.

You'll use five basic mouse actions throughout this book.

When you are directed to	Do this
Point to an item	Move the mouse to place the pointer on the item.
Click an item	Point to the item on your screen, and quickly press and release the left mouse button.
Use the right mouse button to click an item	Point to the item on your screen, and then quickly press and release the right mouse button. Clicking the right mouse button displays a shortcut menu from which you can choose from a list of commands that apply to that item.
Double-click an item	Point to the item, and then quickly press and release the left mouse button twice.
Drag an item	Point to an item, and then hold down the left mouse button as you move the pointer.

Using Window Controls

All programs designed for use on computers that have Windows 95 or Windows NT installed have common controls that you use to scroll, size, move, and close a window.

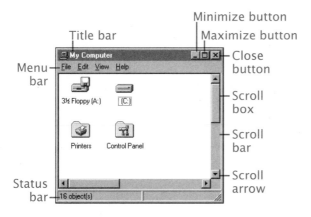

215

To	Do this	Button
Move, or *scroll*, vertically or horizontally through the contents of a window that extends beyond the screen	Click a scroll bar or scroll arrow, or drag the scroll box. The previous illustration identifies these controls.	
Enlarge a window to fill the screen	Click the Maximize button, or double-click the window's title bar.	▣
Restore a window to its previous size	Click the Restore button, or double-click the window title bar. When a window is maximized, the Maximize button changes to the Restore button.	▣
Reduce a window to a button on the taskbar	Click the Minimize button. To display a minimized window, click its button on the taskbar.	▬
Move a window	Drag the window title bar.	
Close a window	Click the Close button.	✕

Using Menus

Just like a restaurant menu, a program menu provides a list of options from which you can choose. On program menus, these options are called *commands*. To select a menu or a menu command, you click the item you want.

 NOTE You can also use the keyboard to make menu selections. Press the ALT key to activate the menu bar, and press the key that corresponds to the highlighted or underlined letter of the menu name. Then press the key that corresponds to the highlighted or underlined letter of the command name.

In the following exercise, you'll open and make selections from a menu.

Open and make selections from a menu

1 On the Desktop, double-click the My Computer icon.

The My Computer window opens.

You can also press ALT+E to open the Edit menu.

2 In the My Computer window, click Edit on the menu bar.

The Edit menu appears. Some commands are dimmed; this means they aren't available.

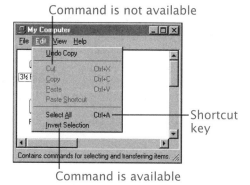

Command is not available

Shortcut key

Command is available

3 Click the Edit menu name to close the menu.

The menu closes.

On a menu, a check mark indicates that multiple items in this group of commands can be selected at one time. A bullet mark indicates that only one item in this group can be selected at one time.

4 Click View on the menu bar to open the View menu.

5 On the View menu, click Toolbar.

The View menu closes, and a toolbar appears below the menu bar.

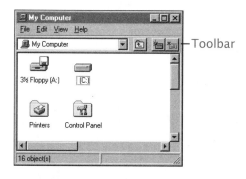

Toolbar

6 On the View menu, click List.

The items in the My Computer window now appear in a list, rather than as icons.

Large Icons

7 On the toolbar, click the Large Icons button.

Clicking a button on a toolbar is a quick way to select a command.

8 On the View menu, point to Arrange Icons.

A cascading menu appears listing additional menu choices. When a right-pointing arrow appears after a command name, it indicates that additional commands are available.

9 Click anywhere outside the menu to close it.

10 On the menu bar, click View, and then click Toolbar again.

The View menu closes, and the toolbar is now hidden.

11 Click the Close button in the upper-right corner of the My Computer window to close the window.

 TIP If you do a lot of typing, you might want to learn the key combinations for commands you use frequently. Pressing the key combination is a quick way to perform a command by using the keyboard. If a key combination is available for a command, it will be listed to the right of the command name on the menu. For example, CTRL+C is listed on the Edit menu as the key combination for the Copy command.

Using Dialog Boxes

When you choose a command name that is followed by an ellipsis (...), a dialog box will appear so that you can provide more information about how the command should be carried out. Dialog boxes have standard features, as shown in the following illustration.

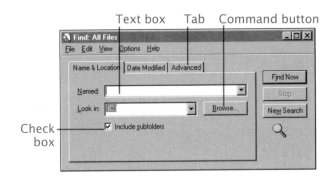

To move around in a dialog box, you click the item you want. You can also use the keyboard to select the item by holding down ALT as you press the underlined letter. Or, you can press TAB to move between items.

Display the Taskbar Properties dialog box

Some dialog boxes provide several categories of options displayed on separate tabs. You click the top of an obscured tab to make it visible.

1 On the taskbar, click the Start button.

The Start menu appears.

2 On the Start menu, point to Settings, and then click Taskbar.

3 In the Taskbar Properties dialog box, click the Start Menu Programs tab.

On this tab, you can customize the list of programs that appears on your Start menu.

4 Click the Taskbar Options tab, and then click the Show Small Icons In Start Menu check box to select it.

When a check box is selected, it displays a check mark.

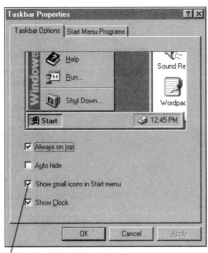

Click here. When you click a check box that is selected, you turn the option off.

5 Click the check box a couple of times, and watch how the display in the dialog box changes.

Clicking any check box will turn the option off or on.

6 Click the Cancel button in the dialog box.

The dialog box closes without changing any settings.

Getting Help with Windows 95 or Windows NT

When you're at work and you want to find out more information about how to do a project, you might ask a co-worker or consult a reference book. To find out more about functions and features in Windows 95 or Windows NT, you can use the online Help system. For example, when you need information about how to print, the Help system is one of the most efficient ways to learn. The Windows 95 or Windows NT Help system is available from the Start menu. After the Help system opens, you can choose the type of help you want from the Help Topics dialog box.

To find instructions about broad categories, you can look on the Contents tab. Or, you can search the Help index to find information about specific topics. The Help information is short and concise, so you can get the exact information you need quickly. There are also shortcut icons in many Help topics that you can use to directly go to or to perform the task you want.

Viewing Help Contents

The Contents tab is organized like a book's table of contents. As you choose top-level topics, called *chapters*, you see a list of more detailed subtopics from which to choose. Many of these chapters have Tips and Tricks sections to help you work more efficiently as well as Troubleshooting sections to help you resolve problems.

Find Help about general categories

Suppose you want to learn more about using Calculator, a program that comes with Windows 95 and Windows NT. In this exercise, you look up information in the online Help system.

1 Click Start. On the Start menu, click Help.

The Help Topics: Windows Help dialog box appears.

2 If necessary, click the Contents tab to make it active.

3 Double-click "Introducing Windows" or "Introducing Windows NT."

A set of subtopics appears.

4 Double-click "Using Windows Accessories."

5 Double-click "For General Use."

6 Double-click "Calculator: for making calculations."

A Help topic window opens.

7 Read the Help information, and then click the Close button to close the Help window.

Finding Help About Specific Topics

You can find specific Help topics by using the Index tab or the Find tab. The Index tab is organized like a book's index. Keywords for topics are organized alphabetically. You can either scroll through the list of keywords or type the keyword you want to find. You can then select from one or more topic choices.

With the Find tab, you can also enter a keyword. The main difference is that you get a list of all Help topics in which that keyword appears, not just the topics that begin with that word.

Find Help about specific topics by using the Help index

In this exercise, you use the Help index to learn how to change the background pattern of your Desktop.

1 Click Start, and on the Start menu, click Help.

The Help Topics dialog box appears.

2 Click the Index tab to make it active.

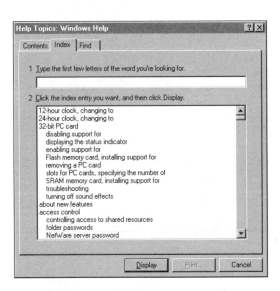

3 In the text box, type **display**

A list of display-related topics appears.

4 Click the topic named "background pictures or patterns, changing," and then click Display.

The Topics Found dialog box appears.

5 Be sure that the topic named "Changing the background of your desktop" is selected, and then click Display.

6 Read the Help topic.

7 Click the shortcut icon in step 1 of the Help topic.

Shortcut

The Display Properties dialog box appears. If you want, you can immediately perform the task you are looking up in Help.

8 Click the Close button in the Display Properties dialog box.

9 Click the Close button in the Windows Help window.

 NOTE You can print any Help topic if you have a printer installed on your computer. Click the Options button in the upper-right corner of any Help topic window, click Print Topic, and then click OK. To continue searching for additional topics, you can click the Help Topics button in any open Help topic window.

Find Help about specific topics by using the Find tab

In this exercise, you use the Find tab to learn how to change your printer's settings.

1 Click Start, and then click Help to display the Help dialog box.

2 Click the Find tab to make it active.

3   If you see a wizard, click Next, and then click Finish to complete and close the wizard.

The wizard creates a search index for your Help files. This might take a few minutes. The next time you use Find, you won't have to wait for the list to be created. The Find tab becomes active.

4   In the text box, type **print**

All topics that have to do with printing appear in the list box at the bottom of the tab.

5   In area 3 of the Help dialog box, click the "Changing printer settings" topic, and then click Display.

The Help topic appears.

6   Read the Help topic, and then click the Close button in the Windows Help window.

Find Help in a dialog box

Almost every dialog box includes a question mark Help button in the upper-right corner of its window. When you click this button and then click any dialog box control, a Help window appears that explains what the control is and how to use it. In this exercise, you'll get help for a dialog box control.

Help

1   Click Start, and then click Run.

The Run dialog box appears.

2   Click the Help button.

The mouse pointer changes to an arrow with a question mark.

3   Click the Open text box.

A Help window appears, providing information about how to use the Open text box.

4   Click anywhere on the Desktop to close the Help window.

The mouse pointer returns to its previous shape.

5   In the Run dialog box, click Cancel.

TIP   You can change the way the Help topics appear on your screen. Click the Options button in any Help topic window, and then point to Font to change the size of the text.

What Is Microsoft Excel?

Microsoft Excel is an electronic spreadsheet that does a lot more than replace the accountant's paper ledger with its neat columns and rows—Microsoft Excel can perform just about any mathematical calculation you want, and changes can be made to your numbers and calculations without having to painstakingly rewrite the entire spreadsheet. A spreadsheet is essentially a large grid that aligns entries into rows and columns so that it is easy to see which numbers you are working with.

Microsoft Excel can also create charts from your numbers much more easily than you can create them by hand, and can exchange information easily with other programs such as Microsoft Word, Microsoft PowerPoint, and Microsoft Access so that your information can be presented to others in nearly any form you choose.

Quit Windows 95 or Windows NT

1   If you are finished using Windows 95 or Windows NT, close any open windows by clicking the Close button in each window.

2   Click Start, and then click Shut Down.

The Shut Down Windows dialog box appears.

3   Click Yes.

A message indicates that it is now safe to turn off your computer.

 WARNING   To avoid loss of data or damage to your operating system, always quit Windows 95 or Windows NT by using the Shut Down command on the Start menu before you turn your computer off.

Matching the Exercises

Microsoft Excel has many optional settings that can affect either the screen display or the operation of certain functions. Some exercise steps, therefore, might not produce exactly the same result on your screen as shown in this book. For example, if your screen does not look like the illustration at a certain point in a lesson, you can turn to this appendix for guidance. Or, if you do not get the outcome described in the lesson, you can use this appendix to determine whether the options you have in effect are the same as the ones used in this book.

 NOTE Each computer system is configured with different hardware and software; therefore, your screen display of icons, folders, and menu options might not exactly match the illustrations in this book. These system differences should not interfere with your ability to perform the exercises in the book.

Installing Windows 95, Windows NT, or Microsoft Excel 97 Components

The exercises in this book assume that a "Typical" setup was used to install Windows 95 or Windows NT on your computer. If a "Portable," "Custom," or "Compact" setup was used, you might not have all the components necessary to complete the lessons. In addition, it is assumed that a "Typical" setup was used to install Microsoft Excel 97.

If you are missing a component, such as an accessory, you can easily add it. If the component is necessary to complete an exercise, a note precedes the exercise to help guide you to install or add the component.

Using the Default Windows 95 or Windows NT Settings

In Windows 95 or Windows NT, it is easy to configure your Desktop to suit your working style and preferences. However, the exercises and corresponding illustrations in this book assume that all Windows options are at their default settings. If you change option settings while working through the exercises, you will restore the default settings by the end of a lesson.

You can easily change your Windows 95 or Windows NT options to match the illustrations in the exercises by using the following procedures.

Show or hide the toolbar

You can show or hide the toolbar in most windows, including the My Computer, Windows Explorer, and Windows NT Explorer windows. The toolbar setting can be different for each window that you open. You can show or hide the toolbar on your screen as appropriate to match the illustrations in this book.

1   In the window, click the View menu.

     If there is a check mark next to the Toolbar command, the toolbar is currently showing; if there is no check mark, the toolbar is hidden.

2   On the View menu, click Toolbar to show or hide the toolbar.

Change window sizes

If the size of your window appears to be different from that of the illustrations in the exercises, you can adjust the window.

1   Position your mouse pointer on any edge of the window until the mouse pointer changes to a double-headed arrow.

2   Drag the edge or corner of the window in or out to make the window smaller or larger.

     You can change the window size horizontally by dragging on a side edge or vertically by dragging on the top or bottom; you can change the height and the width of a window simultaneously by dragging on a corner.

Restore window sizes

If a window fills the entire screen and you want to see other parts of the Desktop, you can restore the window to its previous size.

1 On the taskbar, click the window name button to make it the active
   window.

Restore

2 In the upper-right corner of the maximized window, click the Restore
   button.

   The window is restored to its previous, smaller size.

Change views

If the way files appear in a window are different from the illustrations in this
book, you can easily change the view. The views can be different for each window you open.

➤ In the window, click the View menu, and then click the view you want:
  Large Icons, Small Icons, List, or Details.

Arrange icons on the Desktop

If your Desktop icons are jumbled or in a different order than what you want to
see, you can arrange them.

1 Use the right mouse button to click an empty area of the Desktop.

   A shortcut menu appears.

2 Point to Arrange Icons, and then click Auto Arrange.

   The icons are aligned in a horizontal and vertical format on the left side
   of your Desktop.

3 Use the right mouse button to click an empty area of the Desktop again.

4 On the shortcut menu, point to Arrange Icons, and then click By Name.

   After the default Windows icons on your Desktop, the icons are first arranged by file type, and then in alphabetical order.

Arrange icons in a window

If the icons in a window are jumbled or in a different order than what you want
to see, you can arrange them. The icons for each window that you open can
have a different arrangement.

1 In a window, click the View menu, point to Arrange Icons, and then click
   Auto Arrange.

   The icons are arranged by name in your window.

2 On the View menu, point to Arrange Icons again, and then click By
   Name.

Open cascading My Computer windows

You can set up your display so that a new window appears every time you open a new folder, or you can browse through folders using a single window that changes each time you open a new folder.

1   Double-click the My Computer icon.

2   In the My Computer window, on the View menu, click Options.

    The Options dialog box appears.

3   Be sure that the Folder tab is active, and then click the Browse Folders By Using A Single Window That Changes As You Open Each Folder option button.

4   Click OK.

Matching the Screen Display to the Illustrations

Microsoft Excel makes it easy for you to set up the program window to suit your working style and preferences. If you share your computer with others, previous users might have changed the screen setup. You can easily change it back so that your screen matches the illustrations in the lessons. The following methods can help you control the screen display.

If you change the screen display as part of a lesson and leave Microsoft Excel, the next time you open Microsoft Excel, the screen looks the way you left it in the previous session.

Display toolbars

If toolbars are missing at the top of the screen, previous users might have hidden them to make more room for text. You can easily display the toolbars that contain the buttons you need in the lessons.

1   On the View menu, click the Toolbars command.

2   In the Toolbars dialog box, click the check boxes for the toolbars you need.

    Most of the lessons require that the Standard and Formatting toolbars appear.

Hide extra toolbars

To use specific features in some of the lessons, additional toolbars appear in the program window. If, after completing the lesson, you no longer want these toolbars to appear, you can use the Toolbars shortcut menu to hide toolbars you do not want to see. However, most of the lessons require that the Standard and Formatting toolbars appear.

1   Use the right mouse button to click any toolbar.

2   On the shortcut menu, click the name of the toolbar you do not want to see.

If the vertical or horizontal scroll bars do not appear

If you do not see the vertical or horizontal scroll bars, a previous user might have hidden the scroll bars to make more room for data. You can easily display them again.

1   On the Tools menu, click Options.

The Options dialog box appears.

2   Click the View tab to display the view options in the dialog box.

3   In the Window Options area, select the Vertical Scroll Bar and Horizontal Scroll Bar check boxes.

If either or both of these check boxes were previously selected, skip to step 4.

4   Click the OK button.

If the Microsoft Excel program window does not fill the screen

A previous user might have made the Microsoft Excel program window smaller to allow quick access to another program. You can enlarge the document window by doing the following.

Maximize

➤   Click the Maximize button.

If the right edge of the Microsoft Excel window is hidden so that you cannot see the Maximize button, point to "Microsoft Excel" in the title bar at the top of the screen, and then drag the title bar to the left until you see the Maximize button.

If your chart on a chart sheet does not fill the window

A previous user might have displayed charts at a smaller size. To see your chart at full size, use the Sized With Window command on the View menu.

➤   On the View menu, click Sized With Window.

If the document does not fill the space that Microsoft Excel allows

A previous user might have displayed the workbook in a smaller size to get an overview of a worksheet. To see your workbook at the normal size, use the Zoom Control down arrow on the Standard toolbar.

➤   Click the Zoom Control down arrow, and then select 100%.

If the sheet tabs do not appear in your workbook

A previous user might have hidden the sheet tabs to see more of the worksheets. To view the sheet tabs, you use the Options command on the Tools menu.

1   On the Tools menu, click Options.
2   In the Options dialog box, click the View tab.
3   In the Window Options area, select the Sheet Tabs check box, and then click OK.

If you see number signs rather than numbers in your practice files

If you see number signs (#) instead of numbers in your practice files, your column width might not be wide enough. To display the numbers, you resize the columns.

➤   Select the affected columns, and then double-click the column header border between two of the selected columns.

If gridlines do not appear in your workbook

A previous user might have hidden the gridlines to see a cleaner view of the data. To view the gridlines again, you use the Options command on the Tools menu.

1   On the Tools menu, click Options.
2   In the Options dialog box, select the View tab.
3   In the Window Options area, click the Gridlines check box, and then click OK.

If your columns are identified by numbers instead of letters

A previous user might have changed the reference style to R1C1. To change to the A1 reference style, you use the Options command on the Tools menu.

1   On the Tools menu, click Options, and then click the General tab.

2   In the Reference Style area, click the A1 option button, and then click OK.

If the File Properties dialog box does not open when you save a document

A previous user might have turned off the File Properties option. To turn the Prompt For File Properties option on again, use the Options command on the Tools menu.

1   On the Tools menu, click Options, and then click the General tab.

2   Select the Prompt For File Properties check box, and then click OK.

Changing Other Options

If you are not getting the results described in the lessons, you can follow the instructions in this section to verify that the options set in your program are the same as the ones used in this book.

Review each of the following dialog boxes to compare settings for those options that users change most often and that are most likely to account for different results. You can view these dialog boxes by clicking the Options command on the Tools menu. Then click the tab corresponding to the options you want to see. The following illustrations show the option settings used in this book.

View options

Click the View tab to change options that affect the appearance of the document window.

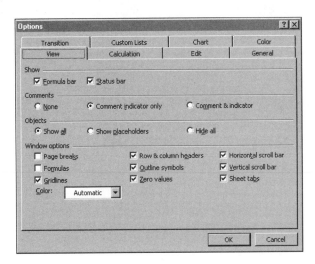

Calculation options

*Click the Calcu-
lations tab to
change options
that affect the
calculations of
your formulas.*

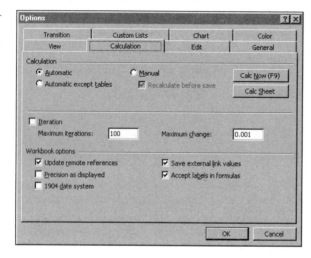

Edit options

*Click the Edit
tab to change
options that af-
fect how editing
operations are
performed.*

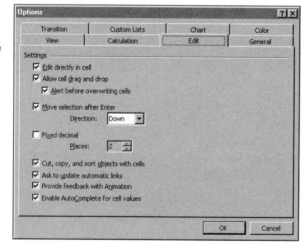

General options

Click the General tab to change options that affect the operation of Microsoft Excel in general.

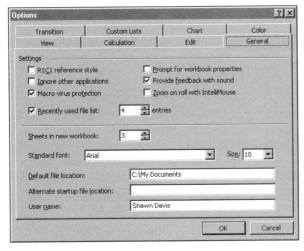

Chart options

Click the Chart tab to change options that affect how charts appear in Microsoft Excel. (Chart tab options are available only when a chart is active.)

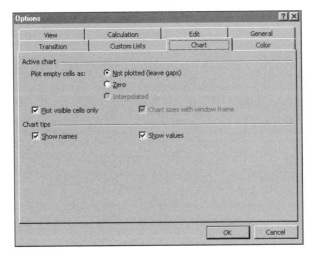

Customizing Your Workspace

When you are working on a big project with several workbooks full of information, you need some way to arrange your workspace so that the information you need is more accessible. You also need quick access to any toolbar buttons you might want to use.

In this appendix, you'll learn how to customize your Microsoft Excel screen to meet your needs, and how to change your toolbars so that the buttons you need most are easy to find. In addition, you'll find out how to view and arrange worksheets so that you can see the information you need on all of your sheets. You'll also view your sheets at different magnifications and split your window into panes to display different parts of your sheet in each pane.

Making Your Toolbars Work for You

Microsoft Excel comes with several built-in toolbars containing buttons that can save you time and effort. When you first start the program, you'll see two toolbars by default, the Standard and Formatting toolbars.

In addition to these toolbars, there are several others that you can use as you work with Microsoft Excel. If you use scenarios often, you'll probably find it convenient to use the Workgroup toolbar. If you work with graphic elements, you'll become familiar with the Drawing toolbar.

You can customize your toolbars to make them work better for you. For example, if you rarely use the sorting buttons on the Standard toolbar or use only the Sort Descending (and not the Sort Ascending) button, you can easily remove the buttons you don't need from the toolbar. Or, if you often need to turn worksheet gridlines on and off, you can add the Gridlines button to the

Some toolbar buttons, such as the Sort buttons, are multifunctional—for example, to perform an ascending sort, hold down SHIFT and click the Sort Descending button.

Standard toolbar so it is within easy reach. You can create your own customized toolbars that contain only the buttons that you need to use. You can also move buttons around on your existing toolbar to make them easier to use or move the entire toolbar to a new location.

In the following exercises, you'll move toolbars around on your screen, hide and then show a toolbar, change the buttons on a built-in toolbar, and create a new toolbar.

Move a toolbar around on your screen

You can move your toolbars to any position on your screen. When you move a toolbar to the top, bottom, or either side of your window, it will *dock* at that location. When your toolbar docks, it changes its shape to a single vertical row of buttons (on either side of your screen) or a single horizontal row of buttons (at the top or bottom of your screen). If you move a toolbar anywhere near the center of your window, it will *float* there.

 NOTE Drop-down lists, such as the Font box or Font Size box on the Formatting toolbar, will not appear on a toolbar if you dock the toolbar on either side of your screen, because the boxes will not fit.

In this exercise, you move your Formatting toolbar around on your screen to see how it docks in some positions and floats in others. Then, you dock it at the top of your screen, in its original position.

1 Click on the raised double bar on the left end of the Formatting toolbar, and then drag to the center of your worksheet.

Drag this bar.→

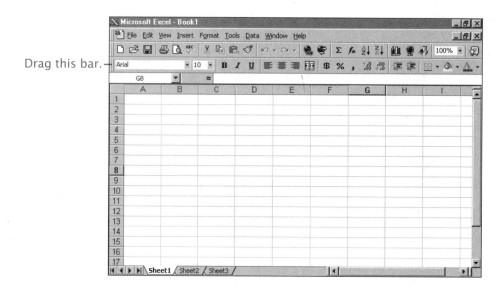

The Formatting toolbar floats in the center of your worksheet, and the toolbar name appears in the toolbar's title bar.

2   Drag the Formatting toolbar by its title bar all the way to the left, until the shape changes from a square to a vertical rectangle, and then drop it.

The toolbar is docked on the left side of your screen.

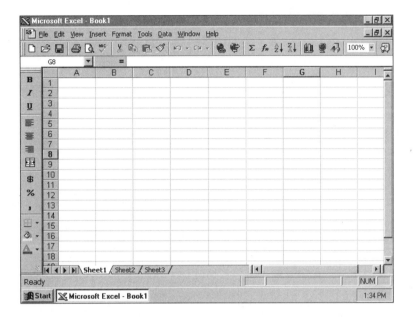

3   Click on the dark horizontal bar at the top of the Formatting toolbar and drag upward until the toolbar shape changes from vertical to horizontal, and then drop it below the Standard toolbar.

The Formatting toolbar is docked below the Standard toolbar.

Hide and show toolbars

You've seen how certain toolbars automatically appear when you perform a certain action or choose a particular command. For example, when you created a chart, and then clicked it to make changes, the Chart toolbar automatically appeared. When you created a PivotTable in Lesson 8, the Query And Pivot toolbar appeared so that you could make changes to the PivotTable easily. But what if you need to use a button located on a toolbar that isn't displayed or if you want to hide a toolbar that is displayed?

In this exercise, you practice hiding and showing different toolbars.

1   Use the right mouse button to click on a toolbar.

A shortcut menu appears with a list of toolbar names. Toolbars that are currently displayed have a check mark next to their names.

237

Toolbars currently displayed

✓	Standard
✓	Formatting
	Chart
	Control Toolbox
	Drawing
	External Data
	Forms
	Picture
	PivotTable
	Reviewing
	Visual Basic
	Web
	WordArt
	Customize...

2   On the shortcut menu, click Formatting.

The Formatting toolbar is hidden.

3   Use the right mouse button to click the Standard toolbar, and then, on the shortcut menu, click Formatting.

The Formatting toolbar appears again.

4   Use the right mouse button to click a toolbar, and then, on the shortcut menu, click Customize.

The Customize dialog box appears. The Toolbars tab contains a list of all the available toolbars.

5   On the Toolbars tab, scroll down, and then click Picture.

The Picture toolbar appears.

6   Click Close.

7   On the Picture toolbar, click the Close button.

Change the buttons displayed on the Formatting toolbar

The default Formatting toolbar contains an assortment of buttons that are useful to most users, but you might have different needs, and therefore, there might be several buttons on the Formatting toolbar that you don't want to show constantly. You can easily remove buttons that you don't use and add buttons that you would like to have available on any toolbars.

In this exercise, you remove the Percent Style and the Currency buttons from the Formatting toolbar and add the Style button.

Percent Style

1   Hold down ALT and drag the Percent Style and Currency buttons away from the Formatting toolbar, and then drop them on the worksheet.

The buttons are removed from the toolbar.

Currency

238

2   Use the right mouse button to click a toolbar, and then, on the shortcut menu, click Customize.

The Customize dialog box appears.

3   Click the Commands tab, and then, in the Categories list, click Format.

4   In the Commands list, select Style.

5   Drag the Style command out of the dialog box, and then drop it on the right end of the Formatting toolbar.

The Style command is added to the Formatting toolbar. Your toolbar should look similar to the following illustration.

6   Click Close.

 TIP   To reset a toolbar to its default configuration, use the right mouse button to click a toolbar, and then click Customize on the shortcut menu. On the Toolbars tab, select the appropriate toolbar, and then click Reset.

Create a new toolbar

As you share your computer with other employees of the Island Tea & Coffee Company, it might be inconvenient to change the configuration of the built-in toolbars to suit your needs. You might also find that there are a few buttons on several toolbars that you use often, but displaying all of these toolbars takes up too much of your screen area. In either case, you can easily resolve these problems by creating a new toolbar that contains only the buttons you want. In this exercise, you create a custom toolbar, and then add some buttons to it.

1   Use the right mouse button to click a toolbar, and then, on the shortcut menu, click Customize.

2   Click the Toolbars tab, and then click New.

The New Toolbar dialog box appears.

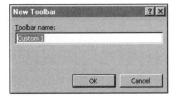

3 Type **My Tools** in the Toolbar Name box, and then click OK or press ENTER.

The name My Tools is added to the list of available toolbars, and a new, empty toolbar appears on top of the Customize dialog box.

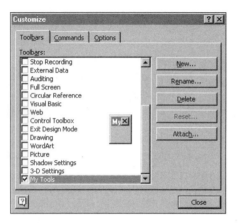

4 Drag the new My Tools toolbar onto the worksheet.

5 In the Customize dialog box, click the Commands tab, and then be sure that Insert is selected in the Categories list.

A list of the buttons contained in the Insert category appears.

6 In the Commands list, select the Worksheet button, and then drag it onto the My Tools toolbar.

The new button appears on the My Tools toolbar. Your toolbar should look similar to the following illustration.

7 Repeat steps 5 and 6 to add the Style button (in the Formatting category) to the My Tools toolbar.

8 Repeat steps 5 and 6 to add the Button and Toggle Grid buttons (in the Forms category) to the My Tools toolbar.

9 Repeat steps 5 and 6 to add the Select Current Region button (in the Edit category) to the My Tools toolbar.

You can rear-range the tools on the toolbar by holding down ALT and drag-ging them to a new location.

10 Close the Customize dialog box.

Your new toolbar should look similar to the following illustration. You can dock it, float it, close it, and open it the same way you would any other toolbar.

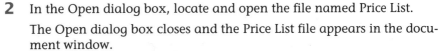

Optimizing Your Screen Display

There might be some screen elements that you don't use frequently. For example, if you find that you don't use the formula bar and status bar often, and you want to see more of your data at one time, you can hide them easily. The Full Screen command on the View menu hides everything except your sheet, sheet tabs, menu bar, and scroll bars.

In order to perform the following exercises, you'll need to open a practice file so that you'll have data with which to practice optimizing your screen display.

Open a file

The practice file you will be using to perform the following exercises is a list of Island Tea & Coffee Company products and price information. You won't make any changes to the practice file, so there is no need to save it with a different name.

Open

1 On the Standard toolbar, click the Open button.

2 In the Open dialog box, locate and open the file named Price List.

The Open dialog box closes and the Price List file appears in the document window.

Hide and display on-screen elements

In this exercise, you practice hiding and showing different elements of your worksheet.

1 On the View menu, click Formula Bar.

The Formula bar is hidden, and a bigger portion of your worksheet is visible.

2 On the View menu, click Status Bar.

The Status bar is hidden, and a bigger portion of your worksheet is visible.

3 On the View menu, click Formula Bar.

The Formula bar appears again.

4 On the View menu, click Status Bar.

The Status bar appears again.

Show a full-screen view for maximum worksheet display

In this exercise, you invoke a full screen view of your worksheet, and then you restore the hidden screen elements to view.

1 On the View menu, click Full Screen.

Everything except the menu bar, row and column headers, scroll bars, and sheet tabs is hidden, and the Full Screen toolbar appears.

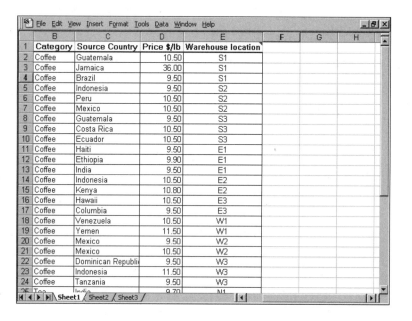

2 Click the Close Full Screen button on the Full Screen toolbar.

The previously hidden screen elements appear again.

Zooming In or Out to View a Worksheet

You've seen how to make more space to display your worksheet by hiding the screen elements, but what if you need to see even more data? For example, the Island Tea & Coffee Company price list is a long worksheet that contains more than one screenful of information. If you want to see the worksheet in its entirety on one screen, you can zoom out to display more cells in the window; if you want to take a closer look at a specific group of cells, you can zoom in.

Zoom in or out on your worksheet

In this exercise, you zoom out to see the entire price list in the window, and then zoom in and out at different magnifications to see the price list from different perspectives.

Select Current Region

1 Click cell A1, and then, on the My Tools toolbar, click the Select Current Region button.

The entire price list table is selected.

2 On the Standard toolbar, click the Zoom down arrow, and then click Selection.

Your view is zoomed out enough to display the entire selection in the available window area.

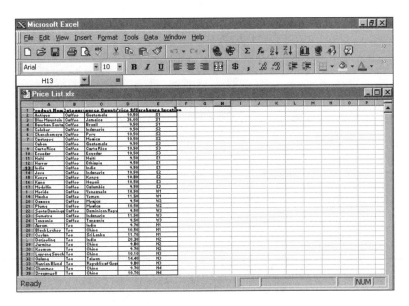

3 Click the Zoom down arrow, and then click 75%.

The view is zoomed to a magnification of 75% of the normal size.

4 Click the Zoom down arrow, and then click 100%.

The view is returned to normal magnification.

Splitting Your Worksheet into Panes

When you work in a large worksheet, you usually have headings at the top and/or the left of your worksheet, with data extending to the right and downward. When you have scrolled past the point where the headings are visible, it can be difficult to remember what they were. One way to keep the headings in view while you work is to freeze panes, as you did in Lesson 1. Another way is to simply split the worksheet into panes without freezing them—this way, you can scroll around in each pane independently.

Split your worksheet into panes

In this exercise, you split the Price List worksheet into two panes, and then remove the split.

1 Point to the small bar at the top of the vertical scroll bar, and when your pointer becomes a two-headed arrow, drag downward, and then drop the split in the middle of the screen.

The worksheet is split horizontally by a *split bar.* You can scroll the entire length of the worksheet in either pane.

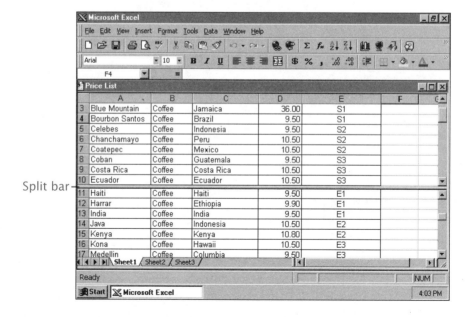

Split bar

2 Double-click the split bar.

The split is removed.

Customizing Your Workbooks

If you find that there are changes you consistently make to your new workbooks, such as changing the font for the entire workbook or inserting five new worksheets, you can change the Microsoft Excel default settings so that your new workbooks always open looking just the way you want.

Change the default font and number of worksheets in all new workbooks

One of your co-workers in the Island Tea & Coffee Company Accounting department has asked you to use a specific font for all of your worksheets, because he finds it easier to read. In the following exercise, you change the default font that will be used with all your new worksheets; this change won't affect existing workbooks.

1 On the Tools menu, click Options.

The Options dialog box appears.

2 In the Options dialog box, click the General tab.

3 Click the Standard Font down arrow, and then select Times New Roman.

4 Change the Sheets In New Workbook number to 8.

5 Click OK.

All new workbooks you open from now on will have eight worksheets and Times New Roman font.

Changing gridline color

If you would prefer another gridline color in your worksheets, such as a pale blue instead of gray, you can change the gridline color for the active worksheet.

1 On the Tools menu, click Options, and then click the View tab.

2 Click the Color down arrow, select a new gridline color, and then click OK.

The gridlines in the active worksheet are the color that you selected.

absolute cell reference   A cell address in a formula that does not change when copied to another cell. An absolute reference has the form A1.

active cell   The selected cell in a worksheet. The active cell is surrounded by a heavy border and is identified by the cell address.

active window   In a multiple-window environment, the window that is currently selected and whose contents will be affected by all mouse actions, commands, and text entry.

alias   A name or label that is used as an alternative means of referring to a file or person. For example, the group alias "Marketing" could be used to send an e-mail message to all the employees in the Marketing department.

alignment   The horizontal position of text within the width of a column or between tab stops.

AND function   A function used to perform multiple tests on the content of cells in a spreadsheet and display a value or text based on whether the overall test is true or false.

application   *See* program.

argument   The information that a function uses to produce a new value or perform an action. For example, a new value is displayed when the SUM function adds the argument (A6:A12). An argument consists of numbers, references, text, operators, arrays, or error values.

arithmetic operator   A symbol used for simple math calculations. For example, the operators for addition and subtraction are the plus sign (+) and the minus sign (–).

arrow keys   The UP ARROW, DOWN ARROW, LEFT ARROW, and RIGHT ARROW keys that are used to move the insertion point or to select from a menu or a list of options.

ascending   A method of ordering a group of items from lowest to highest, such as from A to Z. *See also* sort.

AutoFormat   A feature used to format a range of cells with a predefined set of attributes.

axis title   Text that identifies the horizontal plot line.

binary file   A file type that is encoded using only the binary digits 0 and 1. Binary files are usually programs, graphics, or complex documents, and are readable only by a computer.

bit   A binary digit. The smallest unit of information a computer can handle. A bit can have the value 0 or 1, and is represented physically as a single pulse sent through a circuit, or a single spot on a disk. A group of 8 bits is called a byte.

bitmap A collection of bits that make up a dot pattern or graphic image. Bitmaps with a BMP extension are the default file type for the Paint accessory.

border A line that goes around text or tables. You can assign a variety of widths to a border.

browser Software that can display information found in files posted on the World Wide Web. A browser can also play sound or video files if you have the necessary hardware.

bullet A mark, usually a round or square dot, often used to add emphasis or to distinguish between items in a list.

byte A unit of information consisting of 8 bits. The equivalent of a single character, number, or punctuation mark.

cascading menu A submenu that branches off or cascades from another menu. A command name followed by an arrow indicates that a submenu appears when the command is pointed to.

cell The basic unit of a table or worksheet. The intersection of a row and a column forms one cell. You type text, numbers, or formulas into cells. Each cell is named by its position in the row (1, 2, 3) and column (A, B, C). For example, cell A1 is the first cell in column A, row 1.

cell note A note that explains, identifies, or comments on the information in a specific cell or range of cells.

central processing unit (CPU) The microprocessor chip that interprets and carries out instructions.

character An individual letter, number, or symbol corresponding to a key or key combination. Each character can be formatted individually.

chart A graphic representation of worksheet data. Values from worksheet cells are displayed as bars, lines, or other shapes. Common chart types are pie, bar, line, and area.

chart sheet A chart placed on a separate worksheet instead of on the worksheet where the chart data is stored.

check box A dialog box option that is not mutually exclusive. Clicking a check box inserts or removes an "X."

click To press the primary mouse button once.

Clipboard A temporary holding area in computer memory that stores the last set of information that was cut or copied (such as text or graphics). You transfer data from the Clipboard by using the Paste command. The information remains on the Clipboard until you cut or copy another piece of information, which then replaces the current contents of the Clipboard.

collapse   To reduce the number of rows displayed in a view by showing only categories or by eliminating responses.

column   A vertical section of a worksheet. In Microsoft Excel, there are 256 columns in a worksheet. Columns are usually identified by letters (A–Z, AA–AZ, BA–BZ, IA–IV).

column heading   The lettered gray area at the top of each column that identifies the letter of the column, such as column B.

command   An instruction issued by a user that causes an action to be carried out by the computer program.

comment   A note that explains, identifies, or comments on the information in a specific cell or range of cells.

comparison operators   The flexible criteria used to search for records that are equal to, less than, or greater than a specific value, or for records that are between two values.

context-sensitive help   A type of online help used to identify any screen element in a window or to provide relevant information about the current operation.

Control menu   A menu that appears in each window when you click the Control-menu icon in the upper-left corner of the window.

Control Panel   The set of Windows 95 programs that you can use to change system, hardware, software, and Windows 95 settings.

conventional memory   The memory used to run software under MS-DOS. It is the lowest 640K of the memory.

coprocessor   A separate processor designed to assist in specific functions, such as handling complex mathematics or graphics, and to temporarily reduce the workload of the microprocessor.

copy   To duplicate information from one location to another, either within a file, to another file, or to a file in another program. The copied information is stored on the Clipboard until you cut or copy another piece of information.

criteria   The conditions that control which records to display in a query; the words or values used to determine the data that appears in a data list.

cursor   The pointer on the screen that indicates where characters appear in response to keyboard or mouse input.

cut   To remove selected information from a document so you can paste it to another location within the file, to another file, or to a file in another program. The cut information is stored on the Clipboard until you cut or copy another piece of information.

data points The individual values plotted in a chart and represented by bars, lines, pie slices, dots, and other shapes.

data series One row or column of values (data points) that appears on a chart, such as bars, lines, or pie slices. The orientation of the data series, either in rows or in columns, determines how the data is plotted on the chart.

data type The attribute of a field that determines the kind of data the field can contain.

database A collection of data related to a particular topic or purpose, such as a database of customer information. Can also refer to a type of program, such as Microsoft Access, that you can use to organize and manipulate detailed lists of information.

datasheet A spreadsheet view of rows and columns. A chart is created from the values in a datasheet. Each new datasheet contains a set of default data that you modify to create the chart.

default A predefined setting that is built into a program and is used when you do not specify an alternative setting. For example, a document might have a default setting of one-inch page margins unless you specify another value for the margin settings.

delete To remove information such as a file or text. The user can choose the Delete command, press the DELETE key, or press the BACKSPACE key.

demote In Outline view, an action that changes a heading to body text or a higher heading level to a lower heading level.

descending A method of ordering a group of items from highest to lowest, such as from Z to A. *See also* sort.

Desktop The entire Windows 95 screen that represents your work area. Icons, windows, and the taskbar appear on the Desktop. You can customize the Desktop to suit your preferences and working requirements.

destination A document or program receiving information that was originally generated in another program. *See also* source.

dialog box A window that displays additional options when a command is chosen from a menu.

disk A round, flat piece of flexible plastic (floppy disk) or inflexible metal (hard disk) that stores data. The disk is coated with a magnetic material on which digital information can be recorded. To protect this material, disks are enclosed in plastic or metal casings.

disk drive A hardware mechanism that reads information from a disk and writes information to a disk.

document Any independent unit of information, such as a text file, worksheet, or graphic object, that is created with a program. A document can be saved with a unique filename by which it can be retrieved.

document window A rectangular portion of the screen in which you view and edit a document. A document window is typically a window inside another window. For example, documents in Microsoft Word or Microsoft Excel are displayed in their own window, inside the program window.

double-click To press the primary mouse button twice rapidly. Double-clicking an object performs the default action.

double-density disk Common type of floppy disk for IBM-compatible computers. Capacity is 360K for 5.25-inch disks and 720K for 3.5-inch disks.

download To transfer a file from a remote computer to your local computer. This type of transfer can be performed by using computers on a network or through telecommunication.

drag-and-drop A mouse technique for directly moving or copying a set of information from one location to another. To drag an object, position the pointer over the object, hold down the mouse button while you move the mouse, and then release the mouse button when the object is positioned where you want it.

drive *See* disk drive.

edit To add, delete, or change information, such as text or graphics.

electronic mail Notes, messages, or files sent between different computers using telecommunication or network services. Also referred to as e-mail.

embed To insert an object from a source program into a destination document. When you double-click the object in the destination document, the source program opens and you can edit the object. *See also* link.

embedded chart A chart that exists on a worksheet instead of on a separate chart sheet.

embedded object Data (such as text or graphics) that you can edit using the full resources of its source program while it is in a destination document. *See also* embed.

expand To display all subordinate entries in an outline or in a folder.

expanded memory The additional memory above 640K. Expanded memory exists separately from conventional memory and extended memory. Most personal computers can accommodate expanded memory.

export The process of converting and saving a file to be used in a another program. *See also* import.

field   In a list or database, a column of data that contains a particular type of information, such as Last Name or Phone Number or Quantity.

file   A document that you create or save with a unique filename.

file format   The format in which data is stored in a file. Usually, different programs, such as Microsoft Word or Microsoft Excel, have different file formats.

filter   A set of criteria you can apply to records to show specific tasks, records, or resources. The tasks, records, or resources that match your criteria are listed or highlighted so that you can focus on just the information you want.

floating palette   A palette that can be dragged away from its toolbar. *See also* palette.

floating toolbar   A toolbar that appears in a window with a title bar, stays on top of the other windows, and is not fixed in position.

floppy disk   *See* disk.

folder   A container in which documents, program files, and other folders are stored on your computer disks. Folders can help you organize your documents by grouping them into categories, as you would organize paper documents into file folders. Formerly referred to as a *directory*.

font   A family of type styles, such as Times or Arial. Effects, such as bold or italic, are possible within one font, and various point sizes can be applied to a font.

footer   The text or graphics printed at the bottom of every page in a document.

footnote   An explanation or comment reference inserted at the bottom of the page on which the reference mark is located or at the end of the document.

format   The way text and cells appear on a page. Types of formats include character, number, cell border, color, and more. Styles can contain any of these formats. Format can also refer to preparing a disk to record or retrieve data. Formatting usually erases any information previously stored on the disk.

formula   A sequence of values, cell references, names, functions, or operators that produces a new value from existing values. A formula always begins with an equal sign (=).

function   A built-in formula; a named and stored procedure that performs a specific operation and returns a value. Functions begin with a function command and are followed by a set of parentheses. Inside the parentheses is the argument, which can be a set of cell references, a range, numbers, text, or other functions. Some functions do not use an argument.

gridlines   The horizontal and vertical lines on a chart that help relate a plotted point to a value.

handles   Small black squares located in the lower-right corner of selected cells or around selected graphic objects, chart items, or text. By dragging the handles, you can perform actions such as moving, copying, filling, sizing, or formatting on the selected cells, objects, chart items, or text.

hard disk   *See* disk.

hardware   The physical parts of a computer system, such as the monitor, keyboard, and printer.

header   The text or graphics printed at the top of every page in a document.

high-density disk   A type of floppy disk. A high-density 3.5-inch disk has a capacity of 1.44 MB, and a high-density 5.25-inch disk has a capacity of 1.2 MB.

hyperlink   An object, such as a graphic or colored or underlined text, that represents a link to another location in the same file or in a different file, and that, when clicked, brings up a different Web page. Hyperlinks are one of the key elements of HTML documents.

icon   A small graphic that represents an object, such as a program, a disk drive, or a document. When you double-click an icon, the item the icon represents opens.

IF function   A function that tests the content of the cell, performs a calculation, and displays a value or text based on whether the test is true or false.

import   The process of converting and opening a file that was created in a another program. *See also* export.

indent   The distance between the left or right edge of a block of text and the page margin. A paragraph can have a left, right, and first-line indent. Indents can also be measured relative to columns in a section, table cells, and the boundaries of positioned objects.

index   A table that lists page numbers for topics in a document. The topics are usually listed alphabetically and the index is placed near the end of the document.

input   The information conveyed to a computer using a keyboard or a mouse.

insert   To enter text, data, or a graphic into a document, cell, or dialog box. You can also insert cells, rows, and columns into a worksheet. You insert information at the insertion point. *See also* insertion point.

insertion point   The blinking vertical bar that marks the location where text is entered in a document or a dialog box. You can move the insertion point by clicking the mouse in another location or by using the keyboard arrow keys.

install   To prepare equipment or software for use for the first time.

interface   A point of connection between two elements so that they can work with one another. The connection can be at many levels, including between two types of hardware, between hardware and software, or between software and user.

Internet   A worldwide "network of networks," made up of thousands of computer networks and millions of commercial, education, government, and personal computers, all connected to each other. You connect to the Internet using an Internet service provider, an online service such as CompuServe, or through a corporate network. Also known as the Net.

intranet   A self-contained network that uses the same communications protocols and file formats as the Internet. An intranet can, but doesn't have to, be connected to the Internet. Many businesses use intranets for their internal communications. *See also* Internet.

kilobyte (K)   A unit of measure for computer memory or storage capacity. One kilobyte equals 1024 bytes.

label   A descriptive name that identifies a group of cells, a named value, or a formula.

landscape   The horizontal orientation of a page; opposite of *portrait*, or vertical, orientation.

laser printer   A high-quality printer that uses a laser beam to generate an image and has a resolution of 300 dots per inch (dpi) or higher.

legend   A box containing the name of each data series in a chart.

link   To copy an object, such as a graphic or text, from one file or program to another so that there is a dependent relationship between the object and its source file. *Link* also refers to the connection between a source file and a destination file. Whenever the original information in the source file changes, the information in the linked object is automatically updated. *See also* embed.

margin   The absolute boundary of text and graphics on a page.

marquee   *See* moving border.

megabyte (MB)   A unit of measure for memory or storage. One megabyte equals 1024 kilobytes, or 1,048,576 bytes.

megahertz (MHz)   A measurement of frequency equivalent to 1 million cycles per second; commonly used to measure the clock speed of a computer.

memory   The primary storage in a computer, which is measured in bytes, kilobytes (K), and megabytes (MB).

menu   A list of commands or options available in a program.

merge   To combine items, such as lists, without changing the basic structure of any item.

microprocessor   The central processing chip in a personal computer. Common microprocessors for IBM and IBM-compatible computers include the Intel 386, 486, and Pentium processors.

Microsoft Office 97   An integrated family of business programs. Microsoft Office 97 Standard includes Word, Excel, PowerPoint, and Outlook. Microsoft Office 97 Professional adds Access to the package.

minimize   To contract a window to an icon. This can be reversed by double-clicking the icon, or by using the Restore command or the Maximize command on the Control menu.

move   To transfer information from one location to another, either within a file, to another file, or to a file in another program.

moving border   A moving dotted line that surrounds a cell or range of cells. A moving border appears around a cell or range that has been cut or copied, or around a cell or range you are inserting into a formula.

network   A group of computers and associated devices that are connected with communication links.

object   A table, chart, graphic, equation, or other form of information you create and edit. An object can be inserted, pasted, or copied into any file.

OLE   A Microsoft programming standard that allows a user or a program to communicate with other programs, usually for the purpose of exchanging information. Drag-and-drop and linking and embedding are examples of OLE features. *See also* link *and* embed.

operating system   The software used to control application processing and hardware resources, such as memory, disk space, and peripheral devices.

options   The choices you have in a dialog box.

output   The results of processing that can be sent to a screen or printer, stored on disk as a file, or sent to another computer over a network.

Page Break Preview   A view that displays your document with preset page breaks or allows you to change page breaks by dragging page boundaries.

palette   A dialog box containing choices for color and other special effects that you use when designing a form, report, or other object. A palette appears when you click a toolbar button, such as Border or Fill Color. *See also* floating palette.

paragraph   Any text, graphics, tables, frames, or black lines followed by a paragraph mark. The paragraph mark is treated as part of a paragraph.

password A unique series of characters that you type to gain entry into a restricted network system, messaging system, or protected file or folder.

paste To insert cut or copied text into a document from the temporary storage area called the Clipboard.

path The location of a file within a computer file system. The path indicates the filename preceded by the disk drive, folder, and subfolders in which the file is stored. If the file is on another computer on a network, the path also includes the computer name.

pattern A graphic style that can be used to fill an object.

PivotTable An interactive worksheet table that summarizes data using a selected format and calculations. It is called a pivot table because you can rearrange the table structure around the data.

pointer The representation of the mouse position on the Desktop. You move the pointer on the Desktop by moving the mouse on a smooth, horizontal surface. The pointer changes shape depending on the action.

port A channel for transferring electronic information between the CPU and peripheral devices. The system unit can have several physical ports.

portrait A term used to refer to vertical page orientation; opposite of *landscape*, or horizontal orientation.

Print Preview A view that displays your document as it will appear when you print it. Items, such as text and graphics, appear in their actual positions.

print range A set area of the worksheet to be printed.

printer A peripheral device that produces a paper copy of output. Different types of printers include dot matrix, ink jet, and laser printers.

program A computer software program, such as a word processor, spreadsheet, presentation designer, or relational database, that is designed to do a specific type of work.

promote In Outline view, an action that changes body text to a heading or a lower heading level to a higher heading level.

properties The information about an object, including settings or options for that object. For example, you can look at the properties of a file for information such as the file size, file type, and file attributes.

protocol A communications standard—such as TCP/IP, used on the Internet and intranets, or NETBEUI, used in Microsoft networks—that ensures reliable transmission among the computers and other components on a network.

random access memory (RAM)   The computer's memory, which can be accessed randomly rather than sequentially. RAM allows the computer to store and retrieve information without searching sequentially from the beginning of a location.

range   Two or more adjacent cells on a sheet. You identify a range by the upper-left corner and lower-right corner cell addresses, separated by a colon or by two dots, for example, A1:B10 or A1..C5.

read-only memory (ROM)   Memory containing instructions or data that can be read but not modified. Permanent startup programs and other essential information are stored in ROM.

record   A set of information that belongs together, such as all the information on one job program or one magazine subscription card. A record can also refer to one row in a database. The first row of the database contains the field names. Each additional row of the database is one record. Each record contains the same categories of data, or fields, as every other record in the database.

reference   A cell address used in a formula.

relative cell reference   In formulas, a reference to the address of another cell in relation to a cell that contains a formula.

report   A formatted collection of information that is organized to provide project data related to a specific area of concern.

restore   To expand a minimized application by double-clicking it or to return a window to its previous size.

row   A horizontal section of a worksheet. There are 65,576 rows in a worksheet.

save   To transfer data from temporary memory to a floppy disk or a hard disk.

scroll   To move vertically or horizontally in a window so you can view objects that are not currently visible. You can scroll through a window by clicking the scroll arrows, by dragging the scroll box, or by clicking the scroll bar.

scroll arrow   A button or box with an arrow that appears at each end of a scroll bar. You can scroll through a window in small increments by clicking the scroll arrows. The arrow indicates the direction the document moves when scrolled.

scroll bar   The bar that appears at the right side or the bottom of a window that contains more information than can be displayed. The scroll bar is used to scroll an object or parts of a document into view when the entire object or document does not fit in the window.

scroll box   The rectangle in a scroll bar that indicates the relative position of the current screen to the beginning or end of the file.

select To point to a button, phrase, icon, menu choice, or other object on the screen with the pointer, and then click the primary mouse button once.

shortcut An object that acts as a pointer to a document, folder, Internet address, or program. If you double-click the shortcut, the object opens.

shortcut menu A menu of commands that appears when you click the right mouse button while your mouse pointer is on a toolbar, property sheet, control, or other screen element. The menu of commands depends on the element you click.

software Internal computer programs that instruct the computer to do work. There are two basic categories of software: operating systems and programs.

sort To automatically reorder text or numbers in ascending or descending order, alphabetically, numerically, or by date.

source The document or program in which the data was originally created. *See also* destination.

split bar The double line that indicates where a window is split.

split box The solid box at the end or top of a scroll bar that users drag to split a document window in two, so that each half can be scrolled independently. Users can split a window vertically, horizontally, or both.

spreadsheet A collection of data organized into rows and columns.

status bar A bar at the bottom of the screen that displays information about the currently selected command, the active dialog box, the standard keys on the keyboard, or the current state of the program and the keyboard. You can turn the display of the status bar off and on.

style A named collection of text formatting choices, such as font, size, leading, spacing, and alignment, that can be applied to change the appearance of text. Body Text, Headline, and Subhead are examples of styles that are often used. Styles are also common to word-processing programs. Styles are stored in a document or template.

tab A horizontal setting used to determine the position of text on a line.

table One or more rows of cells commonly used to display numbers and other items for quick reference and analysis. Items in a table are organized into rows (records) and columns (fields).

taskbar The rectangular bar usually located across the bottom of the Windows 95 Desktop. The taskbar includes the Start button as well as buttons for any programs and documents that are open. Its location, size, and visibility can be modified to fit your preferences.

template   A special kind of document that provides basic tools and text for shaping a final document. Templates can contain the following elements: text, styles, glossary items, macros, and menu and key assignments.

text attributes   The characteristics of text, including the font, font style, font size, and color of text.

text box   A box within a dialog box where you type information needed to carry out a command. A text box can also refer to a graphic element that you can use to label parts of a worksheet or chart.

title bar   The horizontal bar at the top of a window that displays the name of the document or program that appears in that window.

toolbar   A bar at the top of Windows-based programs that displays a set of buttons used to carry out common menu commands. The buttons displayed on a toolbar change depending on which window or view is currently selected. Toolbars can be moved, or docked, at any edge of a program window. *See also* floating toolbar.

trendline   A graphic used to study problems of predictions such as future sales. Also called a regression analysis.

view   A set of criteria used to display items in a folder. By applying a different view to a folder, you can change the way the folder contents appear. Views can include specific groups, filters, and sort orders.

Web page   A document, formatted in HTML, that usually contains links that you can use to jump from one page to another or from one location to another. *See also* hyperlink.

widow   The last line of a paragraph forced to the top of the next page of text.

wildcard   Special character used in place of any other characters. An asterisk (*) takes the place of one or more characters; a question mark (?) takes the place of one character.

window   A separate rectangular part of the screen identified by a border. A window represents an open object and displays information. Multiple windows can be open at the same time.

wizard   A tool that guides you through a complex task by asking you questions, and then performing the task based on your responses.

workbook   A Microsoft Excel document in which you can store other documents. A workbook can include multiple worksheets and chart sheets.

worksheet   A set of rows, columns, and cells in which you store and manipulate data. Several worksheets can appear in one workbook, and you can switch among them easily by clicking their tabs with the mouse.

x-axis A line, usually horizontal, along the bottom of a chart. The x-axis shows the labels for the data series. Also called the horizontal axis.

xy chart A chart type that represents one data series. Xy charts include vertical bar, horizontal bar, line, area, high/low/close, and scatter charts.

y-axis A line, usually vertical, along the left side of a chart. The y-axis shows the values for the data series.

Index

Index

Index

Index

Index

status bar, 215
STDEV function, 22
styles
    applying, 60
    creating by example, 59–60
    defined, 59
    modifying, 60–61
    vs. custom number formats, 67
SUBTOTAL function, 104–5
subtotals
    creating, 112–14
    sort using, 110
    nesting, 113–14
    pasting into Word documents, 117
    removing, 113
SUM function, 48, 52, 53
SUMIF function, 105–6
summary information. *See* file properties; reports

T

TAB key, 10, 11, 218
tabs
    in dialog boxes, 218
    worksheet, 6, 230
taskbar, 214
templates
    adding formulas, 46–54
    adding graphics, 39–40
    arranging labels, 34–36
    built-in, 91–97
    controlling data entry in, 37–38
    creating, 32–36
    customizing, 91–97
    editing, 72–73
    entering labels, 32–33
    linking to intranet, 72
    opening copy of, 71–72
    overview, 31–32, 43
    printing, 38–39, 73
    saving, 70–71, 94
    writing instructions for, 36–37
text. *See also* fonts; labels
    aligning in cells, 34–35
    entering in cells, 13–14
text boxes, in dialog boxes, 218
text files, importing, 126–28

tiling windows, 86
title bar, 215, 216
titles. *See* headers and footers, row/column; labels
toolbars
    adding buttons to, 238–39
    closing, 238
    creating, 239–41
    customizing, 238–39
    displaying/hiding, 217–18, 226, 238–39, 242
    docking, 236–37
    in Excel, 235–41
    floating, 236–37
    moving, 236–37
    opening, 238
    overview, 235–36
    rearranging buttons, 241
    removing buttons, 238–39
    resetting to default configuration, 238
    shortcut menu, 237–38
    in Windows 95, 217–18
training. *See* Certified Microsoft Office User
    (CMOU) program; practice files
trendlines, adding to charts, 152
typing, correcting, 17

U

undoing actions, 16, 149
updating linked data, 193, 195
user names, 214

V

values. *See* numbers

W

Web. *See* intranet
"what if" analysis. *See* scenarios
windows. *See also* screen display
    arranging, 85–86
    changing size, 226
    closing, 216
    enlarging, 226
    maximizing, 216
    minimizing, 216
    moving, 216
    multiple, arranging, 85–86

Get
quick, easy
answers—
anywhere!

Microsoft® Excel 97 Field Guide
Stephen L. Nelson
U.S.A. $9.95 ($12.95 Canada)
ISBN: 1-57231-326-9

Microsoft® Word 97 Field Guide
Stephen L. Nelson
U.S.A. $9.95 ($12.95 Canada)
ISBN: 1-57231-325-0

Microsoft® PowerPoint® 97 Field Guide
Stephen L. Nelson
U.S.A. $9.95 ($12.95 Canada)
ISBN: 1-57231-327-7

Microsoft® Outlook™ 97 Field Guide
Stephen L. Nelson
U.S.A. $9.99 ($12.99 Canada)
ISBN: 1-57231-383-8

Microsoft® Access 97 Field Guide
Stephen L. Nelson
U.S.A. $9.95 ($12.95 Canada)
ISBN: 1-57231-328-5

Microsoft Press® Field Guides are a quick, accurate source of information about Microsoft® Office 97 applications. In no time, you'll have the lay of the land, identify toolbar buttons and commands, stay safely out of danger, and have all the tools you need for survival!

Microsoft Press® products are available worldwide wherever quality computer books are sold. For more information, contact your book retailer, computer reseller, or local Microsoft Sales Office.

To locate your nearest source for Microsoft Press products, reach us at www.microsoft.com/mspress/, or call 1-800-MSPRESS in the U.S. (in Canada: 1-800-667-1115 or 416-293-8464).

To order Microsoft Press products, call 1-800-MSPRESS in the U.S. (in Canada: 1-800-667-1115 or 416-293-8464).

Prices and availability dates are subject to change.

Microsoft Press

Keep things **running** smoothly around the **Office.**

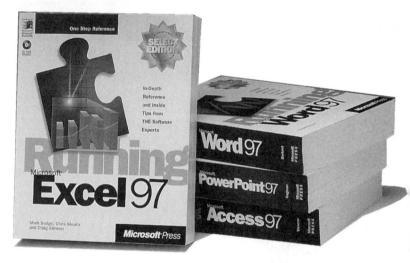

These are *the* answer books for business users of Microsoft® Office 97 applications. They are packed with everything from quick, clear instructions for new users to comprehensive answers for power users. The Microsoft Press® *Running* series features authoritative handbooks you'll keep by your computer and use every day.

Running Microsoft® Excel 97
Mark Dodge, Chris Kinata, and Craig Stinson
U.S.A.   **$39.95**   ($54.95 Canada)
ISBN: 1-57231-321-8

Running Microsoft® Office 97
Michael Halvorson and Michael Young
U.S.A.   **$39.95**   ($54.95 Canada)
ISBN: 1-57231-322-6

Running Microsoft® Word 97
Russell Borland
U.S.A.   **$39.95**   ($54.95 Canada)
ISBN: 1-57231-320-X

Running Microsoft® PowerPoint® 97
Stephen W. Sagman
U.S.A.   **$29.95**   ($39.95 Canada)
ISBN: 1-57231-324-2

Running Microsoft® Access 97
John L. Viescas
U.S.A.   **$39.95**   ($54.95 Canada)
ISBN: 1-57231-323-4

Microsoft® Press

Take
productivity
in stride.

Microsoft Press® *Step by Step* books provide quick and easy self-paced training that will help you learn to use the powerful word processor, spreadsheet, database, desktop information manager and presentation applications of Microsoft® Office 97, both individually and together. In approximately eight hours of instruction prepared by the professional trainers at Catapult, Inc. and Perspection, Inc., the easy-to-follow lessons in each book present clear objectives and real-world business examples, with numerous screen shots and illustrations. Put Microsoft's Office 97 applications to work today, *Step by Step*.

Microsoft Press® products are available worldwide wherever quality computer books are sold. For more information, contact your book retailer, computer reseller, or local Microsoft Sales Office.

To locate your nearest source for Microsoft Press products, reach us at www.microsoft.com/mspress/, or call 1-800-MSPRESS in the U.S. In Canada: 1-800-667-1115 or 416-293-8464).

To order Microsoft Press products, call 1-800-MSPRESS in the U.S. In Canada: 1-800-667-1115 or 416-293-8464).

Prices and availability dates are subject to change.

Microsoft® Excel 97 Step by Step
U.S.A. $29.99   ($39.99 Canada)
ISBN: 1-57231-314-5

Microsoft® Word 97 Step by Step
U.S.A. $29.99   ($39.99 Canada)
ISBN: 1-57231-313-7

Microsoft® PowerPoint® 97
 Step by Step
U.S.A. $29.95   ($39.95 Canada)
ISBN: 1-57231-315-3

Microsoft® Outlook™ 97 Step by Step
U.S.A. $29.99   ($39.99 Canada)
ISBN: 1-57231-382-X

Microsoft® Access 97 Step by Step
U.S.A. $29.95   ($39.95 Canada)
ISBN: 1-57231-316-1

Microsoft® Office 97 Integration
 Step by Step
U.S.A. $29.95   ($39.95 Canada)
ISBN: 1-57231-317-X

***Microsoft*® Press**

IMPORTANT—READ CAREFULLY BEFORE OPENING SOFTWARE PACKET(S). By opening the sealed packet(s) containing the software, you indicate your acceptance of the following Microsoft License Agreement.

MICROSOFT LICENSE AGREEMENT

(Book Companion Disks)

This is a legal agreement between you (either an individual or an entity) and Microsoft Corporation. By opening the sealed software packet(s) you are agreeing to be bound by the terms of this agreement. If you do not agree to the terms of this agreement, promptly return the unopened software packet(s) and any accompanying written materials to the place you obtained them for a full refund.

MICROSOFT SOFTWARE LICENSE

1. GRANT OF LICENSE. Microsoft grants to you the right to use one copy of the Microsoft software program included with this book (the "SOFTWARE") on a single terminal connected to a single computer. The SOFTWARE is in "use" on a computer when it is loaded into the temporary memory (i.e., RAM) or installed into the permanent memory (e.g., hard disk, CD-ROM, or other storage device) of that computer. You may not network the SOFTWARE or otherwise use it on more than one computer or computer terminal at the same time.

For the files and materials referenced in this book which may be obtained from the Internet, Microsoft grants to you the right to use the materials in connection with the book. If you are a member of a corporation or business, you may reproduce the materials and distribute them within your business for internal business purposes in connection with the book. You may not reproduce the materials for further distribution.

2. COPYRIGHT. The SOFTWARE is owned by Microsoft or its suppliers and is protected by United States copyright laws and international treaty provisions. Therefore, you must treat the SOFTWARE like any other copyrighted material (e.g., a book or musical recording) except that you may either (a) make one copy of the SOFTWARE solely for backup or archival purposes, or (b) transfer the SOFTWARE to a single hard disk provided you keep the original solely for backup or archival purposes. You may not copy the written materials accompanying the SOFTWARE.

3. OTHER RESTRICTIONS. You may not rent or lease the SOFTWARE, but you may transfer the SOFTWARE and accompanying written materials on a permanent basis provided you retain no copies and the recipient agrees to the terms of this Agreement. You may not reverse engineer, decompile, or disassemble the SOFTWARE. If the SOFTWARE is an update or has been updated, any transfer must include the most recent update and all prior versions.

4. DUAL MEDIA SOFTWARE. If the SOFTWARE package contains both 3.5" and 5.25" disks, then you may use only the disks appropriate for your single-user computer. You may not use the other disks on another computer or loan, rent, lease, or transfer them to another user except as part of the permanent transfer (as provided above) of all SOFTWARE and written materials.

5. SAMPLE CODE. If the SOFTWARE includes Sample Code, then Microsoft grants you a royalty-free right to reproduce and distribute the sample code of the SOFTWARE provided that you: (a) distribute the sample code only in conjunction with and as a part of your software product; (b) do not use Microsoft's or its authors' names, logos, or trademarks to market your software product; (c) include the copyright notice that appears on the SOFTWARE on your product label and as a part of the sign-on message for your software product; and (d) agree to indemnify, hold harmless, and defend Microsoft and its authors from and against any claims or lawsuits, including attorneys' fees, that arise or result from the use or distribution of your software product.

DISCLAIMER OF WARRANTY

The SOFTWARE (including instructions for its use) is provided "AS IS" WITHOUT WARRANTY OF ANY KIND. MICROSOFT FURTHER DISCLAIMS ALL IMPLIED WARRANTIES INCLUDING WITHOUT LIMITATION ANY IMPLIED WARRANTIES OF MERCHANTABILITY OR OF FITNESS FOR A PARTICULAR PURPOSE. THE ENTIRE RISK ARISING OUT OF THE USE OR PERFORMANCE OF THE SOFTWARE AND DOCUMENTATION REMAINS WITH YOU.

IN NO EVENT SHALL MICROSOFT, ITS AUTHORS, OR ANYONE ELSE INVOLVED IN THE CREATION, PRODUCTION, OR DELIVERY OF THE SOFTWARE BE LIABLE FOR ANY DAMAGES WHATSOEVER (INCLUDING, WITHOUT LIMITATION, DAMAGES FOR LOSS OF BUSINESS PROFITS, BUSINESS INTERRUPTION, LOSS OF BUSINESS INFORMATION, OR OTHER PECUNIARY LOSS) ARISING OUT OF THE USE OF OR INABILITY TO USE THE SOFTWARE OR DOCUMENTATION, EVEN IF MICROSOFT HAS BEEN ADVISED OF THE POSSIBILITY OF SUCH DAMAGES. BECAUSE SOME STATES/COUNTRIES DO NOT ALLOW THE EXCLUSION OR LIMITATION OF LIABILITY FOR CONSEQUENTIAL OR INCIDENTAL DAMAGES, THE ABOVE LIMITATION MAY NOT APPLY TO YOU.

U.S. GOVERNMENT RESTRICTED RIGHTS

The SOFTWARE and documentation are provided with RESTRICTED RIGHTS. Use, duplication, or disclosure by the Government is subject to restrictions as set forth in subparagraph (c)(1)(ii) of The Rights in Technical Data and Computer Software clause at DFARS 252.227-7013 or subparagraphs (c)(1) and (2) of the Commercial Computer Software — Restricted Rights 48 CFR 52.227-19, as applicable. Manufacturer is Microsoft Corporation, One Microsoft Way, Redmond, WA 98052-6399.

If you acquired this product in the United States, this Agreement is governed by the laws of the State of Washington.

Should you have any questions concerning this Agreement, or if you desire to contact Microsoft Press for any reason, please write: Microsoft Press, One Microsoft Way, Redmond, WA 98052-6399.

The
Step by Step
Practice Files Disk

The enclosed 3.5-inch disk contains time-saving, ready-to-use practice files that complement the lessons in this book. To use the practice files, you'll need Microsoft Excel 97 and either the Microsoft Windows 95 operating system or version 3.51 Service Pack 5 or later of the Microsoft Windows NT operating system.

Before you begin the *Step by Step* lessons, read the section of the book titled "Installing and Using the Practice Files." There you'll find a description of each practice file and easy instructions for installing the files on your computer's hard disk.

Please take a few moments to read the license agreement on the previous page before using the enclosed disk.

Register Today!

Return this
Microsoft® Excel 97 Step by Step
registration card today

Microsoft·Press
mspress.microsoft.com

OWNER REGISTRATION CARD   **1-57231-314-5**

Microsoft® Excel 97 Step by Step

_____   _____   _____
FIRST NAME   **MIDDLE INITIAL**   **LAST NAME**

_____
INSTITUTION OR COMPANY NAME

_____
ADDRESS

_____

_____   _____   _____
CITY   **STATE**   **ZIP**

                                                        (   )
_____   _____
E-MAIL ADDRESS   **PHONE NUMBER**

U.S. and Canada addresses only. Fill in information above and mail postage-free.
Please mail only the bottom half of this page.

**For information about Microsoft Press®
products, visit our Web site at
mspress.microsoft.com**

Microsoft·Press